PLAYMAKERS

HOW THE NFL REALLY WORKS
(AND DOESN'T)

MIKE FLORIO

PUBLICAFFAIRS

NEW YORK

PublicAffairs
Hachette Book Group
1290 Avenue of the Americas, New York, NY 10104
www.publicaffairsbooks.com
@Public_Affairs

Printed in the United States of America

First Edition: March 2022

Published by PublicAffairs, an imprint of Perseus Books, LLC, a subsidiary of Hachette Book Group, Inc. The PublicAffairs name and logo is a trademark of the Hachette Book Group.

The Hachette Speakers Bureau provides a wide range of authors for speaking events. To find out more, go to www.hachettespeakersbureau.com or call (866) 376-6591.

The publisher is not responsible for websites (or their content) that are not owned by the publisher.

Print book interior design by Trish Wilkinson.

Library of Congress Cataloging-in-Publication Data

Names: Florio, Mike, author.
Title: Playmakers : how the NFL really works (and doesn't) / Mike Florio.
Description: First edition. | New York, N.Y. : PublicAffairs, 2022.
Identifiers: LCCN 2021033337 | ISBN 9781541700185 (hardcover) |
    ISBN 9781541700178 (ebook)
Subjects: LCSH: National Football League. | National Football League—Corrupt
    practices. | Football—Corrupt practices—United States. | Football players—
    United States—Conduct of life.
Classification: LCC GV955.5.N35 F57 2022 | DDC 796.332/640973—dc23
LC record available at https://lccn.loc.gov/2021033337

ISBNs: 9781541700185 (hardcover), 9781541700178 (e-book)

LSC-H

Printing 1, 2022

In memory of my parents,
Herman "Butch" Florio and Margaret Ann Alexander Florio

CONTENTS

Introduction   1

PART I: THE DRAFT

Tom Brady Proves the Draft Is an Inexact Science   9
At Its Core, the Draft Is Anti-American   12
The Draft Is the Safest Place to Find a Franchise Quarterback   15
The Predraft Process Focuses on All the Wrong Things   18
Draft Picks Have Incredible Value to Teams—before
   They're Used   21
The Temptation to Tank Is Real   24
The Commissioner's Conundrum   27
The Draft Becomes an Accidental Road Show   30
Owners Often Get Involved without Getting Involved   33
There's a Huge Benefit to Discretion   36

PART II: FREE AGENCY

Free Agency Rarely Makes a Huge Difference for Any Team   41
The Franchise Tag Hurts Players More Than Fans Realize   44
Thanks to Free Agency, Players Often Can't Stay Put   47
Players Should Be Celebrated for Trying to Get More   50
The Albert Haynesworth Debacle   54
Running Backs Aren't Valued, and for Good Reason   57
Peyton Manning's Foray into Free Agency   60
Kirk Cousins Cracks the Franchise-Tag Code   63

Le'Veon Bell's Lost Season   66
Tom Brady Leaves Town after Twenty Years   69

PART III: QUARTERBACKS

The Death of Johnny Unitas   75
The Rise of Mike Vick   77
Aaron Rodgers Sits for Three Years   80
The Brett Favre Retirement Odyssey   83
The Donovan McNabb Trade   86
Ben Roethlisberger's Redemption   89
Tebowmania   92
Andrew Luck Retires   95
The College Offense Revolution   98
Patrick Mahomes Changes Everything   101
The Quarterback Takeover   104

PART IV: COACHES

The Jon Gruden Trade   111
The Rooney Rule   115
The Randy Ratio   118
Nick Saban   121
The Peter Principle, on Repeat   124
The Resentment of Bill Belichick   127
The Unreality of the NFL's Reality Show   130
Jim Harbaugh vs. Jim Schwartz   133
The Near Trade of Jim Harbaugh   136
Another Generation of Belichicks   138
Matt Rhule Blows the Salary Curve (and It Doesn't Matter)   140

PART V: OWNERS

The Hiring of Matt Millen   145
The Commissioner   148
Daniel Snyder   151
The Lockout   154
The Misadventures of Jimmy Haslam   157
The Suspension of Jim Irsay   160

Jerry Jones vs. Roger Goodell   163
Robert Kraft Wins One for the Little Guy   166
The Green Bay Dynamic   169
The Rise of Analytics   172

PART VI: HEALTH AND SAFETY

The Death of Korey Stringer   177
The Roy Williams Rule   180
Chris Simms Nearly Dies on the Field   183
The Concussion Epiphany   186
Defenseless Receivers   190
The Concussion Lawsuits   194
The Minimization of the Kickoff   197
Lowering the Helmet   200
The Pro Bowl   203
The In-Game Concussion Conundrum   206
The Pandemic   209

PART VII: OFF-FIELD PLAYER MISCONDUCT

The Whizzinator   215
The Love Boat   218
Reggie Bush   221
Pacman Jones   224
Mike Vick   227
Plaxico Burress   230
Brett Favre   233
Aaron Hernandez   236
Ray Rice   239
Ezekiel Elliott   242
Antonio Brown   245
Deshaun Watson   249

PART VIII: MAJOR SCANDALS

The Janet Jackson Incident   255
Spygate I   259
Spygate II   262

CONTENTS

Bountygate   265
Bullygate   268
Michael Sam   271
Deflategate   274
Colin Kaepernick   279
Jerry Richardson   283
Spygate III   286
Jon Gruden and the WFT Emails   289

PART IX: OFFICIATING

Replay Review   297
The Tuck Rule   300
Super Bowl XL   303
Scott Green's Irrelevant (Not Really) Mistake   306
The Santonio Holmes Missed Call   309
The Fail Mary   312
The Index Card Incident   316
The Catch Rule   319
The Rams-Saints Debacle   322
The Worst Rule in Football   325

PART X: THE FUTURE

The Proliferation of Sports Betting   331
The Injury Report   334
The Tim Donaghy Dynamic   338
Sky Judge   341
Protecting Inside Information   344
The Playoff Seeding Formula   347
Expansion   350
The Best Approach to Overtime   353
Protecting the Mental Health of Players   357
Global Domination   360
Corporate Ownership   363
Alternative Leagues   366

Acknowledgments   369

PLAYMAKERS

INTRODUCTION

PICTURE YOURSELF WALKING out your door after dinner. The air is cooling after a hot day. There's a bit of a breeze. You can feel it pushing your shirt against your lower back.

You're standing in the driveway, seven feet away from the garage. The door is down. It's painted off-white. You see the lines where the rectangular panels will separate as it slides up squeakily on the metal tracks, the dent from where your kid ran into it with his bike and then tried to deny it. A row of windows lines the top of the door, as if you (or anyone else) will ever climb onto a step stool to have a look inside. All you'd find is the Ford Taurus and the Subaru Forester and the weed whacker and the half-filled gasoline can with a rag stuck in the hole because you lost the nozzle. And a smattering of grimy and long-forgotten toys.

Now, run. Run right into the door. Run as hard as you can.

Get up. You OK? Who cares if you're not? Go back and do it again.

Do it again.

And again. And again.

After you've done it about fifty times or so, you'll feel like an NFL player feels after a game.

Now, do it every Sunday (plus maybe a Thursday or a Monday or a Saturday instead) for the next eighteen weeks. Don't worry. You'll get one of those weeks off to rest—until you get to keep doing it some more.

And if you do it really well, you'll get to do it even more. Another three or four weekends.

Do that from September through January, and you'll begin to understand life in the NFL.

We've become conditioned over the years to think it's glitz and it's glamour and it's riches and it's luxury and it's whatever else is good and enviable to play in the NFL. It's not. It's pain and it's agony and it's surgeries and it's pressure and it's stress and it's everyone you know wanting some of what you have, and it's a far cry from the fun, thrilling life that a resentful nation of fans believes it to be.

Now, go back to your driveway. And before you run full speed into the garage door, pretend that you're doing it in front of sixty-five thousand people. Half the time, when you're on the home team, they'll love you (unless they think you suck). The other half the time, when you're on the road team, they'll hate you with a flaming passion (especially if they know you don't suck).

With millions more watching at home. With people who have get-rich-quick cash riding on the outcome of the game. With tens of thousands who "own" you in fantasy football needing you to score a touchdown, or three. With an unlimited number of assholes on social media who will hurl insults at you, your wife, your mother, your kids. Who will threaten to kill you, or them, if you fail to perform in a way that advances their financial interests, their rooting interests, or both.

Welcome to the real life of an NFL player. Welcome to the pain. The stress. The heartache. Welcome to the hours spent trying to mend a broken body to the point that it can keep running into that garage door. Welcome to the challenges of realizing your peak earning potential well before your twenty-fifth birthday and the demands from family and friends who believe that the fountain of cash will last forever, or at least a lot longer than it actually will.

Welcome to life as a candle that burns quickly and has an unknown supply of wax. One year? Two years? Three? Four? Five, maybe. And only a handful can stretch it out much longer than that.

And every year, there's a new crop of players, younger, cheaper, healthier, fresher. They're coming to take what's yours. Eventually, one of them will. Until that happens, you get to worry about the inevitability of it.

Along the way, everyone is watching everything you do. The reward for success is a life led in public, with constant requests for photos and autographs and tickets and phone calls. It sounds great at first, but it gets old quickly. Very quickly.

There's a story that has made the rounds for years in league circles that a female fan once approached Hall of Fame defensive tackle Warren Sapp while he was eating dinner and said, "I hate to bother you, but can I get your autograph?"

Sapp pushed his chair back, as the legend goes, glared at the woman, and pointed at his meal.

"Do you see any peas on my plate?" Sapp said.

The woman, confused by the question, looked at the plate.

"No," she said.

"Do you know why there's no peas on my plate?" Sapp said.

"I don't know," she replied.

"Because I hate peas!" Sapp exclaimed. "So if you hate to bother me, why are you bothering me?"

And that's just a sliver of life as an NFL player. For nearly every player who makes it there, it's the realization of a lifelong dream. That dream in many ways can quickly become a nightmare, especially after the players retire to face decades of worry about potential physical and cognitive problems that they'd never even have thought about if their boyhood wishes had been different. If their circumstances and natural gifts had led them to become chemists, or doctors, or even pro athletes in a far less grueling game.

Although success in any professional sport will invite many of the issues that NFL players confront, few exact a physical toll so extreme that some must wonder whether it was all worth it. Most will say it was, because what else can they say? Deep down, however, many of the men who emerge from a career in the NFL with mangled joints and scarred flesh and empty bank accounts and fingers that point in every direction other than the proper one and memories that, if they're lucky, mix good and bad almost equally know that the reality simply didn't live up to the dream.

So remember all of this the next time you're inclined to heckle an NFL player, or to tweet insults or threats at him, or to otherwise mock or deride his performances. Most if not all NFL players are doing the best they can with the talents they have while facing the most talented football players in the world. For many players, the will required to handle the hatred and abuse without becoming jaded or cynical reflects a much rarer quality than the skill needed to make it to the highest levels of the game.

And be grateful that the lack of supreme physical abilities saved you from the realities of a life playing football. In all probability, it's not the life you think it is.

This book covers a wide variety of topics about life in the NFL, or at least what it's been about for the past twenty years. Although the players are the game and the game is the players, the game is much more than that. The game is a multibillion-dollar business that continues to thrive in many respects because of itself, and in many more despite itself.

The NFL loves to say, "Football is family." Football isn't family. Football is business, and it's good for business to say, "Football is family." This book is about the game, the business, the players, the coaches, and all other important aspects of the NFL.

Pro football has grown into a gigantic business, and at times it can be a strange one. Every other industry respects the notion that the customer is always right. For the NFL, the supplier has so little product (and the product has so much value) that if the customer does something the supplier doesn't like, the supplier smoothly pivots to a new customer.

The networks that broadcast NFL games have learned that lesson, sometimes the hard way. In 2003, ESPN debuted its first-ever fictional show. The network, then and still now an NFL broadcast partner, called it *Playmakers*. It generated solid ratings and decent reviews. Given, however, the way it depicted controversies and misconduct involving pro football players, the league hated it.

"Everyone feels that it's a gross mischaracterization of our sport," then Commissioner Paul Tagliabue told CNN at the time. So the league huffed and it puffed, and ESPN blew its own house down, canceling the series in direct response to relentless pressure from the NFL. Since then, Tagliabue's statement has often been proved prescient; the TV show was a gross mischaracterization of the sport because, in some respects, it was far too tame.

This version of *Playmakers* isn't fictional. It represents, in many ways, a history of the NFL over the past twenty years. The sections are organized by broad subjects, and each one unfolds chronologically. The book looks at what the league gets right and gets wrong, driven largely by the individuals who have played significant roles, whether they realized it or not, in the events of the past two decades. It focuses on how the NFL has evolved and how change has happened more swiftly. It's a series of anecdotes, surprises, and opinions. It focuses on a league that never stops making more and more money but that also never seems to be very far from actual or potential scandals—scandals that never seem to do much damage to the ever-rising bottom line.

The NFL does plenty of things well, as this book shows. The book also reveals some of the things the NFL doesn't do well. Hopefully, it will nudge the league toward finding a way, over the next twenty years, to do things even better.

PART I
THE DRAFT

TOM BRADY PROVES THE
DRAFT IS AN INEXACT SCIENCE

FOR ALL THE time and money and effort and anxiety devoted to determining the selection of incoming players by NFL teams, the process remains a crapshoot. The best proof of that comes not from the many high-profile busts but from the fact that the greatest quarterback of all time, and arguably the greatest player at any position of all time, fell all the way to round six, selection No. 199, in 2000.

Anyone who has paid any attention to the NFL over the past two decades knows that Tom Brady entered the league amid hardly any fanfare. A poor performance at the Scouting Combine, where he stood for a legendary photo that looks less like a future Hall of Famer and more like a middle-aged dad who had stumbled out of bed with a raging prostate, didn't help matters. Indeed, it's not as if the Patriots knew that they'd eventually pilfer an all-time great in the penultimate round of the draft. If they'd known who and what Brady would become, he would have been selected before their other draftees, such as Antwan Harris (round six), Jeff Marriott (five), Dave Stachelski (five), Greg Randall (four), J. R. Redmond (three), and Adrian Klemm (two).

Some have tried to say publicly that they knew what Brady would be. Hall of Fame Bills, Panthers, and Colts general manager (GM) Bill Polian, for example, has insisted that he had a first-round grade on Brady. Fine, so why not draft Brady before round six, keep him for a year or two as a Peyton Manning insurance policy, and then trade him? Privately, former Ravens offensive coordinator Matt Cavanaugh stood on the table for Brady to come to Baltimore—but former Ravens head coach Brian Billick ignored Cavanaugh. While the Ravens won a Super Bowl with Trent Dilfer that year, the ill-fated Elvis Grbac experiment happened in 2001, and the Ravens drifted at the position until they used a first-round pick on Joe Flacco the year after Billick was fired.

Brady's case (beyond a level of confidence and a superhuman work ethic that didn't register and likely didn't exist when teams sifted through prospects in 2000) was ultimately aided by the fact that new coach Bill Belichick wanted to pivot from Drew Bledsoe, the team's franchise quarterback, who had recently signed a market-setting nine-figure contract, in the hopes of finding someone who would consume less cap space and attention. Belichick found it in Brady, who for years took less money than he could have gotten, even long after he had supplanted Bledsoe as the face of the team and anyone/everyone else as the face of the NFL.

Many think Brady did it because he wanted to ensure that the Patriots always had sufficient cash and salary cap space to afford a roster full of competent starters and, more importantly, accomplished backups not consisting of low-level free agents who would be paid, and who would perform, accordingly. The truth, as told by multiple people with a thorough understanding of the dynamics in New England, resides elsewhere. Brady never wanted Belichick to feel compelled to get rid of him, so he never wanted to have the kind of salary-cap commitment that would cause Belichick to make an objective, dispassionate assessment of the roster and decide that the time had come to look elsewhere for a quarterback.

Whatever the dynamic, it worked. For two decades, it worked. And it delivered nearly perennial playoff appearances (they made it every year from 2001 through 2019 with the exception of 2002 and 2008, when Brady suffered a season-ending knee injury in Week One), nine Super Bowl appearances, and six NFL championships.

It all started because every team—including the Patriots—repeatedly overlooked the fact that the player who would go on to become the GOAT sat in plain sight, while six other quarterbacks (Chad Pennington, Giovanni Carmazzi, Chris Redman, Tee Martin, Marc Bulger, and Spergon Wynn) exited the draft board. Look at those names again.

While Pennington and Bulger had decent careers, they don't even begin to mimic Brady. As for the other four, their NFL careers will be remembered for only one thing: a team needed a quarterback, and the team drafted one of them instead of Brady.

And so, as the hype and the pomp and the circumstance unfold in every given April, as the NFL uses the draft as a vehicle for selling plausible hope to every fan of every team that every pick can become a player who will change the franchise for years to come, well, that's accurate. The problem continues to be that those franchise saviors won't necessarily come from the first thirty-two names called. Or the next thirty-two. Or the thirty-two after that. Lurking at the bottom of the process could be a player about whom no one is talking and in whom no one has a high degree of faith.

The fact that a player like that could become one of the best players of all time proves conclusively that no one knows whether any of these players will thrive at the next level and that no one will know until they get there and start playing against NFL-caliber competition. For every Brady, there are hundreds, if not thousands, of guys who aren't. The fact that a Tom Brady became buried so deep in the process shows that ultimately no one really knows what they're getting when it's time to put names on draft cards.

AT ITS CORE, THE DRAFT
IS ANTI-AMERICAN

I DON'T LIKE the draft. Yep. I said it. I'll say it again.

I don't like the draft. I've come to hate the draft.

I'm supposed to like the draft since I make my living covering all things football, including the process for selecting incoming players and the incessant February-to-April run-up to it. Actually, I'm supposed to love the draft. Sure, it's fun to watch round one play out. And covering how round one will unfold in the weeks, days, and hours before the draft has helped pay the bills for years.

I still don't like it.

I don't like the draft because young men embarking on their professional careers in any industry should have the right to choose where they will work, for whom they will work, and with whom they will work. In nearly every industry, the new wave of workers has that ability. When picking their colleges, football players have that ability. When it comes to professional football (and all pro sports, for that matter), the league always has utilized, and always will utilize, a process of allowing various independent companies to call dibs.

Despite the inherently American characteristics of sports leagues such as the NFL, the draft reflects anti-American values. It restrains movement and flexibility and the inherent realities of self-determination. It forces men not long removed from being boys to move to places they otherwise would never choose to live, often hundreds if not thousands of miles from the places they'd prefer to start their professional lives for any and all possible reasons.

The NFL nevertheless has crafted over the years a sense that it's a privilege to be told where your playing career will begin. That it's an honor to get a phone call from one of thirty-two teams and to have your name announced from a podium in whichever NFL city is hosting the draft that year. That it's a good thing, not a bad thing, to be whisked away to a place where you would never reside and perhaps never even visit.

For most players, submission becomes necessary because the process provides no alternative. Rarely, and not nearly often enough, a player forces a different path by making it clear that he doesn't want to play for the team that plans to draft him. The examples, however, can be counted on two fingers: John Elway in 1983 and, most recently, Eli Manning in 2004.

Both made a power play, and for both, it worked. It happens so rarely because it invites widespread criticism from fans, who have become even more conditioned than the players to accepting that the movement of the pawns on the chessboard is never controlled by the individual pieces.

For Manning, it helped to have a father who had played in the NFL and who was willing to take the flak on his youngest son's behalf. When Archie, who had been drafted to a bad Saints team and therefore had never enjoyed the success his skills deserved, made it clear that Eli had no desire to play for the then San Diego Chargers, the Chargers eventually blinked. The truth was that Eli had visited the Chargers and sensed that the mortal enemies who ran the team—GM A.J. Smith and coach Marty Schottenheimer—didn't agree on whether they wanted to pick Eli. He sensed that Smith did and Schottenheimer didn't, so he found a way to take a stand.

The fact that no one has tried to do it since Eli Manning shows how hard it is to buck the system. (In early 2020, Bengals quarterback Joe Burrow definitely considered the possibility. As one person with knowledge of the situation explained it, "If Joe was from Athens, Georgia, and not Athens, Ohio, he would have refused to play in Cincinnati.") Not long before Eli, former Ohio State running back Maurice Clarett tried to disrupt the draft not by fighting it directly but by attacking the artificial barrier to entry, a mandatory three-year waiting period after high school graduation, arguing that this makes college football a de facto minor-league system for which the players don't get paid.

Clarett, who had been suspended by Ohio State for all of the 2003 season for receiving benefits beyond room, board, and tuition, sued the NFL for early entry to pro football through the 2004 draft. At the federal district court level, he won. At the appeals court level, he lost. Along the way, the NFL and the NFL Players Association (NFLPA) formalized the three-year rule, strengthening the perception/reality that anyone who wants to play pro football must simply accept that he will play wherever he's drafted to play.

The many who blindly support the status quo say that any other system would allow NFL teams to stock their rosters with talent, rounding up all the best new players and skewing the balance of power. This argument ignores the fact that great players won't choose a team that will not give them a clear path to the starting lineup. Likewise, a hard salary cap for rookies, with the worst teams having more money than the best teams to sign college players, would equalize the playing field by allowing them to lure the best rookies by offering them better financial packages.

Those counterarguments fall on deaf ears as the draft becomes increasingly popular. The NFL will never abandon one of its primary off-season tent-pole events, and with only one player or so per generation becoming the aberration, the average football fan will never take a step back, stand in the shoes of a twenty-one-year-old who deserves options, and realize that the entire system contradicts the basic principles on which America was founded.

Even though it most definitely does.

THE DRAFT IS THE SAFEST PLACE TO FIND A FRANCHISE QUARTERBACK

THE NFL HAS three types of teams: those with a franchise quarterback, those desperately looking for a franchise quarterback, and those with a quarterback who may (or may not) become a franchise quarterback. For those teams hoping to find a franchise quarterback, the draft represents the best option for obtaining one.

Even though the draft has been, is, and always will be a crapshoot, every season of college football creates a new crop of high-level talent who emerge as consensus candidates for franchise quarterbacks. Over the span of a quarter century, the Pittsburgh Steelers learned this lesson both the easy way and the hard way.

In 1970, Terry Bradshaw arrived from Louisiana Tech as the first overall pick in the draft. Although it took him a while to find his footing (and to fend off the likes of Terry Hanratty and Joe Gilliam), Bradshaw eventually led the Steelers to four Super Bowl wins en route to the Hall of Fame.

Thirteen years after drafting Bradshaw, the Steelers had an opportunity to land Pittsburgh native Dan Marino, who plummeted to the bottom of the first round amid a haze of rumors that (insert gasp) he enjoyed partying, possibly with certain substances that enhanced the party experience. The Steelers, as those who know the story tell it, opted not to create an awkward transition year or two from Bradshaw to Marino. So

15

Marino landed in Miami, and then Bradshaw suffered a career-ending injury later that season.

Over the next twenty years, the Steelers had a revolving door of so-so quarterbacks, never going all in for a franchise guy. Sure, players like Neil O'Donnell and Kordell Stewart had their moments, but neither became franchise quarterbacks.

To their credit (but for draft purposes to their detriment), the Steelers rarely bottomed out in the standings and, conversely, rarely climbed to the top of the draft order. A 5–11 record in 1988 gave the Steelers the seventh overall pick the next year, but after top pick Troy Aikman (drafted by the Cowboys), the 1989 draft had no potential franchise quarterbacks. In 1999, a 6–10 mark again put the Steelers at No. 7; however, they selected receiver Plaxico Burress, passing on the only first-round quarterback taken that year (Chad Pennington, who never became a true franchise quarterback) and ultimately selecting Tee Martin one round before Tom Brady landed in New England. (It's not as bad as when the Steelers cut Johnny Unitas in the 1950s, but it's close.)

Then came 2004. A 6–10 season put the Steelers in the eleventh spot in a draft that had three highly regarded quarterbacks. The Chargers took Eli Manning, over his objection, and then traded him to the Giants, who had taken Philip Rivers with the intention of sending him to San Diego.

The third high-level prospect, Ben Roethlisberger from Miami (Ohio), remained on the board. And the slide began. At No. 5, Washington opted for safety Sean Taylor. (Washington had drafted quarterback Patrick Ramsey in the first round two years earlier.) At No. 6, the Browns went with tight end Kellen Winslow II. (Cleveland had the prior month given Jeff Garcia a four-year, $25 million deal to supplant 1999 first overall pick Tim Couch.) The Lions at No. 7 had taken Joey Harrington a year earlier with a top-three pick, the Falcons at No. 8 had Mike Vick, the Jaguars at No. 9 had selected Byron Leftwich a year earlier, and the Texans at No. 10 had made David Carr the first overall pick in 2002.

The Steelers pounced on the man known as Big Ben. (As it turned out, only the Steelers had brought Roethlisberger to town for a predraft visit.) It paid off. An injury to Tommy Maddox thrust Roethlisberger into the starting lineup in September. The Steelers won fifteen of sixteen games and made it to the brink of the Super Bowl that season. They won it the next year, they won it in 2008, they returned in 2010 (losing to the Packers), and they generally benefited from the presence of a franchise quarterback for a full generation.

Again, taking a top quarterback prospect high in the draft doesn't guarantee the arrival of a franchise quarterback. However, with the 2011 rookie wage scale dramatically reducing the financial investment associated with top-ten picks, a team that lands near the top of the draft and needs a franchise quarterback should roll the dice. If it doesn't work, that team will return to the top of the draft soon enough, and it can then roll the dice for another franchise quarterback.

The importance of the position more than justifies the risk. The potential longevity of a franchise quarterback makes it even more worthwhile, especially as quarterbacks increasingly play deep into their thirties and now into their forties, a dynamic that previously applied only to kickers.

Thus, the lesson for every team that needs a franchise quarterback becomes clear: hope to land near the top of the draft, and then take one of the best quarterbacks available. And if at first you don't succeed, try, try (and if necessary try) again. Every year, another crop of potential franchise quarterbacks comes to the NFL. Every year, that quarterback taken in the upper portion of round one could become the answer at the position for up to two decades.

THE PREDRAFT PROCESS FOCUSES
ON ALL THE WRONG THINGS

BY THE TIME the latest wave of players graduates to the NFL after three, four, or five years of college football, the thirty-two franchises have exactly what they need to assess the players. Specifically, they have anywhere from one to four years of game film.

But that's never enough—because it's never been enough. Yes, the NFL picked players with far less information decades ago, before the game became what it is now. Over time, teams have found a way to use every minute, and to spend every dollar, looking at things that, in many cases, just don't matter.

The thing that matters the least requires players to answer fifty questions in twelve minutes in an effort to determine their intelligence. The NFL has used this method, dubbed the Wonderlic test, at the Scouting Combine since the mid-1970s. (Teams such as the Cowboys started using it much earlier than that.) Given the obsession of all teams with comparing all classes of draft picks on an apples-to-apples basis, the NFL continues to make taking the test one of the various activities in which incoming players engage, simply because the NFL has done so for nearly fifty years.

After all that time, no one knows what the scores mean. A really low score becomes a red flag—especially for quarterbacks and offensive linemen. For some teams, a really high score also becomes a red flag because some teams don't want players in the locker room who are smarter than the coaches.

Low scores arise for various reasons, however. Plenty of players don't test well. Plenty of players don't even know they'll be tested until they're given the test. Plenty of players don't care about the test, viewing it as irrelevant to their football abilities.

The most notorious example involving the Wonderlic test happened in 2006, when former Texas quarterback Vince Young initially scored 6 out of 50 and then, after the result was leaked and created a media sensation, received a chance to take the test again and boosted his score to 11. Young, who exited the draft board with the third overall pick to the Titans and won the NFL's Offensive Rookie of the Year award, never truly panned out. It's nevertheless impossible to attribute his ultimate struggles to a fifty-question intelligence test.

Scouts will say that for any player, it's just another data point. But if the value of the data remains undetermined after all these years, what's the point?

The potential for cheating makes the value even less certain. Some scouts or executives give various versions of the Wonderlic test to certain agents, who then use the tests to prepare their clients for the real thing. Plenty of football people shrug at this reality, reasoning that if a player can process and remember the answers to up to six different versions of a fifty-question test, the player will be able to learn and recall the various pages of an offensive or defensive playbook.

Some of the physical aspects of the predraft process have questionable value, too. Although the 40-yard dash generates the most interest for fans and media, in part because it feels the most like a real sporting event, the speed generated by running in a straight line without pads and while neither chasing nor being chased doesn't say much about football ability. Indeed, a time-honored adage in football circles encapsulates the true utility of the event: a football player only ever runs forty yards in a straight line during a football game when something very good is happening or when something very bad is happening.

The intrusive process of gathering exhaustive personal information about a player also has, at times, questionable relevance. Multiple teams over the years have tried to bait prospects into reacting angrily or violently to rude or hostile questions. Issues have arisen when players have told stories to reporters or radio hosts about questions involving sexual orientation.

Perhaps the most notable instance of an executive crossing the line came when then Dolphins GM Jeff Ireland asked receiver Dez Bryant whether his mother was a prostitute. "No, my mom is not a prostitute," Bryant told Yahoo Sports at the time. "I got mad—really mad—but I didn't show it. I got a lot of questions like that. Does she still do drugs? I sat and answered all of them."

Ireland publicly apologized, saying in a statement released by the team that he had used "poor judgment." But Ireland apologized only after the information came to light. Most scouts and executives would never proactively apologize for using any and all information at their disposal to see whether a prospect will keep his cool under stress, because he'll be under extreme stress on an NFL football field.

Still, the best way to see how a player will handle stress at the next level is to see how he handled it at the college level. Which takes us back to the game film generated by the player's college career. From studying the performances to talking to coaches and teammates and otherwise gaining information about what the player has already done, NFL teams obtain much more reliable and useful information than they do from the more media-friendly activities that are routinely publicized. The next time you hear about a player's intelligence tests, his performance at the made-for-TV underwear Olympics (better known as the Scouting Combine), that controversial comment he made while meeting with a team, or that tweet he posted when he was twelve, remember that it's all a sideshow. The real scouting flows from things far less interesting but far more important.

DRAFT PICKS HAVE INCREDIBLE VALUE TO TEAMS—BEFORE THEY'RE USED

GO TO THE store and buy a scratch-off lottery ticket. (I'll wait.) Now that you have it, hold it up. Look at it. Beneath that metallic acrylic paint hides, potentially, a jackpot. Or, more likely, nothing at all. (Go ahead and scratch off the silver stuff. If it's a winner, you're welcome.)

For NFL teams, every single draft pick in every single round has the same limitless potential as that unscratched lottery ticket. It may become something. It may become nothing. Until the edge of the quarter exposes what lies beneath, no one knows.

For that reason, teams love to stockpile draft picks. In any round. In every round. Pick the right one, and the player becomes a consistent starter or a perennial Pro Bowler or maybe even a Hall of Famer, securing the careers of everyone in the organization who can claim credit for turning possibility into reality.

Indeed, an unused lottery ticket can become even more powerful when entrusted to the right evaluators of talent. While no one has managed to crack the code decisively and consistently, some (such as the Ravens of the past twenty-plus years) do better than others when it comes to bending the winning tickets their way. But even the least skilled scout knows that with a little luck, that unused lottery ticket can indeed become a superstar.

Other teams, such as the Rams in recent years, would rather trade first-round draft picks for proven players. Many believe the reason is simple: the Rams don't want to risk being criticized for getting a high-value pick wrong.

Before 2011, the system of paying rookies complicated this lottery dynamic, converting the most valuable draft picks into the most costly investments. The value of the contracts grew every year, and at the very top, the growth outpaced the expansion of the salary cap. As a result, picking the wrong ticket tied a team's hands, forcing it to keep an underperforming player or swallow a massive cap charge to dump him.

It got so bad that in 2008, the Miami Dolphins considered choosing no one with the first overall pick in the draft, letting the clock expire and allowing the team with the second pick (the Rams) to make the first selection and so on until the Dolphins felt comfortable taking a player and paying him according to the corresponding slot in round one. It's unclear how seriously the Miami organization, led at the time in an executive role by Hall of Fame coach Bill Parcells, considered not using the first pick; the handful of agents who tend to represent the top picks in the draft planned to push for Miami to pay its first pick commensurate with the first overall selection, no matter when the Dolphins actually used it. Likewise, the league would have frowned upon a gaming of the system that would have caused the draft to lose some of its luster.

The concern about the cost of high draft picks nevertheless remained, culminating in an effort by the NFL to impose a rookie wage scale that prevented high-profile busts (such as Raiders quarterback JaMarcus Russell, the first overall pick in 2007) from taking millions out of the system without ever earning it—millions that ostensibly would be available to other players, primarily veterans. Since the rookie wage scale did not hurt (at least not directly) any of the players currently in the league, the players agreed to it as part of the 2011 labor deal that resolved an offseason lockout.

The rookie wage scale changed everything, allowing teams (as noted earlier) to take their chances on a franchise quarterback one year and then do it again as soon as the next year, as the Cardinals did by trading up to the tenth spot in 2018 to take Josh Rosen before earning the No. 1 position in 2019 and selecting Kyler Murray.

The rookie wage scale actually made those unused picks even more valuable because from 2011 onward, they became a device for landing young talent at a relatively low cost and keeping them on the team for four years (as to rounds two through seven) or five years (as to round one). This dynamic in turn makes the threat of stripping draft picks in any round the best device for the league office to punish teams that violate the rules. Teams often regard fines, even significant ones, as a cost of doing business. However, teams regard the potential loss of draft picks as a serious penalty because it takes away that unused lottery ticket that usually has far more value before it's used than after.

This hasn't stopped plenty of teams from using draft picks for trades, often giving up multiple selections for veteran players or for the opportunity to move higher in the draft, which happens not for the privilege of drafting higher but because the team making the move hopes to get a specific player. The best teams tread lightly in that regard, resisting the urge to make an all-in move by sacrificing multiple unused lottery tickets for one specific veteran or rookie. The not-best teams, however, continue to willingly throw away those lottery tickets because they believe the player they'll get represents more of a sure thing.

Sometimes they're right. Sometimes they're wrong. But one thing is clear: more picks mean more chances. More chances to get it right. More chances to fix a broken team. More chances for the GM or the head coach to keep their jobs.

THE TEMPTATION TO TANK IS REAL

WHEN YOUR FAVORITE team falls to 3–10 with four games to play, it has two options: try like hell to finish strong, or embrace (if not enhance) the path on which the team is already stumbling. The best-case scenario becomes a 7–10 finish and no playoffs—unless the team happens to be in a division with four horrible teams. The worst-case scenario becomes 3–14 and no playoffs.

Either way, there will be no playoffs.

So the season ends, and the standings become locked. Most importantly, the NFL determines the draft order based on record, with the worst team getting the first pick, the Super Bowl champion getting the last pick, and the other thirty teams falling in line (second-worst team getting second overall pick, and so on).

Who will remember whether a nonplayoff team finished 7–10 or 6–11 or 5–12 or 4–13 or 3–14? Many will remember if the nonplayoff team lands high enough in the draft to get a franchise-altering cornerstone. To get there, the nonplayoff team wins by losing.

These realities create a definite temptation to tank, to lose deliberately in order to enhance draft status. It never happens at the player level; they don't care about draft order, especially since they may not even be employed the next year. Sometimes the coach or GM are involved, if either or both has sufficient job security to stick around for a higher pick. Usually the tanking occurs when owners instruct those who run the football operation to "evaluate" young players who otherwise occupy lower spots on the depth chart.

The commissioner has said the league doesn't see evidence of tanking. It doesn't see it because it doesn't want to see it. It also doesn't see it because it's rarely obvious. In 2011, the not-so-subtle "Suck for Luck" campaign helped the Colts sink to the bottom and in turn surge to the top, allowing them to replace Peyton Manning with Andrew Luck. In 2014, the Buccaneers removed roughly half of their starters during the second half of a game in which Tampa Bay led by 11 points, setting the stage for the lead to be blown and the first overall pick to be secured. As one player who wasn't benched in the effort to allow the Saints to come back and win told me, "I wasn't sure what to think when they pulled everyone and I remained. I learned a lot about myself that day."

In the end, the loss by the Buccaneers allowed them to land quarterback Jameis Winston with the first pick in the 2015 draft. Arguably, they got what they deserved.

Regardless, playing to lose after a season is lost has obvious value. In the same year that the Colts secured dibs on Luck, Washington gave up three first-round picks and a second-round pick for a shot at quarterback Robert Griffin III. In most years, teams give up plenty of draft capital for the privilege of jumping the line to get a preferred player. If those teams had simply lost more games in the prior season, the player could have been acquired without giving up anything more than the pick used to select him.

The league wants fans and media to never notice the allure of the tank. The league wants fans and media to believe that every single team tries its damnedest to win every single game. The league wants the obvious connection not to be made so badly that it has consistently resisted any type of lottery system that would minimize the temptation to tank, since it would acknowledge the temptation to tank.

The NFL currently has multiple significant offseason tent poles, from the Scouting Combine to free agency to the schedule release to the draft. A draft lottery would become a fifth significant event during the non-playing season, one that would generate millions of eyeballs, and dollars.

The powers that be don't want a lottery because they don't want to acknowledge the strategic advantage that comes from not trying to win games, a dynamic that necessarily undermines the integrity of those games. Absent a system that puts all nonplayoff teams into the same pot with an equal chance at the first overall pick, the formula for allocating ping-pong balls or whatever will reward teams for finishing poorly, acknowledging and legitimizing the temptation to not try to win games in an effort to obtain more chances to secure the highest possible draft pick.

So the system won't change. And the current system invites tanking. And tanking will happen, subtly, artfully, and skillfully (and sometimes not). In a lost season, there's only one thing left to achieve. Winning a late-season game serves only to screw that up.

Case in point: in Week Sixteen of the 2019 season, Washington and the Giants played an exciting game that went to overtime. It was a game that few will remember for the quality of the football because both teams stunk. The Giants won, Washington lost, and then Washington won since the loss delivered for it the second overall pick in the 2020 draft—a pick that became Defensive Rookie of the Year and promising pass rusher Chase Young.

THE COMMISSIONER'S CONUNDRUM

IN 2010, THE NFL moved the first round of the draft from Saturday afternoon to Thursday night. "Welcome to Primetime" became the mantra for the week. Radio City Music Hall, on the first night of the draft, oozed electricity and excitement. The crowd celebrated football and everything about it, including a then popular commissioner of the sport, Roger Goodell.

A year later, things changed.

The NFL launched a long-anticipated lockout in March 2011, but the league nevertheless proceeded with the draft amid the ownership-imposed work stoppage. Although fans appreciated the three-day respite from posturing and preening and negotiation and litigation, the fans also received their chance to give loud and prominent voice to their displeasure with the overall situation when Goodell took the stage for the first time as he declared the draft open.

They booed Goodell. They booed him loudly. The booing lasted well beyond the point of awkwardness.

They booed, and they chanted. "*We want football! We want football!*"

"I hear you," Goodell repeatedly said. "I agree with you. . . . Me, too."

League officials privately brushed off the hostile reception, arguing that the same individuals who would boo from within the anonymity of a mob would jostle to be photographed with Goodell when he approached. Regardless, it has become a trend, a ritual, an inescapable price for the commissioner to pay for the annual opportunity to provide a face and a voice for the NFL shield.

Every year, the commissioner continues to take the podium for each pick of the first round of the draft and sometimes beyond. Every year, the booing happens.

He has tried to make a sport of it, at times urging them, "Bring it on." The league has tried to protect him with human booing shields. When the draft visited Philadelphia in 2017, for example, Goodell brought former Eagles quarterback Ron Jaworski to the stage for the first pick of the second round. The crowd cheered Jaworski. The crowd booed Goodell.

The following year, in Dallas, Cowboys legends Roger Staubach, Troy Aikman, and Jason Witten joined Goodell at the outset of the draft. That didn't work, either.

"I can't believe you guys are booing the Cowboys," Goodell said in a humanizing (and all too rare) moment of self-awareness.

Owners have felt growing discomfort over this dynamic. Although Goodell serves in large part as a high-priced pin cushion for the policies and practices of billionaires who prefer to remain behind the curtain, the owners become uncomfortable when their liaison to the public receives such a negative reception because it creates the inescapable perception/reality of a negative reaction to the league and everything for which it stands. The owners are obsessed with the NFL's "shield," and the league's image becomes significantly undermined when booing the man in charge of the entire sport morphs into a time-honored tradition similar to playing games on Thanksgiving.

It would be easy to fix the situation. Goodell, during the draft, should retreat behind the curtain with his thirty-two bosses, allowing a local icon or an actor with a memorable voice (and the ability to correctly pronounce surnames such as "Mariota," which Goodell failed to do for the second overall pick in the 2015 draft) to handle the duties of calling the picks. Someone like a Sam Elliott or a James Earl Jones. A long list of people who would be welcomed with universal applause and zero boos could easily be compiled.

The commissioner refuses to even consider the possibility. The draft has become his moment to enter the spotlight and to dispense bear hugs to the incoming players who accept the invitation to attend the draft in person. Even with the booing, Goodell declines to stand down.

He received a respite from the jeering in 2020, when the pandemic forced the draft to become a virtual event. That year, the league and the commissioner tried to muscle in on the joke, turning booing into an online fundraiser that triggered a $1 donation from Bud Light for every social-media video of fans booing the commissioner.

The end result was awkwardness. It wasn't nearly as awkward as the booing that returned in April 2021 in Cleveland, when the commissioner started the draft by making the walk to the podium on the stage that he stubbornly refuses to surrender.

THE DRAFT BECOMES
AN ACCIDENTAL ROAD SHOW

THE NFL NOTORIOUSLY resists change. When change is thrust upon it, however, it sometimes discovers plutonium by accident.

In 2014, an Easter event at Radio City Music Hall forced the league to move the draft from late April to early May. The indignity also compelled it to consider doing something it hadn't done since 1964: hold the draft elsewhere.

"I think one of the things we'll have to do at some point is start looking at other cities," a resigned Roger Goodell said in 2013 when he first acknowledged the possibility of relocation out of Manhattan.

So the league indeed started looking at other cities. And it found other cities. It first found Chicago, where the draft became a great success in 2015 and 2016. The next year, the league found Philadelphia, which on the first night of the event provided jarring images of thousands of fans in and around the city's Museum of Art. In that moment, the draft somehow became a much bigger deal than it ever had been.

The next year, Dallas had its turn with the draft. The scenes didn't feel quite as compelling as those from Philadelphia, but the draft lost none of its new luster. In 2019, Nashville made the draft a three-day street fair, generating a combined crowd of 600,000. Those in that crowd spent nearly $133 million, according to the *Tennessean*.

Las Vegas, the City of Sin with which the NFL not long ago swore it would never do business, prepared to host the ultimate reality show about nothing before the pandemic turned the world upside down in March 2020. It didn't happen. In April 2022, it will. When it does, the draft will reach another new level.

But it won't become an annual event in any one NFL city, not with nearly every NFL city bending over backward (and opening the coffers) for the opportunity to host the three-day event. The fact that the draft happens in the spring qualifies places that would never host a Super Bowl—especially not after the NFL's one-time-only dalliance with an outdoor championship game in New Jersey. The draft will keep moving. The draft will keep getting bigger. And the NFL will continue making more and more money from events that happen in the middle of what is otherwise a void on the football calendar.

Although the latest level of sustained success for the draft happened accidentally, the league knows how to market itself. The fact that it can so effectively market something that amounts to a business meeting highlights the strength of the sport.

What is the draft? It's a commencement ceremony with a long lag between the reading of names. Names that could be communicated via a group text, with no centralized location at which the rest of the world learns the identity of the next pick.

And it's entirely true that every team knows the name of the next pick, often ten minutes or more before the commissioner announces it during the draft. In 2012, we turned the quick-change dressing room at Radio City Music Hall into an interview area for the various first-round picks who had been selected, and at times we knew, simply from being behind the stage, the names of the next three or four players to be picked as the league tried to slow the process down in order to make for better TV.

That's ultimately what it's all about: good television. The players who show up without an appearance fee (they should each demand one) are props. The thousands of fans are props. The commissioner, ultimately, is a prop. The league takes those various props, sprinkles in the reading off of a list of names that most viewers don't even recognize, and puts it all on TV, and millions tune in.

At its core, the NFL draft truly is the ultimate reality show about nothing. But the gradual disclosure of names, the incessant praise heaped on every pick by on-air analysts (you'll never hear during the first round of the draft that half of the selected players will become busts), and the incessant selling of plausible hope to every fan of every team that this year could be *the year* moves the needle, rings the cash register, and makes the accidental road show that the NFL draft has become a permanent fixture of the American sports landscape.

OWNERS OFTEN GET INVOLVED
WITHOUT GETTING INVOLVED

FANS HATE WHEN team owners meddle. As a result, most team own-ers who meddle find a way to do so without creating the impression that they have meddled.

Then there's Jerry Jones. He made himself the GM of the Dallas Cowboys when he bought the team in 1989, years before sports talk radio, the Internet, or social media had the wherewithal to shout him down. It's now inconceivable that another billionaire could buy a team and simultaneously put himself in charge of the football operation.

The past twenty years in the NFL have included plenty of examples of owners other than Jerry Jones influencing draft picks. When the Falcons tried to rebuild the franchise after Mike Vick's arrest, prosecution, and guilty plea in 2007, a year that included first-year coach Bobby Petrino abruptly quitting in December, owner Arthur Blank nudged the football operation toward taking quarterback Matt Ryan with the third pick in the 2008 draft. To Blank's credit, the roll of the dice paid off, giving the Falcons a franchise quarterback, and an eventual league MVP, for well over a decade. Similar efforts haven't yielded the same results.

The most prominent example came in 2014, when former Texas A&M quarterback Johnny Manziel left school early for the draft. Manziel came with red flags, however. He'd gotten in trouble in College Station, including an arrest that had culminated in a shirtless mugshot. Texas A&M initially planned to suspend him for the entire 2012 season before relenting. The decision paved the way for Manziel to win the Heisman Trophy that season as a redshirt freshman.

Evaluators had mixed opinions about Manziel as an NFL quarterback. At the time, small quarterbacks had a hard time persuading scouts to stick their necks out, prompting many to remain in the safe harbor of advocating men of more prototypical stature. Manziel's off-field issues made it harder for him to generate top-of-the-draft buzz, along with concerns that he'd be more inclined to wing it (something he had done well at the college level) than to put in the work and stay out of trouble as an NFL quarterback.

Two owners had become particularly smitten with Manziel. The first, whose team held the sixteenth pick in the first round, was Jones. The owner/GM wanted to groom the man known as Johnny Football to be Tony Romo's eventual successor.

Even with the final say and the keys to the franchise, Jerry found sufficient resistance to persuade him to back off. His son, Cowboys executive Stephen Jones, explained at the time that, as their pick approached, "Jerry said, 'Let's go through the [prospects] again, make sure we all see eye to eye on how we've got 'em ranked.'" As they scanned the available prospects and came to Manziel, Jerry said (according to Stephen), "I assume we'd take him—wouldn't we?"

Stephen said in response, "Well, I don't think we would."

When the Cowboys prepared to make their selection, the name placed on the card wasn't Manziel but Martin. Zack Martin, a Notre Dame tackle who, after sliding inside to guard, would quickly become a cornerstone of a great offensive line.

Manziel's slide continued through the teens and into the twenties. The Browns, who had two picks in the first round in 2014 thanks to a trade that had sent running back Trent Richardson (the failed third overall pick in 2012) to the Colts, had already traded down from No. 4 to No. 9 then back to No. 8 to get cornerback Justin Gilbert, who became a bust. Thus, the Browns also held the twenty-sixth pick, which otherwise would have belonged to Indianapolis. As Manziel fell, owner Jimmy Haslam's intrigue grew.

Yes, the Browns had a GM, Ray Farmer, whose job it was to make the picks. But staying employed by a billionaire, especially one who had already installed a revolving door at key positions in the organization, required picking up the billionaire's signals. Indeed, one of the benefits of being a billionaire is never having to be anything more than subtle. If, for example, the receptionist places a bowl of mini-Twix bars in the lobby and the owner unwraps one, takes a bite, and exclaims that this is the best damn candy bar he's ever had, mini-Twixes will soon be flowing from every drawer and cabinet in the facility.

When it comes to players, the owner can be equally nuanced. Officially, the pick is usually made by the GM. Unofficially, the GM hopes to continue to be the GM. So when the owner, who in almost every instance has absolutely no qualifications or experience when it comes to evaluating football talent, starts dropping hints, a GM with any semblance of a survival instinct acts accordingly.

That was what Farmer did, abandoning a plan to take Louisville quarterback Teddy Bridgewater with the twenty-sixth pick and trading up for Manziel. Haslam insisted that he had nothing to do with the pick. However, by explaining to ESPN reporter Sal Paolantonio that a homeless man had recently urged Haslam to "draft Manziel," Haslam inadvertently disclosed the truth.

Haslam, for all practical purposes, picked Manziel. And if Manziel hadn't become the latest in a long line of Cleveland first-round quarterback busts (from Tim Couch to Brady Quinn to Brandon Weeden), Haslam surely would have claimed credit for the selection at some point.

But a bust Manziel became, and when Haslam inevitably fired Farmer after two failed seasons with Manziel at quarterback, the selection would officially and permanently remain on Farmer's record, not Haslam's.

THERE'S A HUGE BENEFIT
TO DISCRETION

AS THE FIRST round of the 2017 draft unfolded, Saints coach Sean Payton became increasingly intrigued. Although one of the all-time great quarterbacks in league history remained on his roster, then thirty-eight-year-old Drew Brees, a quarterback who could become a future all-time great had begun to slide. And the Saints, after a third straight losing season, held the eleventh overall pick in the draft.

The Bears, after trading up from the third pick to the second with San Francisco, had taken a different quarterback, Mitchell Trubisky. The 49ers didn't take a quarterback at No. 3. Neither did the Jaguars at No. 4, the Titans at No. 5, the Jets at No. 6, the Chargers at No. 7, the Panthers at No. 8, or the Bengals at No. 9.

Payton began to think that the Saints would have a chance to select the quarterback the Super Bowl–winning offensive wizard secretly coveted. As the process inched closer and closer to pick No. 11, Payton began to become convinced that Patrick Mahomes would still be on the board.

At that point, Payton prepared to officially make Mahomes the team's pick.

Then, the door to the draft room opened, and in walked Drew Brees along with a group of guests. Eyes instantly widening, Payton advised Saints GM Mickey Loomis to tell Brees that the team could indeed be picking a quarterback so that the team's current franchise quarterback wouldn't be embarrassed in front of his friends. The message was delivered, the Buffalo Bills entered the selection window just one selection in front of the Saints, and then it all fell apart.

The Chiefs, led by coach Andy Reid and at the incessant urging of Brett Veach, who would become the team's GM after the draft, moved all the way up from No. 27 to No. 10, cutting in front of the Saints and snatching Mahomes.

No one knew the Chiefs wanted Mahomes. No one knew the Saints wanted Mahomes. No one knew because both teams had managed to keep their desires quiet.

It's not easy to do that in the NFL. People in any organization talk. They tell secrets. Don't we all tell one other person that one thing in confidence that we were told in confidence in exchange for a promise not to tell anyone? Some coaches, whether because of ego or insecurity, share secrets with those who can't be trusted, and before anyone knows it, the cat is out of the bag and pissing all over the furniture.

The Chiefs definitely hadn't blabbed. The Saints hadn't, either; the Chiefs simply knew they needed to move as high as they could, and the Bills were the first team willing to move so far down.

The ability of both teams to keep their lips zipped is even more stunning given that the predraft process rarely entails a vacuum. For every top player, both good and bad opinions percolate. Often a team that actually wants a player spreads negativity in the hope that the player will fall—and a team that doesn't want that player excessively praises him so that some sucker with a higher pick will take him, pushing other prospects farther down the board.

In 2017, Mahomes became a true wild card. Because the teams that secretly wanted Mahomes said nothing, the draft experts—who frequently claim to craft their draft boards based on their own scouting skills but who mainly shape their rankings based on information gleaned from scouts and coaches—didn't push Mahomes as a top prospect, contributing to his slide to No. 10.

A similar dynamic played out the very next year. With five quarterbacks regarded as first-round prospects, four found homes within the first ten selections. The Ravens, however, coveted Lamar Jackson.

Baltimore held the sixteenth overall pick. Team owner Steve Bisciotti wanted to take Jackson then and there. The Ravens, however, knew that they could wait.

So they traded down from No. 16 to No. 22. They next traded from No. 22 to No. 25. And at No. 25, they didn't take Jackson; the Ravens instead selected tight end Hayden Hurst.

Then they waited, confident that none of the teams picking from No. 26 to No. 31 would take Jackson—and that no one else would move up from the second round to get him. When the thirty-second selection, held by the Eagles, went on the clock, the Ravens made their move, trading back into the first round and making Jackson the final selection of the opening night of the draft.

It worked, both in 2017 for the Chiefs and in 2018 for the Ravens. Mahomes became the league MVP in his second season, and Jackson became the league MVP the following year, in his second season. For both teams, it happened because they followed one of the critical life rules communicated by Jimmy Conway to a young Henry Hill in *Goodfellas*: they kept their mouths shut.

PART II
FREE AGENCY

FREE AGENCY RARELY MAKES A HUGE DIFFERENCE FOR ANY TEAM

PLAYERS FOUGHT FOR decades to secure the ability to move from team to team. For nearly thirty years, they've had that power. It has made plenty of players and their families rich—some very rich. It rarely has made a team that throws money at free agents into a champion or even into a consistent contender.

Consider the context in which a player becomes a free agent. He has played for his current team for four and sometimes five years. That team knows him well, far better than it ever knows a player in whom a draft pick is invested. And that team has decided, after four or five years of constantly being around him, to let the player walk away.

The mere fact that a player even becomes a free agent should be regarded as a red flag. Sometimes the player simply has had enough, refuses all opportunities to sign a new contract, and makes his exit. Usually, however, if a team wants to keep a player, it finds a way to sign him to a new contract. If all else fails, the team uses the franchise tag (which usually results in the player leaving only if a trade happens) or the transition tag (which gives the current team the right to match an offer sheet that the player signs with a new team but no compensation from that team).

This nuance is often lost on a team with cash to burn and salary-cap space to allocate to a player who has shown that he can perform capably or better at the NFL level. Some teams splurge because they must, given the minimum spending requirements of the labor deal. Others break open the piggy bank to create positive buzz locally and nationally. What better way to attract attention and in turn to sell tickets and/or merchandise in March? Whether the player actually fits the offense, the defense, the culture, or whatever doesn't matter at a time on the calendar when no one keeps track of points scored. Teams need people to part ways with their money, and spending money on a quality player who has played for another team can be an effective crowbar for a customer's wallet.

Still, great teams rarely if ever come from free-agency spending sprees. The smart franchises build and rebuild through the draft, where players can be obtained for far less money than free agents command. The best of those players then get second (and sometimes third) contracts, graduating from a core of young talent to a nucleus of experienced leaders to the heart and soul of the team.

The not-smart franchises do the opposite, constantly searching the rosters of other teams for players who can be pilfered and never rewarding home-grown talent, forcing them to find payment elsewhere. This practice sends a horrible message to young players looking for a linear path to a payday. The smart teams provide clear, bright lines that lead from Point A to Point $. The not-smart teams constantly reward new players from other teams.

The smartest of the smart teams persuade their veteran players to stay put without demanding huge money, consciously leaving cash and cap space on the table in order to ensure that enough will remain to build and maintain a high-quality team. The Patriots became the one team to crack that code, using Tom Brady's constant willingness to take less as the "Who do you think you are?" leverage to convince players not named Tom Brady to take what they could get. Rarely have the Patriots paid market value to keep their own players or to sign players from other teams. While exceptions exist (paying big money to keep linebacker Dont'a Hightower and to land Bills cornerback Stephon Gilmore, along with an uncharacteristic drunken sailor spending spree in 2021, fueled by an extreme need for quality players and plenty of cap space to sign them), the Patriots have managed to maintain a nucleus of highly talented players who consumed sufficiently little of the salary cap to permit a robust middle class of quality backups, allowing the team to not have to rely on an unproven rookie or a street free agent when a starter is injured.

In a similar, but hardly the same, vein reside the Cowboys. If uncon-strained by a salary cap, owner Jerry Jones would buy up every player he could find, outbidding anyone and everyone to obtain the players he covets. Because of the cap, the Cowboys pay good money to good players, but the team also uses the allure of playing for the Cowboys to persuade them to take a little less so that the Cowboys have a little more to throw at another star player or two. The approach worked incredibly well until it didn't—first with running back Ezekiel Elliott (who held out until he received top-of-market value in 2019) and then with quarterback Dak Prescott (who repeatedly refused major offers in search of what he de-served, even after he suffered a badly broken ankle, and eventually signed an incredibly player-friendly contract).

When it comes to spending big money, it's almost always better to do it with current players, paying them for performance and loyalty and showing young players that a similar reward waits for them, too. When-ever a team chases a stranger to the organization with the kind of cash it takes to attract him in the early days of free agency, the obvious ex-citement aroused by the new arrival should be tempered by the reality that when all is said and done, the player likely won't have done much to deliver a championship.

THE FRANCHISE TAG HURTS
PLAYERS MORE THAN FANS REALIZE

FROM TIME TO time, a specific argument surfaces from those who advocate for the rights of players (and not nearly enough fans or media advocate for the rights of players). The argument is simple, clear, and direct: the franchise tag must go.

But the franchise tag won't go away. Ever.

Established in 1993 as part of the settlement of the antitrust litigation filed by a group of players (led by Hall of Famer Reggie White) after the failed strike of 1987, the franchise tag gives every team the ability to squat on one otherwise unrestricted free agent every year. In exchange for a significant (but in most cases not life-changing) one-year salary, the team can deprive the player of his shot at the open market, temporarily if not permanently delaying his chance to enjoy the first-day-of-free-agency windfall.

The league has tried, much as it did with the draft, to craft a narrative that receiving the franchise tag represents some sort of honor or distinction. That's a much tougher sell because all players whose rights become restricted by the franchise tag see lesser players who hit the open market receive much more significant contracts.

Fans shed few tears for franchise-tagged players, who after all make millions of dollars for one more season of football. But the franchise tag comes with a different sort of price. It forces the player to wait for a generational haul of guaranteed money, an amount that brings far more security and prosperity than the one-season salary. And if the franchise-tagged player suffers a serious injury while playing on the franchise tag, that big payday may never come.

Really, why else would teams use it? They want to keep the player, and they don't want to have to compete with other teams that possibly would offer more for a long-term deal. It's that simple: the franchise tag short-circuits free agency by allowing each team to prevent one player per year from having the opportunity to shop his services to someone who would offer more than his current team wants to pay.

For that reason alone, the league will never sacrifice the franchise tag. Even if the teams had any inclination to entertain the idea of giving up the ability to squat on great players for less than they'd be worth if they could determine their worth through the forces of free enterprise, the league would demand a major concession from the NFLPA at the back-and-forth of the bargaining table. The union as a whole would never want to make the collective sacrifice necessary to help the relatively few players per year who find themselves prevented from becoming free agents.

This overlooks the reality, of course, that the expansion of the market value of the best players at a given position tends to boost the compensation given to lesser players, driving up the average salaries for veteran players at every layer and level of value. It's difficult if not impossible, however, to convince most players to see it that way. For the average player, the franchise tag keeps the richest from getting even richer, necessarily leaving more salary-cap dollars behind for the rest.

That's why players who find themselves subject to the franchise tag must be willing to take advantage of their own rights under the Collective Bargaining Agreement (CBA). Franchise-tagged players who haven't accepted the one-year offer have no obligation to report for mandatory offseason workouts or training camp. They can wait until days before the start of the regular season, show up, accept the franchise salary, and collect every penny of it.

That strategy entails a calculated risk, however. As first learned by Eagles linebacker Jeremiah Trotter in 2002 (and then by Eagles defensive tackle Corey Simon in 2005 and Panthers cornerback Josh Norman in 2016), the team can rescind the franchise tag at any time before it's accepted, making the franchise player a free agent after most of the major free-agency money has evaporated from team budgets. Right or wrong, fair or unfair, teams have the ability under the CBA to apply the franchise tag and, until it's accepted, to take it back.

Players have rights, too. As mentioned above, they can hold out without violating a contract because until they accept the franchise tender, they're not under contract. As mentioned later, they can choose to play on a year-to-year basis, eventually forcing their way to the open market (if they can avoid injury and/or a significant decline in their skills). Regardless, the franchise tag gives a huge advantage to teams that hope to keep their best players in place, and for that reason, the franchise tag will never go away despite the random and occasional shouts to get rid of it for good.

THANKS TO FREE AGENCY, PLAYERS OFTEN CAN'T STAY PUT

THE GOOD NEWS for players as of 1993 was that they finally secured actual free agency. Despite limitations such as the franchise tag, they achieved the ability to change teams when their contracts expired. The bad news for players as of 1993 was the system through which free agency would operate.

In order to prevent certain owners (Jerry Jones, Jerry Jones, and . . . let's see . . . Jerry Jones) from spending themselves and other teams into oblivion or bankruptcy, the league adopted a salary cap. Teams could now spend only so much per year on players, with various exceptions and loopholes that allowed them to work around the cap in any given year. But only so many games could be played before the reckoning arrived.

This reality created an important unintended consequence for the realization of free agency. Players who wanted to stay with a given team sometimes became so-called cap casualties, cut not because of skill or injury but because their contracts consumed more cap space than the team could justify based on other available options for the player's roster spot.

Although teams have routinely dumped players and their contracts for cap reasons with no questions asked, some will try to leverage the player into taking less to stay put. If the player's contract does not include a term that forces a team-initiated cap squeeze to happen early in the off-season, when a termination would give the player a much greater chance to land elsewhere before rosters become set for the coming campaign, teams often will wait past free agency, the draft, the offseason program, training camp, and the preseason. Then, a week or so before the start of the regular season, the team will make the player an offer it knows he won't refuse: take a pay cut or take a hike.

Some players will call the team's bluff, either as a matter of principle or because their agents know that someone else will pay more if the player is released. (It's technically tampering for other teams to supply that information. It nevertheless happens all the time.) Others will realize that the best decision is taking less than they were supposed to make since it means staying where they want to continue to play, in a city where they and their family want to continue to live.

One of the most prominent examples of a player taking less to stay put happened in Pittsburgh, where running back Jerome Bettis accepted significant pay cuts in consecutive years in order to pursue a chance at a Super Bowl championship. In 2004, he agreed to drop his pay from $3.757 million to $900,000. The next year, Bettis agreed to cut his scheduled pay from $4.484 million to $1.5 million.

The pay cuts eventually paid off. The 2004 season got Bettis to the AFC Championship. The 2005 season took him over the top, allowing him to walk away into retirement with a Super Bowl win and eventually into the Hall of Fame.

In 2003, a veteran player opted to say no when faced with a request to take less just before Week One. Entering the fourth season of a seven-year, $35 million deal, Patriots safety Lawyer Milloy balked at the idea of reducing his pay below $4.5 million.

The Patriots cut Milloy. Teammates such as linebacker Tedy Bruschi and cornerback Ty Law broke free from the usual do-your-job silence in New England to express amazement at the development.

"I think 'shocked' is the word," Bruschi said at the time. "You sort of just shake your head and ask yourself, 'Why?'"

Milloy received an offer from the Buffalo Bills, and he decided, "Why not?" Only days later, Milloy suited up for the Bills in a season-opening game against the Patriots. Buffalo shut out New England, 31–0. ESPN analyst Tom Jackson proclaimed of the Patriots at the time, "They hate their coach."

Bill Belichick and the Patriots had the last laugh: they'd win the Super Bowl that season. After the game, Belichick climbed onto ESPN's field set in Houston and said directly to Jackson, "Fuck you."

Plenty of players believe that's the sentiment teams necessarily convey when tearing up contracts due to the salary cap. It's not inaccurate, and it's definitely one of the realities of life in a free-agency system that includes real restraints on the ability of teams to gobble up as many free agents as they can.

PLAYERS SHOULD BE CELEBRATED FOR TRYING TO GET MORE

WHEN THE BILLIONAIRES who own NFL teams square off against the millionaires who play for NFL teams, fans routinely line up behind the billionaires. On the surface, it makes no sense. Most NFL players come from modest backgrounds, and they've managed through some combination of God-given ability and hard work to rise to a level of the profession that gives them a limited window for maximizing their earnings.

Still, fans want players to *play*. Given the temporary (in the grand scheme of things) and transient (thanks to free agency) nature of any player's relationship with a team, fans who won't be swapping out their loyalty for a new franchise tend to more closely identify with the people who likewise will be sticking around indefinitely. No matter how good or bad a team becomes, ownership remains in place until owners decide to sell. As 49ers CEO Jed York once said during a period of protracted dysfunction, "I own this football team. You don't dismiss owners."

And so when a player who will be assuming the risk of short-term injury and long-term health consequences makes the conscious decision to withhold services in an effort to leverage a better compensation package, most fans get mad at the player. The situation becomes far worse when a player holds out despite having years left on his existing commitment to the team.

"He signed a contract!" they'll scream into a phone or furiously type onto a social-media platform. And they almost always find support from those in the media who blindly recite a mantra that is only partially accurate.

Yes, plenty of players who decide to stay away from training camp and (at times) regular-season games are disregarding a valid, binding contract. A second contract applies to the relationship, however. The CBA, negotiated and executed by and between the NFL and the NFLPA, gives all players the right to withhold services under certain circumstances. Significant daily fines apply, and in recent years, the numbers have increased. Service time toward free agency becomes sacrificed. But the player has the right under the CBA to take a stand, regardless of the terms of his individual contract.

It's an important factor that fans and media must always remember before passing judgment and/or casting aspersions on players who have the right to stay away. Thanks to the CBA, they have the power to not show up in an effort to get more.

That said, the CBA places clear limitations on players' rights. For example, draft picks can't get a new contract until after the completion of the final game of their third regular season. Holding out before then has no benefit. Likewise, a player who shows up for training camp and then leaves has a much harder time applying leverage than one who never shows up for training camp at all, given the team's right to eventually place the player on the "left squad" list and shut down his entire season with no pay.

Some players have tried to get more without holding out. In 2004, for example, 49ers receiver Terrell Owens landed with the Eagles via a convoluted legal process sparked by his agent's failure to file paperwork voiding the remainder of his San Francisco contract. Owens eventually signed a long-term deal with the Eagles, and during his first season he took the league by storm, turning the Eagles into a Super Bowl contender and, along the way, participating in a controversial *Monday Night Football* cold open that had *Desperate Housewives* star Nicolette Sheridan, donning only a bath towel and a smile, persuading T. O. to skip the game by dropping one of the two.

ABC quickly apologized, but Owens made no apologies after suffering a late-season broken leg and returning to play in the Super Bowl before it had fully healed. Arguably the best player on the field for either team in a game the Patriots eventually won, Owens decided after his first season in Philadelphia that he wanted more money—and more security.

The Eagles said, essentially, "You signed a contract!" Instead of holding out, incurring fines, and potentially being forced to give up a season of salary, Owens showed up. And he sulked and he pouted and he otherwise expressed his displeasure in a calculated strategy to get the Eagles to pay him, trade him, or cut him.

They did none of the three, opting to take a hard line and kicking him out of training camp. He returned after shirtless driveway sit-ups and a front-lawn press conference during which his agent, Drew Rosenhaus, answered nearly every question by asking for the "next question."

The impasse lingered, with Owens generating 763 receiving yards in seven games while continuing to pursue his strategy of disruption. In early November, after he said during an interview that the team would be better off with Brett Favre at quarterback than with Donovan McNabb and complained that the organization had done nothing to commemorate Owens's one hundredth career receiving touchdown, the Eagles suspended him for the rest of the season. They successfully withheld four game checks under the CBA, and then they paid him to stay away.

Owens finally got what he wanted after the season, with the Eagles cutting him and the Cowboys signing him to a three-year, $25 million contract. Through it all, Owens incurred the wrath of fans and media. However, while his tactics were far from ideal, the underlying objective had merit. Owens showed that he had far more value to the Eagles than his original contract suggested, and he wanted to secure full value for his rare skills and abilities, given the ever-present risk that he'd suffer another broken leg or some other injury that would prompt the team to exercise its right to tear up his contract whenever it wanted and move on.

In the years since Owens took his stand, the underlying wisdom of his effort to get more has become increasingly clear. Again, he could have handled the situation better. His effort to get as much money as he could while he still had significant on-field value ultimately should have been understood and appreciated.

NFL owners continue to print money year after year while assuming no real physical or financial jeopardy. The men who assume all of the risks and who have only so many prime earning years should always be respected for trying to get what they deserve before they, like every other player, are inevitably cast aside as the owners continue raking in more and more and more cash through an endless stream of players.

Those owners always get what they can while they can. The players have every right to get what they can while they can, too.

THE ALBERT HAYNESWORTH
DEBACLE

MOST NFL TEAMS have made mistakes in free agency. Even the Patriots, the franchise that has done it better than any other, made a rare decision to pay market value to linebacker Adalius Thomas in the 2007 free-agency cycle—and blew it. Few teams have made a mistake quite as glaring as the Albert Haynesworth contract, however.

A first-round pick of the Titans in 2002, Haynesworth became a solid defensive lineman, specializing at tackle in the 4–3 defense, one of the interior havoc creators of a four-man line. Haynesworth became nationally known for all the wrong reasons early in his fifth season after ripping off the helmet of Cowboys center Andre Gurode and stomping on his forehead with a cleat. Haynesworth received a five-game suspension for behavior that, if he'd committed it outside a football stadium, would have put him in prison.

After Haynesworth completed a six-year rookie contract (as of 2011, first-round contracts became limited to five years), the Titans used the franchise tag to keep him in place. To convince him to agree to the one-year franchise tender, the team agreed not to use it again in 2009 if he qualified for the Pro Bowl. He did, which unlocked the potential for him to get paid a ton of money.

And a ton of money Haynesworth got paid, thanks to Daniel Snyder and the Washington franchise. In 2009, the free-agency market opened at midnight on Friday morning, February 27. Within just a few hours, the two sides had negotiated a nine-figure contract, supposedly from scratch.

The negotiation most definitely didn't happen from scratch. Every year, teams openly haggle with agents representing impending free agents before the window for such discussions opens. Regarding Haynesworth, the speed with which the two sides hammered out a seven-year, $100 million contract raised eyebrows. The fact that Snyder and Haynesworth's agent, Chad Speck, had recently been spotted having dinner in Indianapolis at the Scouting Combine prompted an official (and rare) tampering investigation. Based on the fact that Speck represented Washington receiver Malcolm Kelly (a second-round bust who'd had three total catches the prior year), the team crafted a cockamamie excuse that Speck had met with Snyder to discuss Kelly, not Haynesworth.

They said enough to keep Washington out of trouble with the league, but the trouble with Haynesworth was only beginning. After a disappointing initial season in Washington, one that definitely did not justify the massive investment, Snyder fired Jim Zorn and hired Mike Shanahan to coach the team. Shanahan changed the defense from a 4–3 to a 3–4, converting Haynesworth to nose tackle, a position he didn't want to play.

Shanahan gave Haynesworth an out, offering to allow him to leave the team if he forfeited a $21 million guaranteed payment due on April 1. Haynesworth opted for the money.

Apart from the $21 million payment, Haynesworth had a tumultuous offseason that included litigation over unpaid loans, a lawsuit arising from an automobile accident, allegations from his ex-wife regarding unpaid bills, and a claim that he had gotten a stripper pregnant. From a football perspective, Haynesworth stayed away from all pretraining camp workouts, both voluntary and mandatory.

When Haynesworth finally showed up for the start of training camp, Shanahan made Haynesworth a second-stringer. Haynesworth then repeatedly failed the team's conditioning test, which kept him from practicing. He cleared the conditioning test after ten days, but the dysfunction continued, with Haynesworth missing more practice time, Shanahan making it clear that Haynesworth wouldn't play if he didn't practice, and the two men publicly clashing over the reasons for the missed practices.

Haynesworth and Shanahan never really clicked, with Haynesworth appearing in only eight games during the 2010 season and starting none. The team suspended him without pay for the final four games of the campaign.

While Haynesworth bears the vast majority of the blame for the way things unfolded, Washington made a major investment in someone who didn't deserve it. The franchise should have or could have learned enough about Haynesworth, whom Shanahan several years later called "lazy," before giving him such a big contract.

The coaching change became the kicker. Shanahan chose a defensive system that didn't fit Haynesworth's playing style. Haynesworth, emboldened by the contract he had received in 2009, rebelled.

The 2011 offseason went no better for Haynesworth. He faced claims of road rage and sexual abuse, the latter arising from an allegation that he had fondled a waitress at a hotel bar. When the lockout ended in late July, Washington unloaded Haynesworth onto the Patriots for a fifth-round pick in the 2013 draft. As part of the deal, Haynesworth agreed to reduce his salary to $1.5 million.

And so ended one of the worst free-agent arrangements in league history. Haynesworth departed with far less than $100 million and even less than the $41 million he had supposedly been guaranteed to make. He lasted six games with the Patriots before being waived, and then he finished the year with the Buccaneers.

After the 2011 season, less than three years after signing that massive contract, Haynesworth never played again.

RUNNING BACKS AREN'T VALUED, AND FOR GOOD REASON

FOR MOST POSITIONS on an NFL team, demand for capable players outpaces supply. When it comes to the running back position, supply far outweighs demand.

Every major college every single year has a running back with the skills to thrive at the next level. If his NFL team can give him adequate blocking, if he can hold on to the football when it's attacked by defenders as he's never seen the ball attacked before, and if he can be trusted to pick up blitzing linebackers and other defenders who blow past the wall of offensive linemen in pass protection, the player can make it as a professional football player.

As a result, teams can acquire competent tailbacks in every round of the draft and even after the draft has ended. Texans running back Arian Foster, undrafted in 2009, became not just the team's leading rusher but the league's leading rusher in 2010. Every year, quality running backs emerge anywhere and everywhere, and a huge gap rarely exists between the best in the game and the many others trying to prove themselves on the practice field or in special-teams duties in order to earn reps with the first-string offense.

For that reason, teams don't like to pay big money to running backs. They sometimes have to bite the bullet and write the check, however, if that young tailback becomes a fan favorite and a fantasy football star, racking up yards and touchdowns and winning the kind of customer loyalty that makes it hard, from a business perspective, for the team to let him go.

That's precisely what happened to the Seahawks in 2006. The prior year, running back Shaun Alexander became the league's MVP and led the team to a Super Bowl. How could the Seahawks not keep him? So he received an eight-year, $62 million contract, making him by far the highest-paid running back in league history.

The Seahawks immediately regretted it. Injuries limited Alexander to ten games during the first year of his new contract. His rushing yardage plummeted by nearly a thousand yards, from 1,880 to 896. His rushing touchdowns free-fell from twenty-eight to seven. As a result, the Seahawks kicked the can through 2007 (when his yardage and touchdowns dropped even further) before cutting Alexander loose.

At about the same time, other teams hatched a different plan. Instead of making one running back into a workhorse who churns up yardage and touchdowns and fame and eventually a whole lot of money, some teams began using a platoon system, with multiple running backs sharing the load and none of them ever becoming bigger than the team. This approach makes it cheaper to keep the player when his rookie contract expires because he never has a chance to rack up Shaun Alexander–style numbers.

The ready availability of young, cheap running backs with full tread on the tires makes teams far less likely to splurge on a free-agent tailback in the rare instances that a star player hits the market. Most great running backs end up staying put with contracts that, like Shaun Alexander's, won't last long if the player doesn't keep playing at a high level. In 2020, for example, five different teams (Panthers, Titans, Bengals, Saints, and Vikings) secured long-term deals with running backs (Christian McCaffrey, Derrick Henry, Joe Mixon, Alvin Kamara, and Dalvin Cook, respectively) who arguably had played their best football before they got paid. (Three of them, Henry, Kamara, and Cook, had solid years.)

For all other running backs, the big money rarely comes. Le'Veon Bell (more on him later) eventually snagged a major contract on the open market from the Jets, but the deal that paid $27 million guaranteed over the first two years (he was cut midway through the second) became not a benchmark but a cautionary tale. Melvin Gordon, in contrast, held out in

2019 for more from the Chargers, didn't get it, caved, became a free agent in 2020, and signed a deal in Denver worth significantly less than what the Chargers had been willing to pay him.

It all comes back to supply and demand. Despite the importance of the running back position, the college game produces too many competent players at the position each and every year. Throw in the fact that the position takes a significant physical toll on tailbacks, and many regret ever letting their talents take them in that direction during the days of youth football, when the best athlete often ends up being given the football and receiving one simple coaching point: run past, around, over, and/or through anyone who tries to tackle you.

Although not many say it out loud, former NFL running back Ben Tate once did. Speaking to *Sports Illustrated*, Tate made an obvious admission. "I would've been something else, for sure," he said. "I'd have been a safety. I had the opportunity to play it in college, but I wanted to be the guy to get the ball."

At the NFL level, the guy who gets the ball usually doesn't get the money. Even when he does, it's nothing compared to the money paid to the most important positions, quarterback and pass rusher.

PEYTON MANNING'S FORAY
INTO FREE AGENCY

EVEN FRANCHISE QUARTERBACKS change teams, a dynamic that has unfolded plenty of times when a well-known quarterback wants to keep playing but his team wants to move on. The most significant example of a franchise quarterback switching franchises and finding success elsewhere happened in 2012.

Colts quarterback Peyton Manning, the first overall draft pick in 1998 and undeniably a Hall of Famer based on his accomplishments through 2010, had a neck problem that required four surgeries, wiping out his 2011 season. The Colts, for whatever reason (possibly Peyton's justifiably oversized ego), had never kept a high-end backup quarterback on the roster. So when Peyton couldn't play, the Colts turned to Curtis Painter, Dan Orlovsky, and Kerry Collins and bottomed out in the standings, which in turn put them at the top of the draft order. Which meant they ultimately landed Stanford quarterback Andrew Luck.

That mission accomplished (whether they tried to "Suck for Luck" or not), the Colts cleaned house, firing coach Jim Caldwell and GM Bill Polian and waiting/hoping/praying that Manning would retire. At one point, someone (presumably team owner Jim Irsay) leaked to actor Rob Lowe that Manning would be calling it quits. Lowe "reported" the news, making him 0-for-1 as an NFL insider. Manning wanted to play, forcing the Colts to dump his salary and salary-cap number as they prepared for a long, fruitful relationship and (so they hoped) multiple Super Bowl championships with Luck.

Amid real questions about Manning's ability to throw the football the way he previously had, teams lined up for a chance to sign him for his second act. He interviewed them, screened them, and eventually picked his new team with financial expectations ($18 million per year) implied at the time the teams joined the pursuit.

Despite the physical risks, teams desperate to chase one or more championships went all in on the pursuit of Peyton. The Cardinals spent hours with him. The Titans desperately wanted to bring him back to Tennessee, where he had gone to college. The Seahawks (who would later draft Russell Wilson, which worked out fairly well for them) couldn't even get a meeting with him. The Dolphins wanted him, too, but he didn't want the Dolphins.

Manning had an interest in the Texans, but the Texans didn't have an interest in him, opting to stick with Matt Schaub. (Yes, Matt Schaub.) Manning also had an interest in playing for head coach Mike Shanahan and his son, offensive coordinator Kyle Shanahan, in Washington. As Manning met with the Shanahans, however, word broke that Washington had traded up from No. 6 to No. 2 in the 2012 draft, with designs on drafting quarterback Robert Griffin III.

Manning eventually selected the Broncos, thanks in large part to the common language spoken between a pair of all-time great quarterbacks: Manning and unlikely Broncos chief personnel executive John Elway, who had won two Super Bowls as the team's quarterback in the late 1990s. The move laid the foundation for four seasons of contention, two Super Bowl appearances, a walk-off Super Bowl win to cap Manning's career, and (perhaps most importantly) a convenient exit ramp for quarterback Tim Tebow, a first-round pick who predated Elway's return and who had become an unlikely superstar thanks to a propensity for practicing and playing poorly but then for finding a way to pull it all together with the game on the line and will the team to victory.

Elway, whose inner thoughts had been betrayed by a telling golf clap when Tebow had worked his bizarre brand of magic on a Thursday night during the 2011 season against the Jets, wanted to get rid of the streaky and ultimately unreliable quarterback. Manning's arrival allowed Elway to dump Tebow onto the Jets, where he'd spend a year before sliding into oblivion, eventually resurfacing to pursue a belated baseball career.

A Super Bowl win to cap the 2015 season justified Elway's all-in move for Manning, even though the team's defense had won the championship game over the Panthers. As one source who knows Manning well explains it, Manning's decision-making at the line of scrimmage during a divisional round win over the Steelers, when he changed several plays that wouldn't have worked into plays that did, helped the Broncos get there in the first place. Thus, even though Brock Osweiler (who replaced a broken-down Manning for a long stretch of the 2015 season) may have won the Super Bowl if he'd played in the game, Osweiler wouldn't have gotten the team there.

Manning did, and it all dates back to his willingness to eschew retirement and to keep playing, embracing the rare occasion of a franchise quarterback with enough gas still in the tank getting to finally pick his next NFL destination.

KIRK COUSINS CRACKS
THE FRANCHISE-TAG CODE

WASHINGTON OWNER DANIEL Snyder got the first laugh, trading up from the sixth pick in the 2012 draft to the second overall selection (and giving up two other first-round picks and a second-round pick along the way) to land quarterback Robert Griffin III without first telling Washington coach Mike Shanahan. The head coach got the last laugh, taking quarterback Kirk Cousins at the top of the fourth round.

Initially, it seemed that Griffin would more than justify the investment. He exploded onto the scene with a Week One win in New Orleans and ultimately led Washington to a playoff berth. But a knee injury against the Ravens in December knocked him out for a game and ultimately resulted in a torn ACL during a playoff loss to the Seahawks. (Actually, Griffin partially tore the critically important ligament against Baltimore; it went the rest of the way against Seattle.) Despite winning the NFL's Offensive Rookie of the Year award for his debut, Griffin never recaptured the magic of his first season, playing two more years before being relegated to the bench in the fourth year of his first contract.

Enter Cousins. He became the Washington starter in the fourth year of his own rookie contract, and he led the team to the playoffs. Along the way, the front office made multiple contract offers that Cousins and his agent, Mike McCartney, deemed insufficient.

With the team proposing a long-term deal with a value in the range of $16 million per year, Cousins opted to force Washington to use the franchise tag. And why not? At a guaranteed salary of $19.95 million for the 2016 season, he'd make much more on a per-year basis than the average value of the package the team had put on the table.

Cousins would then demonstrate to all current and future players the power of ignoring the team's offers and going year to year. By rule, the second application of the franchise tag in 2017 gave him a 20 percent raise, pushing his salary from $19.95 million to $23.94 million, a two-year haul of $43.89 million.

Next came the potential third application of the tag. For Cousins, that meant a 44 percent raise, which would have pushed his franchise salary for 2018 from $23.94 million to $34.47 million. For Washington, the price tag became too high. They reluctantly let him become a free agent, two years after he originally would have been. Cousins then hit the market, becoming the highest-paid player in league history (at least for a little while) with a three-year, $84 million contract, an average value of $28 million per year, from the Vikings.

He had cracked the franchise-tag code. In so doing, Cousins had shown all future players that after two applications of the franchise tag, the price for a third franchise tag will become too much. For most players, going one year at a time under the franchise tag means two more years before he gets out for good.

Cousins wasn't the only player to do it in 2016–2017. Rams cornerback Trumaine Johnson also played under the franchise tag for two years. Instead of giving Johnson what for nonquarterbacks is the average of the five highest-paid players in the league (typically, the five highest-paid quarterbacks), the Rams let him become a free agent. Like Cousins, Johnson cashed in on the open market.

Johnson ultimately didn't work out with the Jets, who gave him a five-year, $72.5 million contract. But that's not the point. The point is that Johnson, like Cousins, stood firm on the franchise tag for two years and forced his way out.

It's an important lesson for all players who find themselves blocked from free agency by the franchise tag. If they are willing to spend two more years with their current teams, to reject any and all long-term offers from those teams, and to assume the risk of injury or ineffectiveness, the path to free agency eventually will clear.

For some positions (such as running back and defensive tackle), the injury risk may be too great. For quarterbacks, it makes plenty of sense to hold firm, receive a significant salary for two seasons, and then achieve the freedom to choose that which free agency in theory promises to all players but, thanks to the franchise tag, in practice simply doesn't.

LE'VEON BELL'S LOST SEASON

THE MESSAGE CAME from, of all places, the lyrics of a rap song dropped on the Fourth of July 2016: "I'm at the top and if not I'm the closest, I'm'a need 15 a year and they know this."

Although Steelers running back Le'Veon Bell quickly tried to retreat from the perception that the money line (literally) from a track titled "Focus" conveyed a desire to be paid $15 million per year for his dual-threat skills as a ball carrier and pass catcher, the battle loomed. With one year left on the contract he'd signed as a second-round pick from Michigan State, would the Steelers re-sign Bell before the deal expired, let him become a free agent, or apply the franchise tag?

They chose, after talks failed to produce a long-term deal, the franchise tag. It guaranteed Bell $12.1 million for 2017. But, as the lyrics made clear, $12.1 million wouldn't get it done.

The two sides negotiated until the mid-July deadline for signing franchise-tagged players to long-term deals. Because the Steelers (unlike the vast majority of teams) won't fully guarantee cash beyond the first year of a long-term contract, Bell had no reason to take their offers seriously. Because he hadn't officially accepted the franchise tender, he had every right to stay away from the team until just before the start of the regular season. So he did, showing up for the first time in 2017 days before Week One.

The Steelers didn't like it. But the Steelers chose to initiate the franchise-tag dance in order to keep Bell from shopping his services to other teams. The same rules that allowed the Steelers to apply the tag empowered Bell to stay away for all of the offseason, training camp, and preseason while still collecting every penny of $12.1 million for the regular season.

After another solid year, with more than 1,900 yards from scrimmage and 11 touchdowns in 15 games, the dance began again. Bell later explained to *Sports Illustrated* that the team initially told him that it would use the franchise tag for a second time, at a 20 percent raise (per the labor agreement) to $14.5 million, but that it would work with him on a long-term deal. With the Steelers ultimately offering a five-year, $70 million contract and Bell sticking to his "15 a year and they know this" lyrical vow, another mid-July deadline passed with no multiyear contract.

Everyone assumed that Bell would do what he had done the prior year, showing up just before the start of the regular season, making $14.5 million, and pushing his two-year haul to $26.6 million. Everyone assumed wrong.

Bell skipped the first week of the regular season, giving up one of seventeen weekly checks (one for each game plus a bye week) worth more than $855,000. Then he skipped the second week. And the third. And so on until the window closed for good after Week Ten on his ability to play in 2018.

Although some believe Bell's agent didn't realize it at the time, the strategy guaranteed the player a crack at the open market. Despite the fact that Bell didn't play at all in 2018, the team's use of the franchise tag for a second time counted toward the formula that makes it prohibitively expensive to use the franchise tag a third time. Once the Steelers learned that even the transition tag (which gives the team only a right to match an offer from another team) would cost the same $14.5 million Bell had eschewed the prior year, they threw in the Terrible Towel on a player whom most expected to be a cornerstone of the Pittsburgh offense for years to come.

That was when it got even more interesting. As Bell approached free agency in 2019, a substantial market for his skills as a runner and receiver appeared slow to materialize. Once the two-day so-called legal tampering window opened, during which teams can negotiate directly with agents, no one put $15 million per year or anything close to it on the table.

Ultimately, Bell's camp duped Jets GM Mike Maccagnan into thinking that the Ravens had targeted Bell and that the Ravens were prepared to pay top dollar. In reality, *the Ravens hadn't even called*. But all's fair in love, war, and contracts. The Jets swallowed the hook, offering Bell a four-year, $52 million contract that paid out $27 million fully guaranteed over the first two years. In reality, the next-best offer for Bell would have come from the 49ers, in the range of $8 million per year. (Less than two months later, Maccagnan would be fired.)

The fact that Bell fell short of his goal prompted a curious number of fans and media members to do a victory lap, claiming that Bell had erred by not playing in 2018 for $14.5 million or accepting Pittsburgh's five-year, $70 million offer. It's impossible, however, to resolve the question of whether he did the right thing without knowing what would have happened if he'd played in 2018. By sitting out the year, he traded a $14.5 million bird in the hand on a one-year deal for $27 million over two. Throw in the fact that things never clicked between him and the Jets, which resulted in Bell being cut during his second season, and it's hard not to say Bell won his battle against the Steelers, since he got his $27 million for two years plus a chance to become a free agent during the 2020 season and in the 2021 offseason.

TOM BRADY LEAVES TOWN
AFTER TWENTY YEARS

TOM BRADY SPENT two decades worrying that coach Bill Belichick would one day decide to move on. Before that could happen, Brady decided to move on.

The departure came only after Belichick had had every chance to keep it from happening. He didn't, making Brady's decision to leave much more mutual than it would appear on the surface.

Like most coaches, Belichick stays distanced from his players. He does so because he knows that for the vast majority of his players, the decision to end the relationship comes not from the player but from the team. Whether it's a young player who isn't getting it done or an older player who, dollar for dollar, no longer justifies the investment, Belichick needs space in order to quickly and easily remove the Band-Aid when needed, especially since he usually parts ways with a veteran player a year too early for fear of doing it a year too late.

Throughout the 2019 season, the signs of a divorce loomed. Brady, after twenty years of tiptoeing around a notoriously cold-blooded coach, had had enough. Ultimately, that's the only flaw in the so-called Patriot Way—for the players who manage to survive it, there's a point where it gets to be too much.

Brady wanted to feel appreciated for a change. He also wanted to have a better array of weapons than the collection of underachieving receivers and tight ends that Belichick the de facto GM had accumulated for

Belichick the coach. For all his skills in the sport of football, Belichick's job as a coach has always been complicated by his job as an evaluator of talent. In recent years, those shortcomings have caught up with Belichick in the form of numerous draft picks that never should have been made, given that they never really developed. (It's possible that Belichick and his coaching staff also have failed to develop players who otherwise would have thrived elsewhere.)

And so, by 2020 and after twenty years together, the time had come for Tommy to move on. The Patriots knew that it could happen. They welcomed the annual ritual of tampering so that Brady would know what other teams would offer before having to decide whether to stay. Although owner Robert Kraft, who regards Brady as a fifth son, hoped Brady would finish his career in New England, Kraft knew that it made much more sense to pick the coach who might remain with the team for another decade or longer (Kraft once told me he wants Belichick to work deep into his eighties, like Warren Buffet or Rupert Murdoch) over the quarterback whose train necessarily was pulling into the station.

Brady thus began looking weeks before the rules officially permitted it. He wanted to return to California and play for the 49ers, the team for which he had grown up rooting. (As a four-year-old, he had attended the 1981 NFC Championship, where "The Catch" by receiver Dwight Clark delivered San Francisco's first Super Bowl appearance.) The 49ers, who had Brady's former understudy Jimmy Garoppolo as their starter, considered the possibility and passed.

Others (such as the Raiders) quietly passed, too, realizing that Brady's career had moved far closer to the end than the beginning and that he could at any time endure the inevitable defeat at the hands of Father Time. That didn't deter the Buccaneers, who made a huge push for Brady before the window for doing so opened and then acted as if they hadn't. With Jameis Winston, the team's first overall pick in 2015, throwing thirty interceptions in 2019, Tampa Bay believed it wouldn't take much of an upgrade to improve on a 7–9 finish. (It was right.)

Brady, in turn, was smitten by an array of weapons far better than anything the Patriots had acquired since the days of Randy Moss and Wes Welker. With receivers Mike Evans and Chris Godwin and tight ends O. J. Howard and Cameron Brate, Brady knew he could do much more with the Buccaneers than he had done with the Patriots in a final season that had ended in a home playoff loss, punctuated by an interception return for a touchdown by Titans cornerback (and former Brady teammate) Logan Ryan. Throw in tight end Rob Gronkowski, who emerged from retirement to reunite with Brady in Tampa, and the midseason arrival of receiver Antonio Brown, and Brady had what he thought he needed to eventually surpass Michael Jordan's six championships.

Many believe that was what Brady coveted more than anything else. Seven league championships, a feat that no other modern athlete had ever accomplished and that presumably none would ever match. For their part, the Patriots didn't mind letting him try to get No. 7 elsewhere because they had concluded that they wouldn't win a record-setting seventh Super Bowl if Brady stayed.

It's not about comparing apples to apples. The Patriots knew that at some point, they wouldn't have Brady. Instead of hoping (as the Colts had with Peyton Manning) that Brady would opt for retirement, they realized that after twenty years, he had the right to choose where he wanted to finish his career.

Frankly, players should have that right long before they register two decades of service with the same team. Hopefully, the time will come sooner rather than later when players have much more say over where they play and when they choose to play somewhere else. They take the physical risks. They put everything they have, twelve months per year, into pursuing their goals. A system that has given much more power to the teams for decades must eventually recognize that the men who play the game make the game what it is and that those men shouldn't have to wait a full generation to receive the courtesy of choice.

PART III

QUARTERBACKS

THE DEATH OF JOHNNY UNITAS

THE TERM GOAT gets used all too often when describing modern-day pro athletes. Arguably, the true GOAT played football in an era that placed far less emphasis on the forward pass.

John Unitas. *Johnny Unitas*. The name evokes a shudder, a gasp, a palpitation from those who remember witnessing his exploits. For everyone else, it's a mythology that, unlike most tall tales handed down from one generation to the next, has deep roots in the fleetingly fertile soil of truth.

Unitas, in any other era, would have set every passing record. Unitas, in his own era, was the player every kid on every field in every community wanted to be. Although plenty of great quarterbacks came before him, Unitas became the first gunslinger of the television era, which vaulted pro football from something akin to pro wrestling into the greatest sport on the planet.

Unitas. At a time when the league tolerated if not embraced maximum violence and before the league realized that certain rule changes could enhance passing and, in turn, scoring and, in turn, the popularity of the sport, Unitas found a way to rack up yards and touchdowns and wins and fame, and he helped lift the sport into a stratosphere it had never before occupied.

Unitas. A ninth-round pick from Louisville who lost a numbers game with the Steelers and kept his skills sharp by playing for the semipro Bloomfield Rams in Pittsburgh, then found his footing with the Baltimore Colts and never looked back. He led his team to victory in the so-called Greatest Game Ever Played, an overtime win over the New York Giants for the NFL title in 1958, set every career passing record, and threw touchdown passes in forty-seven straight games from 1956 through 1960, a record that somehow remained on the books until 2012.

Unitas last played in 1973 (a final season with the Chargers after seventeen with the Colts), but his impact endured. When he died in 2002, Colts quarterback Peyton Manning wanted to wear a pair of black high-top cleats in homage to the standard Johnny U. footwear.

"He was one of the most influential guys at the quarterback position," Manning said after Unitas passed. "Maybe every quarterback ought to wear black high-top cleats this week."

Enter the NFL in one of its many No Fun League moments. Inexplicably, the league threatened to impose a $25,000 fine on Manning for paying tribute to Unitas because the Colts uniformly wore white cleats—and because the rules at the time required all players on a given team to wear shoes of the same color. (Baltimore Ravens quarterback Chris Redman wore black cleats that week and received only a $5,000 fine because he hadn't inquired in advance, proving that it's always better to seek forgiveness than to request permission.)

Fortunately, the league has since softened its strict tendencies when it comes to footwear. Unfortunately, the league robbed its fans (especially the younger ones) of a moment that could have caused them to learn more about the OG GOAT, the player who if fate had dropped him into a different era arguably would have been better than any quarterback who ever played the game. Given what he accomplished at a time when the rules made it much harder to pass the ball efficiently and effectively, maybe Unitas, and not Tom Brady or anyone else, is the greatest quarterback of all time.

THE RISE OF MIKE VICK

THE NFL NEEDED decades to finally embrace the notion of Black men playing quarterback. It became conspicuous to the point of shameful that coaches, executives, and owners didn't trust players of a certain skin color to handle the most important position in football.

From Marlin Briscoe onward, the modern era of football had far too few Black quarterbacks. While this problem was in some respects a product of the reality that the lower levels of the sport also weren't embracing the concept, the NFL still insisted on moving accomplished Black quarterbacks, such as University of Minnesota standout Tony Dungy, to other positions at the pro level.

Things changed most notably with Warren Moon, who initially found no NFL takers but then became a hot commodity after developing into one of the best quarterbacks the CFL had ever seen. Although players such as James Harris and Doug Williams, the first Black quarterback to win a Super Bowl, moved the needle of mainstream acceptance, Moon's sustained excellence helped nudge the NFL away from its goofy, backward reluctance to entrust the critical position of quarterback to a minority player.

By the turn of the century, the NFL had finally pivoted toward making the quarterback position color-blind. In the 2000 season, a pair of Black quarterbacks (Daunte Culpepper and Shaun King) and a pair of Black head coaches (Dennis Green and Dungy) squared off for the first time. Other Black starting quarterbacks in 2000 included Donovan McNabb of the Eagles, Jeff Blake of the Saints, Kordell Stewart of the

Steelers, Charlie Batch of the Lions, Akili Smith of the Bengals, and Tony Banks of the Ravens.

The narrative changed, possibly for good, once Virginia Tech quarterback Mike Vick entered the draft. Widely known at the time as Michael (he eventually made it clear that he prefers Mike), Vick became the first Black quarterback taken with the first overall pick in the draft.

Vick was believed to be headed for the Chargers, but the Falcons drafted him after trading up to No. 1 to get him. (The Chargers came out of the 2001 draft with Hall of Fame running back LaDainian Tomlinson in round one and future Hall of Fame quarterback Drew Brees, who would eventually become a Canton-caliber player in New Orleans.) Vick played sparingly as a rookie. He became the starter in 2002, leading the Falcons to an 8–6–1 record in fifteen games and, more importantly, establishing himself as the most exciting young quarterback in the league thanks to a 46-yard, walk-off overtime touchdown run for the ages against the Vikings, capping a 173-yard rushing performance and making Minnesota's defense look less like Vikings than like Keystone Cops.

A broken leg during the 2003 preseason sidelined Vick for the year. In 2004, Vick took the Falcons to the NFC Championship game, winning eleven of fifteen starts and cementing his status as the face of the league. Late in the season, he signed a then record ten-year, $130 million contract.

"I'm a winner," Vick said at the press conference announcing his new deal. "All I want to do is win, and that's what I try to continue to do. And one thing I do know is we will get better."

As it turns out, they didn't. The Falcons regressed. Vick later admitted that he had failed to properly study, allowing DVDs with game film to pile up in his car. (Some teams have been known to hide pornographic images in film assignments, using players' reaction or lack thereof to gauge whether they actually did their homework.)

In 2006, Vick set the single-season quarterback rushing record with 1,039 yards, but he was wildly erratic. The team fired coach Jim Mora following an ill-advised radio interview during which he mused about quitting the Falcons to coach the University of Washington.

Things would soon get much worse for Vick and the Falcons (the fall of Mike Vick will be addressed later), but the first six years of his career helped tear down the lingering remnants of the wall that prompted old-school football types to view Black quarterbacks differently. In a league where job security is tied directly to winning, coaches and executives risked ignoring at their own peril the potential of Black quarterbacks—to say nothing of the broader impact of their bias. While it took many years to get there, Vick conclusively ushered in a truly modern era in which quarterbacks succeed or fail based on their skills and abilities alone, with no artificial barrier based on race.

AARON RODGERS SITS
FOR THREE YEARS

ONE OF THE greatest quarterbacks in NFL history could have been even greater if he hadn't been stuck behind one of the greatest quarterbacks in NFL history.

It happened largely by accident in 2005. After more than two years of Hall of Fame quarterback Brett Favre musing publicly about the possibility of retiring, the Packers weren't actively looking for his successor, but they weren't not looking for his replacement, either.

Enter Aaron Rodgers. The former Cal quarterback and Bay Area native, who had hoped to be taken by the 49ers with the first overall pick, saw Utah quarterback Alex Smith head to San Francisco. Then the fun, or the exact opposite of it, began.

Rodgers slid. And slid. And slid some more. Through the top ten. Through the top twenty. ESPN breathlessly chronicled the plummet, a humiliating tactic that televised coverage of the NFL draft eventually abandoned.

As Rodgers fell, the Packers began to pay attention. Although they hadn't performed the full and complete predraft workup for Rodgers, the possibility of getting a player who had been in the conversation for the first overall selection with the twenty-fourth overall pick couldn't be ignored, especially with Favre recently opting, for whatever reason, to thrust the remaining years of his career into a reality-show-style, will-he-or-won't-he? drama.

When Rodgers remained on the board as the Packers went on the clock, the Packers made their move. Favre didn't like it (as explained in Jeff Pearlman's unauthorized biography, *Gunslinger*, Favre initially treated Rodgers like crap), but Favre couldn't do anything about it—other than keep playing at a high level.

That was what Favre did. In 2005, 2006, and 2007. Through it all, Rodgers sat on the bench with never a suggestion that he should get a chance to do that which he clearly had been drafted to do: replace Favre.

Even with the obvious threat posed by Rodgers's presence, Favre continued to ponder the possibility of retirement. He agitated in early 2006 for the team to make a high-impact free-agency move and eventually got it when the draft-and-develop Packers broke character and signed cornerback Charles Woodson away from the Raiders.

When Rodgers arrived in Green Bay, teams tended to sit first-round quarterbacks for at least one full year. Starting in 2008, with first-rounders Matt Ryan and Joe Flacco becoming wire-to-wire starters in Atlanta and Baltimore, respectively, the presumption flipped. The idea that a player with the real potential to be among the best quarterbacks in football would sit for three seasons has truly become inconceivable.

Of course, there's Jordan Love, a first-round choice in 2020 who has two years on the bench and counting behind (coincidentally) Aaron Rodgers. Few teams can afford to use a first-round pick on a player who won't be playing, especially at the quarterback position. If Love had been regarded as a clear-cut potential franchise quarterback (like Rodgers), maybe he would have landed in a place where he would have played sooner.

Football for three seasons lost the benefit of witnessing Rodgers's skills and abilities because he languished on the bench behind Brett Favre. To Rodgers's credit, he never created a stir, opting instead to work on his craft, keep his mouth shut, and wait for his opportunity.

His opportunity would come in 2008—whether Favre liked it or not.

After an unexpectedly great 2007 season capped by a not-great NFC Championship loss on well-frozen tundra to the Giants and coach Tom Coughlin, who lost layers of skin from his face in the freezing temperatures of Lambeau Field, the Packers' powers that be decided to force

Favre's hand. Aware that he would have far less inclination to commit to playing football in February than in August, the team approached Favre not long after the season ended, seeking a firm decision, then and there, as to whether he'd play in 2008.

The Packers timed their approach perfectly. Faced that early in the offseason with an up-or-down decision, Favre chose to retire. The press conference oozed emotion. Favre cried. The relationship ended. The door closed. For good measure, the Packers barricaded the pathway with furniture, drafting not one but two quarterbacks two months later: Brian Brohm and Matt Flynn.

So concluded Favre's tenure with the Packers, and so started Rodgers's time as the team's starter. If only it had turned out to be that simple and easy for Favre.

THE BRETT FAVRE
RETIREMENT ODYSSEY

THE INITIAL INDICATION that Brett Favre's first crack at retirement wouldn't take came in late April, when Favre visited David Letterman's late-night program. Asked whether Favre would miss football, he dropped what turned out to be much more than a hint.

"I think when training camp gets close, I will—something's bound to happen," Favre told Letterman.

Something definitely happened. With the offseason program, which Favre had come to regard as drudgery, firmly in the rearview mirror and training camp approaching, Favre decided that he wanted to play.

The Packers, who had spent nearly a generation working with Favre, surely anticipated his change of heart, as evidenced by their effort to get him to make a clear decision in February and hopefully to stick with it. The team wanted him to adhere to the commitment he'd made, but Favre wanted to play—ideally for the Packers. If not for the Packers, he wanted to play for someone in the Packers' division, the NFC North.

No matter how hard the Packers tried to dissuade Favre from unretiring, unretire Favre did, returning to Green Bay, showing up at camp, and essentially saying, "Deal with me." Because the team had more than enough salary-cap space, absorbing Favre's $12 million salary figure didn't pose a problem. The problem came from the prospect of having Favre on a team that had pivoted to Rodgers.

Favre could have held firm, insisting that the team keep him at $12 million or cut him. Although his contract lacked a no-trade clause, no new team would want to blindly trade for a franchise quarterback who didn't want to be there. The Packers didn't want to hand Favre to a rival such as the Vikings, so the Packers negotiated with the Jets and the Buccaneers, hopeful that they could persuade Favre to agree to continue his career with one of those teams.

Eventually, the Packers sent Favre to the Jets for a conditional fourth-round pick in 2009 along with a commitment that the price would skyrocket to three first-round picks if the Jets traded Favre to one of Green Bay's rivals in Chicago, Detroit, or Minnesota.

The first Jets franchise quarterback since the days of Joe Namath, Favre led the Jets to an 8–3 start that sparked visions of a potential return to the Super Bowl for the first time since the 1969 season. The season then quickly fell apart, however, ending in a disappointing 9–7 finish. The implosion was fueled by a partially torn biceps tendon that the Jets hadn't properly disclosed to the league—and for which the Jets would be severely punished financially the following year after Favre kept citing it as the excuse for his poor play down the stretch.

Favre kept talking about the injury because, like his first annual retirement, his second annual retirement didn't take. The Jets chose to release him, making him a free agent. Then, after avoiding a full offseason of workouts and minicamps (and part of training camp), Favre decided to join the Vikings, partially because they had a contending team and partially because he wanted to stick it to the Packers.

Favre got both of his wishes. Despite a reported "schism" in Minnesota over the question of whether players wanted to roll with incumbent starter Tarvaris Jackson, Vikings players instantly warmed up to the clearly superior skills and abilities of Favre. He led the Vikings to a division title, a convincing playoff win over the Cowboys, and ultimately a close-but-no-cigar NFC Championship game during which the Vikings significantly outplayed the Saints but made just enough mistakes (including an ill-advised throw by Favre that cost them a chance to win in regulation) to end a promising Super Bowl run.

That was probably when Favre should have retired for good. Instead, he temporarily retired for a third time, eventually unretired for a third time, and then returned for a lackluster final season clouded by an off-field issue (more on that later) and a rash of injuries that ended his record streak of 297 consecutive starts, wrapping up his career with far more whimper than wallop.

The Vikings slammed the door on a fourth Favre unretirement, drafting Christian Ponder in the first round of the 2011 draft and later acquiring Donovan McNabb from Washington. While Favre may have liked to have given it one more whirl, he no longer had any takers, and after nearly a decade of retirement chatter and three prior retirements that didn't last, his twenty-year NFL career finally, and in some respects mercifully, came to an end.

THE DONOVAN MCNABB TRADE

THE NEWS CAME in the waning hours of Easter Sunday afternoon, 2010. After eleven seasons as the Philadelphia franchise quarterback, Donovan McNabb would play elsewhere. The destination made the trade even more significant.

The Eagles had shipped McNabb to another team in the same division: Washington. A team with which the Eagles directly competed twice per year on the field and every week in the standings.

The move had bright red flags for the team that wears burgundy uniforms. Apart from the fact that Eagles coach Andy Reid has a long history of making quarterbacks seem better than they are (and thus getting more value for them than perhaps he should), the relationship between Reid and McNabb had been moving toward a conclusion. In 2008, Reid had angered McNabb by benching the veteran for second-year second-rounder Kevin Kolb during a road loss to the Ravens. Even though McNabb quickly regained his job (and responded by taking the Eagles all the way to the NFC Championship), reports that McNabb wanted a "financial apology" for the temporary exile to the sideline suggested that the Reid-McNabb coupling had moved far closer to the end than the beginning.

Then came the decision to give convicted felon Mike Vick a second chance following the conclusion of his federal prison term for dogfighting. Tensions became obvious from the 2009 preseason, when Reid inserted Vick into a wildcat-style package and McNabb made the "cut" gesture with his hand after being removed from action for Vick.

McNabb responded to the preseason drama with one of his best seasons statistically and another playoff berth. But the year ended with consecutive losses to the Cowboys in Week Seventeen and in the wild-card round by a combined score of 58–14. Reid decided that it was time to move on to Kolb or to Vick, or basically to anyone other than McNabb.

Washington surely knew the risk, but the potential upside apparently justified the investment of a second-round pick in 2010 and a conditional pick in 2011—even though the organization had to wonder why Reid would have no qualms about sending McNabb to a division rival. Some have reported that Mike Shanahan made the trade over the objection of his son, offensive coordinator Kyle Shanahan, and that Mike Shanahan believed that Philadelphia's decision to cut the cord would make McNabb willing to do whatever the Shanahans wanted. The truth, however, is that the McNabb trade happened at the behest of owner Daniel Snyder, a well-known meddler.

The Shanahans actually wanted Rams quarterback Marc Bulger. Snyder, however, preferred McNabb. Coincidentally (or not), the Rams retained Bulger's rights until the day after Washington traded for McNabb, cutting Bulger and making him a free agent at a time when Washington had just acquired its starter for the 2010 season.

Unsurprisingly, the move to bring McNabb to DC didn't work. Mike Shanahan and Donovan McNabb got along almost as poorly as Mike Shanahan and defensive tackle Albert Haynesworth. But Shanahan had inherited Haynesworth, whereas McNabb arrived on Shanahan's watch.

McNabb refused to embrace new ways, with his recalcitrance most evident in the much-publicized refusal to wear a wristband containing the plays to be used during a given game. The story created the impression that McNabb wasn't smart enough to know the plays and was too stubborn to change his ways, especially since many quarterbacks used wristbands containing the plays. McNabb would later describe the manner in which he was treated by the Shanahans as "disrespectful and disgraceful."

Mike Shanahan benched McNabb in December for first-rounder-turned-journeyman Rex Grossman, with Shanahan explaining to reporters at the time, "If I do make a mistake, I admit it and move on."

It's a smart approach, although the smartest approach is to not make a mistake in the first place. Still, too many coaches and executives compound their mistakes by refusing to admit them. Doubling down ultimately makes the situation worse for everyone involved because the hope/wish/prayer that a bad situation will improve rarely works.

Thus, even though Washington lost the McNabb trade by burning multiple draft picks on a player from whom the team got thirteen starts, it could have been worse. The team could have kept McNabb into 2011 rather than getting what it could for him after the 2010 season in a trade to Minnesota that yielded a sixth-round pick.

The Vikings, like Washington, would quickly realize the error of their ways, benching McNabb during the 2011 season after five losses in six starts and eventually releasing him. He hoped at the time to sign with another team, but none of the NFL's other franchises were willing to put themselves in the position of eventually having to admit their own mistake.

BEN ROETHLISBERGER'S REDEMPTION

PITTSBURGH'S FIRST FRANCHISE quarterback since Terry Bradshaw didn't need long to become one of the most accomplished players in football. He then didn't need long to become a pariah.

Thrust into the lineup as a rookie, despite publicly voiced concerns from players such as veteran guard Alan Faneca ("Do you want to go work with some little young kid who's just out of college?" Faneca said when Roethlisberger replaced an injured Tommy Maddox), Roethlisberger led the Steelers to a 15–1 record and a berth in the AFC Championship. After the Steelers lost to the Patriots, Roethlisberger's legend as an embellisher of injuries was born. He claimed that he had played the game with multiple broken toes. Coach Bill Cowher responded by telling reporters that Roethlisberger had precisely zero broken toes.

Roethlisberger and the Steelers achieved the long-coveted "one for the thumb" the next year, capturing Pittsburgh's fifth Super Bowl win a full twenty-six years after the team's fourth. But then problems began to come to light.

Roethlisberger was regarded by his teammates as petulant, aloof, and standoffish, and those familiar with the situation say he skipped the Las Vegas retirement party of running back Jerome Bettis, even though Roethlisberger happened to be in Las Vegas at the time. There were also tales of teammates seeking autographs for charities and other good causes, requests that Roethlisberger regularly and at times boorishly refused.

Months after the Super Bowl win, Roethlisberger found himself (as he would tell it) in a near-death experience, riding a motorcycle without a helmet and colliding with a Chrysler. He later claimed that he was "seconds, maybe a minute away from dying" due to blood pouring into his stomach, a claim that was never formally debunked but that also was never widely accepted as truthful. He nevertheless recovered from what was clearly a serious situation and two years later led the Steelers to another Super Bowl victory with a last-second throw to receiver Santonio Holmes for a touchdown that beat the Arizona Cardinals. (Holmes, not Roethlisberger, was named the game's MVP.)

Then came a different sort of wreck for Roethlisberger. In early July 2009, only months after he had reached the top of the NFL mountain for a second time, a Lake Tahoe hotel worker sued Roethlisberger for rape, alleging that he had lured her into his room by claiming that his TV needed to be fixed during a 2008 golf tournament. While the litigation was pending, Roethlisberger had another incident in Milledgeville, Georgia.

The second situation, which happened in March 2010, resulted in the involvement of local authorities, who investigated and considered prosecuting Roethlisberger. Ultimately, no criminal charges were filed, possibly because Roethlisberger reached a financial settlement with the alleged victim.

The NFL did not drop its own case. Roethlisberger eventually received a six-game suspension to start the 2010 season. Fans reacted harshly. Pittsburgh talk radio buzzed with callers who shared tales of insults and other indignities (largely petty and trivial, but why stop a good feeding frenzy?) experienced when encountering Roethlisberger locally during his first six seasons with the team. The Steelers became ambivalent at best about the man known as Big Ben, reportedly exploring opportunities to trade Roethlisberger if a sufficiently high draft pick could be secured for his services. The Steelers claimed that they weren't actively shopping Roethlisberger, but ESPN reported that they had called the Rams, 49ers, Raiders, Bills, Jaguars, Seahawks, and Browns to gauge their interest.

Eventually, and obviously, no trade happened. Roethlisberger complied with the league's directives, and the six-game suspension was dropped to four.

Then came the ultimate basis for forgiving and forgetting—perhaps not for Roethlisberger's alleged victims but definitely for Steelers fans. The Steelers won. They won enough games to get to the playoffs and eventually to return to the Super Bowl in the same season that he served the suspension.

The Super Bowl in Dallas, against the Packers, gave Roethlisberger a chance to win his third Super Bowl title. Even though it ultimately didn't work out—some contend that former offensive coordinator Bruce Arians undermined the effort by trying too hard to position Roethlisberger to win his first-ever Super Bowl MVP award—the ugliness of the suspension and the behavior that had caused it quickly became a footnote, an afterthought, an aberration. In time, as the Steelers continued to field contending teams and as Roethlisberger continued to play like one of the best quarterbacks in the league, the episode largely became overlooked by fans and by the media before it faded away like the memories of the motorcycle wreck.

But not for everyone. Redemption notwithstanding, those who spent multiple years with Roethlisberger remained leery about the supposed transformation, which some thought was more about saving his career than actually growing, maturing, and changing. One former teammate put it plainly and directly when asked about Ben Roethlisberger in the years after the supposed redemption that followed the various events and incidents that dotted his early days in Pittsburgh.

Said the teammate, "He a turd."

TEBOWMANIA

NO QUARTERBACK EVER captured so much of the American imagination with so little quarterbacking ability as Tim Tebow. Even today, legions of Tebowmaniacs refuse to believe that he simply wasn't good enough, clinging instead to the notion that his time in the NFL ended prematurely for other reasons, with the most popular argument being that his devout Christianity ended his career—as if the ranks of NFL players and coaches aren't rife with devout Christians.

It wasn't that Tebow had no ability. It was that his ability seemed to surface only in the closing minutes of a close game. For whatever reason, that was when Tebow mustered the magic that made him one of the biggest stories of the 2011 season.

The former Florida quarterback, a Heisman Trophy winner and one of the best college quarterbacks of all time, became the starter in Denver's sixth game, a bizarre University of Florida reunion game played in the stadium that the Dolphins share with the University of Miami. To get to the top of the depth chart, Tebow leapfrogged Brady Quinn, a failed former first-round pick of the Browns who had earned the backup job.

"I felt like the fans had a lot to do with that," Quinn told GQ in 2012. "Just 'cause they were chanting his name. There was a big calling for him. No, I didn't have any billboards. That would have been nice."

Though Quinn may have deserved the chance to supplant Kyle Orton, Denver's struggling starter at the time, Tebow turned Denver's season around. Against the Dolphins, Tebow led the Broncos back from a 15–0 fourth-quarter deficit. Blown out the next week by the Lions, Tebow and the Broncos thereafter racked up six straight wins, with Tebow typically finding a way to make a big play when the team needed it most despite any and all struggles earlier in any game.

At times, it was laughable. In a 17–10 win over the Chiefs, Tebow completed only two of eight passes. But one of the two connections happened on a long pass that happened to land in the arms of receiver Eric Decker for a 56-yard touchdown.

That was how it went for Tebow. At times embarrassingly inaccurate, he'd somehow pull it together when he had to. That actually tracked with his time in Gainesville; as one person with knowledge of the dynamics explained it while Tebowmania flourished, the Gators coaching staff often would express dismay at Tebow's horrible practice sessions in the days preceding a game. Come Saturday, he'd somehow get it together.

His improbable winning streak became just enough to get the Broncos to the playoffs. Despite three straight losses to end the season, Denver's 8–8 record secured the crown in a subpar AFC West, giving the Broncos a wild-card home game against the 12–4 Steelers.

Pittsburgh's game plan hinged on daring Tebow to win the game with his arm. And he did, generating 236 yards in regulation and connecting with receiver Demaryius Thomas on an 80-yard catch and run for the game-winning touchdown on the first snap of overtime. Tebow's final passing yardage of 316 (3:16) fascinated certain religious types, who regarded the performance as some sort of divine message. (Although I'm a lifelong Catholic, I'm not big on the idea that God sends messages through random items of football statistics, or potato chips. And I may have expressed that skepticism in the days after the game by saying to someone who was blown away by the 316 passing yards, "What if he throws for 666 this week?")

The next round of the playoffs brought a rematch with the Patriots, and coach Bill Belichick knew precisely how to overcome Tebowmania. Tebow couldn't shine in the clutch if there was no clutch. So the Patriots made it their business to blow the Broncos out in both December and January. They scored early, they scored often, and they ran up the score to the point where no amount of late-game heroics could come close to closing the gap.

The Broncos knew that Tebow's antics could never sustain his unlikely achievements of 2011. That was why Hall of Fame quarterback
John Elway, who had been given the reins of the football operation a year
earlier, aggressively pursued future Hall of Fame quarterback Peyton
Manning for the 2012 season. The acquisition of Manning meant that
Tebow could be unloaded onto another team. The Jets offered a fourth-
and sixth-round pick for Tebow, and the Broncos happily cut the cord.

Equally happily, Tebow joined the Jets, uttering the term "excited" or
some variation thereof more than forty times in his introductory press
conference. Few were excited by Tebow's lone season in New York, which
featured cameo appearances and never anything close to the excitement
he had created the prior year.

He spent time with the Eagles and Patriots in 2013 and 2015, respectively, before failing to make the fifty-three-man roster with either
team. He refused opportunities to play in the CFL, possibly to avoid
losing the benefit of the argument that he was indeed good enough to
play in the NFL but that for whatever reason, the NFL had wrongfully
shunned him.

Eventually, Tebow decided to launch a belated baseball career. Although he lacked the chops to make it, the Mets organization realized
the value of Tebowmania and nudged him up the ladder of the various
levels of the minor-league system with an eye toward eventually seizing
the revenue that would come from giving him a spot on the big-league
club. Injury, the pandemic, and age ultimately conspired to keep that
from happening.

And so Tebowmania fizzled in two different sports leagues. In the
NFL, however, Tebowmania had its fifteen minutes of fame.

Or, as the case may be, its three minutes and sixteen seconds. Plus
a blink-and-you-missed-it second NFL act as a tight end playing for his
former college coach, Urban Meyer, in Jacksonville.

ANDREW LUCK RETIRES

FEW ITEMS OF NFL news trigger the "I remember exactly where I was when I heard it" reaction that major world events will often spark. The sudden and abrupt retirement of Colts quarterback Andrew Luck just days before the start of the 2019 regular season prompted many football fans and media members to have the surrounding circumstances seared permanently into their brains.

The night it happened, my wife and I slowly made our way out of a Broadway theater (my memory isn't sufficiently clear to include the show we'd seen, which probably means the show wasn't very good). After nearly three hours of playhouse-mandated offline time, I powered up my phone and pulled up the ProFootballTalk.com (PFT) Twitter profile to see if I'd missed anything.

I had missed something. Something so big that I initially thought the account had been hacked. Andrew Luck? Retiring? At twenty-nine? Once I confirmed that it was true, I did what any NFL fan in an upscale theater would do. I cursed a little too loudly and immediately caught a glare from my wife.

It made no sense. Luck had signed a long-term contract just three years earlier that had made him the highest-paid player in league history. Although he'd since been leapfrogged multiple times as the bar moved north of $30 million per year, Luck was earning $25 million per year on average at the time he walked away. Given the position he played, he could have continued to receive a compensation package at the going rate and higher for another decade.

The Colts had happily nudged Peyton Manning out of town seven years earlier because they'd earned dibs on Luck, perhaps the best quarterback prospect since Manning himself. Initially, it appeared that the Colts would eventually develop into the same type of consistent contender that they had been from 1999 (Manning's second season) through 2010 (Manning's last healthy one).

During Luck's rookie year, and despite a leukemia diagnosis that sidelined first-year head coach Chuck Pagano for most of the season, the Colts went 11–5 and made it to the playoffs. The next year, the Colts again went 11–5, returned to the playoffs, and had a postseason comeback for the ages, turning a 38–10 second-half deficit against the Chiefs into a victory. The next year, the Colts once again won eleven of sixteen regular-season games before making it all the way to the AFC Championship. (The franchise continues to be derided for hanging a banner from the rafters of its home stadium acknowledging that the Colts were a "2014 AFC Finalist.")

Then the trouble started. With a subpar wall of linemen to block for him, Luck began to take a pounding. He missed nine games in 2015. He was injured throughout 2016. He missed all of 2017 with a shoulder injury that many believe began with a snowboarding mishap.

In 2018, Luck managed to play in all sixteen regular-season games, leading the Colts to a 10–6 record, a wild-card win, and a date with the Chiefs in the divisional round. No one who attended or watched the game realized that it would be the last time Luck would wear an NFL uniform.

Officially, Luck suffered a calf injury while working out on his own after the 2018 season. Officially, the calf injury lingered, keeping him from participating in offseason workouts, training camp, or the preseason. Through it all, the Colts projected optimism and confidence that he'd return and that he'd be back by the start of the games that count.

Then came the Saturday-night news that Luck planned to announce his retirement the next day at a press conference. Some believed then (and still believe now) that someone with the Colts deliberately leaked the news during a home preseason game. If so, the move showed diabolical brilliance; the crowd at Lucas Oil Stadium gradually became aware that Luck, who had attended the game in street clothes, would walk away from football. As he walked off the field for the final time, Luck heard boos.

The truth regarding Luck's decision to walk away from multiple hundreds of millions in future earnings remains elusive. Some say he'd grown weary of the injuries. Some believe his then future spouse feared long-term cognitive issues. Few, in the time since Luck has retired, have suggested that Luck would ever return.

He still could. Only thirty-two at the time these words were printed on this page, Luck could come back and play another ten years, especially since he has avoided three seasons of football wear and tear. Unlike others who made a sport out of retiring and unretiring, however, Luck has always seemed to have made a final and permanent decision. Even as more great young quarterbacks enter the NFL through each and every draft, the last thing the NFL needs is an exodus of the best throwers of the football during what should have been the prime of their careers.

Luck likely will be the aberration. But the swift and sudden shock that came from his walking away should at a minimum make everyone wary of the nagging possibility that at any time, any player (regardless of age, talent, or accomplishments) could decide that he's had enough of the game long before the game decides that it's had enough of him.

THE COLLEGE OFFENSE REVOLUTION

GOOD COACHING CONSISTS of figuring out what the available players do well and doing it plus figuring out what the available players don't do well and not doing it. This simple proposition, however, often yields to the egos of coaches who have developed their own "systems" into which the available players must fit, or other players who fit the system will be found.

For decades, that stubborn insistence possibly contributed to college quarterbacks not achieving the kind of success at the NFL level that they could or should have experienced. Instead of embracing the things those quarterbacks did in college to attract the attention of the NFL, pro coaches tried to force them into being something they weren't, making an already challenging adjustment to the NFL even more difficult.

While the eventual failure of a supposed can't-miss quarterback prospect is possibly tied to many factors, embracing the offense the player ran at the college level tends to boost the player's chances for professional success. Eventually, NFL coaches have figured that out.

The Panthers helped prove the value of adapting a pro offense to a college offense with Cam Newton. In 2013, Newton's third NFL season, first-year Carolina offensive coordinator Mike Shula studied Newton's film from Auburn to find things that had worked well for him in college. Other coaches have decided not to insist that a young quarterback adapt to the existing NFL system but have instead adapted the existing system to the young quarterback. Simple yet brilliant, the newfound flexibility of previously hardheaded NFL coaches has helped them to get more out of their young quarterbacks and to allow them to become great players sooner rather than later at the professional level.

It's no coincidence that, for several straight years, young quarterbacks have emerged as league MVP candidates. In 2017, Eagles quarterback Carson Wentz—in only his second season—became the favorite for the top individual regular-season award until he suffered a December knee injury. In 2018, Chiefs quarterback Patrick Mahomes—in only his second season—took the league by storm and became the MVP. In 2019, Ravens quarterback Lamar Jackson—in only his second season—took the league by storm and became the MVP. In 2020, Cardinals quarterback Kyler Murray—in only his second season—took the league by storm and injected himself into the field of MVP finalists before fading down the stretch, largely due to a shoulder injury.

The end result has in many instances turned the notion of a "pro-style" offense on its head. If a quarterback thrived in the shotgun formation at the college level, why force him to take snaps under center in the NFL? Kyler Murray has become just as effective operating almost exclusively out of the shotgun as any quarterback who receives the ball in the more traditional way.

If a quarterback produced significant results for a college offense by running the ball, why prevent him from running the ball in the pros? Although the risk of injury remains ever present (especially with larger, faster, and stronger defensive players), a quarterback such as Lamar Jackson has become as effective as a runner in the NFL as he was in college. It makes sense to let him do it instead of trying to force him to become something he isn't.

That's ultimately the key to getting the most out of a football player: have him do the things he does best and have him not do the things he does worst. And always try to find someone who can do as many of the things a quarterback does as well as anyone can.

Those quarterbacks are hard to find. Great runners often aren't the best passers, and the best passers often aren't the best runners. But the threat of a great runner running the ball makes it easier to pass, and vice versa.

Ultimately, the quality that separates the best quarterbacks from the not-best quarterbacks comes from the ability to run the so-called second play. The first play gets called in the huddle. If/when the first play falls apart, as it often does, can the quarterback turn failure into success?

The key to making the second play work on the fly is often tied to mobility and speed, but it also requires the kind of cool head that many quarterbacks simply don't have. For them, when the first play goes to hell, the best move becomes throwing the ball away or hitting the deck before getting hit, the proverbial sacrifice aimed at living to play another day. For the best quarterbacks, the moment the first play falls apart becomes an opportunity to show what they can do, moving laterally until a receiver pops open or taking off vertically, running to where the defensive players aren't and moving the chains or scoring points.

Plenty of coaches can't stomach that kind of uncertainty. They want their systems run the way they're meant to be run, with the plays followed precisely and with little or no discretion exercised by the quarterback. Those coaches don't want someone who can turn chaos into success, fearful that from time to time the result will be failure.

Still, the best quarterbacks keep their heads and use their legs and arms to salvage a first play that has gone to pot. For them, it's no different than what they did in college. It's ultimately no different than what they did on a sandlot when they first realized that they possessed physical skills far superior to those of their peers.

For all the strategic nuances of football, there's no replacement for having the best possible athletes. The best coaches of the modern NFL fully embrace that reality, recognizing that the best way to get the most out of their players is to rely on the truly best athletes to transcend playbooks and circumstances and make good things happen, even when everything has otherwise turned bad.

PATRICK MAHOMES
CHANGES EVERYTHING

ATTENTION, ASPIRING NFL quarterbacks. Play baseball. Specifically, play shortstop.

Shortstopping skills have become the secret ingredient for the NFL's version of the Michael Jordan college-to-pro transformation. Patrick Mahomes, an above-average quarterback at Texas Tech regarded vaguely as a potential first-round pick but not as a superstar, has become one of the biggest superstars the NFL has ever seen. He's so good and so consistent that many fans and media have already become bored by his antics.

Mahomes can make every throw from every arm angle and body position, passing posture and mechanics be damned. He told me during 2018, his first year as a starter and his first of many MVP seasons, that playing baseball has helped him become a quarterback who doesn't need to stand a certain way with his hips positioned a certain way and his shoulders pointing a certain way and his arm moving a certain way. A shortstop who fields a grounder, rips the horsehide sphere from his glove, grips the stitches however they may be positioned, and fires the ball to first base lacks the luxury of worrying about form or technique. It's all about getting the ball there ASAFP, legs and butt and torso and shoulders and arms and head be damned.

Mahomes has become the first quarterback to fully embrace a shortstop's approach to playing football. The receivers play the role of first basemen, and Mahomes plays the infielder who seizes the opportunity to spin the ball however he can from wherever he is. In 2018, he'd already shown us everything he can do, from sidearm throws to no-look throws to cross-body throws to falling-out-of-bounds throws to falling-down throws to everything but a behind-the-back throw, which is in his arsenal but which (through 2020) he has yet to use in a game.

Of course, Mahomes isn't the first infielder to play quarterback at an extremely high level. Seahawks quarterback Russell Wilson has that get-it-to-first-now experience, and he routinely shows it. The difference comes from the buildup. Wilson does it so quickly and effortlessly that it's hard to notice the cobra strike that results in the ball leaving his hand and landing in the grip of a receiver.

Mahomes has a hair-on-fire quality as he weaves through and around larger, stronger, and faster football players who are trying (and usually failing) to catch him. That serves as the pledge and the turn, with the prestige completing what to any observer does indeed look like a magic trick.

Mahomes's adjustment to the NFL accelerated as a result of his experiences as a child. His father, Pat, played professional baseball. Patrick spent plenty of time in the clubhouse, watching and learning and losing the sense of awe and intimidation that comes from being around a group of elite professional athletes. And so, when he sauntered into a pro football locker room for the first time, it wasn't foreign soil—it was home.

In hindsight, it's stunning that the Chiefs didn't make him the starter sooner. Teammates including tight end Travis Kelce told me during Mahomes's rookie season that he was doing "amazing" things in practice. The football-watching world got a quick glimpse of that in the 2017 preseason when Mahomes (after looking behind him to see if the referee had thrown a flag for holding) rolled to his right, waited for a receiver to get open deep down the field, and fired a piss missile into the nighttime sky and into the hands of the intended target, taking a hit to the chops after he released the ball. When the Kansas City offense struggled, however, during the regular season, coach Andy Reid decided to let Alex Smith finish what he'd started, waiting to embrace Mahomes in 2018.

As special as that 2018 season became, it ended with Mahomes standing on the sideline while the Patriots, after winning the overtime toss, took the ball the length of the field for a walk-off touchdown. The next year entailed similarly spectacular performances until Mahomes suffered a knee injury on a Thursday night in Denver that knocked him out for multiple games and, consequently, resulted in most of the league forgetting what he and the Chiefs could do. After a snow-globe rematch with the Broncos in December in which Mahomes performed as if he'd been born to throw in a blizzard, Mahomes told me that he liked the fact that he and his team had been overlooked.

What followed may take many years to fully appreciate. Down 24 to Houston in the first half of the divisional round of the playoffs, Mahomes and the Chiefs came back and easily won. Down 10 twice to Tennessee in the first half of the AFC Championship, Mahomes and the Chiefs came back and easily won. Down 10 to San Francisco with seven minutes left in Super Bowl LIV, Mahomes connected with receiver Tyreek Hill on a long throw that changed everything in a flash, setting the stage for the first Kansas City Super Bowl win in exactly fifty years, with a final margin of 11 points.

Fifty years from now, football historians quite possibly will look back on the career of Mahomes as the thing that sparked a generation of kids who tried to do the many things he can do with a football—and that resulted in plenty of them realizing that they possessed the skills to do it, sparking a slew of NFL quarterbacks who eventually will play the game just as he did. If it happens, it will be great for the game, and it will prove that Patrick Mahomes did indeed change everything.

THE QUARTERBACK TAKEOVER

IT STARTED WITH Tom Brady leaving the Patriots for the Buccaneers. It continued with Brady's new team gladly bringing along his friends and former teammates, trading a fourth-round draft pick for retired tight end Rob Gronkowski plus a seventh-round pick and signing star-receiver-turned-pariah Antonio Brown. It accelerated with Brady commandeering offseason workouts during the early months of the pandemic, ignoring a recommendation from the NFLPA that players avoid get-togethers before training camp and quoting FDR on social media, proclaiming that the "only thing we have to fear is fear itself." And it culminated in the Buccaneers willingly allowing a six-time Super Bowl champion to take full and complete leadership of the locker room, propelling the team from a 7–5 start to an 8–0 finish and Brady's seventh NFL championship.

Other quarterbacks took notice. More importantly, other quarterbacks took action. Before the postseason ended, Texans quarterback Deshaun Watson—only four months after signing a four-year, $156 million contract—made it clear he wanted out. The tipping point for Watson was the team's broken promise to include him in the search for a new coach and GM, ignoring his suggestion that the Texans interview Chiefs offensive coordinator Eric Bieniemy and 49ers defensive coordinator Robert Saleh. Although an off-field situation (more on that later) complicated his quest to be traded, the Texans took the situation seriously and promptly began planning to move forward with someone else under center.

Only days after a Brady Super Bowl win that Seahawks quarterback Russell Wilson witnessed from a luxury suite (TV cameras showed him looking miserable as a spectator), Wilson explained that he wanted more involvement in personnel matters during an interview with Dan Patrick. Wilson voiced concern about the number of sacks he has taken, a not-so-subtle knock against his offensive line. He also made it clear that, after nine years in the NFL, he wants to play for more championships than the single Super Bowl he won to cap the 2013 season.

"You know what I hate?" Wilson said at the time. "I hate sitting there watching other guys play the game."

He also hates being treated like a mere employee. Other quarterbacks feel the same way and for good reason. Teams expect quarterbacks to arrive early, to stay late, to set the example for other players. Teams expect quarterbacks to hold teammates accountable, to serve as the representative of the coaching staff in the locker room, to essentially be a boss on the shop floor. But then, when the quarterback shows up for a management meeting, he's told to wait outside. It shouldn't be that way.

Wilson's frustration reportedly came in part from the fact that, after a pair of losses during the 2020 season and days before a short-week contest against the Cardinals, he suggested some tweaks to the offense. He was told, politely or otherwise, to mind his own business.

A different type of disrespect fractured the relationship between the Packers and franchise quarterback Aaron Rodgers. During the first round of the 2020 draft, Green Bay (holding the thirtieth pick) wanted to select receiver Justin Jefferson. The Vikings took Jefferson with the twenty-second overall selection. Next, the Packers targeted receiver Brandon Aiyuk. The 49ers jumped the line to get him, trading up from No. 31 to No. 25. Shell-shocked by missing out on their top two players, the Packers traded up to No. 26—and picked not a receiver but a quarterback, Jordan Love. To make matters worse, the Packers failed to tell Rodgers that they planned to use a first-round pick on his potential successor.

Rodgers didn't like it. In a private conversation with former Packers quarterback Brett Favre (the starter when the Packers had picked Rodgers in round one fifteen years earlier), Rodgers admitted that he felt like the "odd man out." He internalized his frustration, putting together one of the best seasons of his career and winning the NFL MVP award for the third time. After losing to Brady's Buccaneers at home in an NFC Championship game that the Packers were favored to win, Rodgers spoke like a guy who didn't know whether he'd be back in Green Bay, admitting that plenty of players' future with the team was "uncertain, myself included." He later tried, during his weekly appearance on Pat McAfee's show, to downplay the comment as an acknowledgment that there are "not many absolutes" in this business.

That successfully calmed things down (but for a report that the Rams tried to trade for Rodgers before acquiring quarterback Matthew Stafford from the Lions). Eventually, it all blew up again.

Hours before the commencement of the 2021 draft, Paul Allen of KFAN in Minneapolis reported that the 49ers had tried to trade for Rodgers. Then, ESPN reported that Rodgers wanted out of Green Bay. Then, a cascade of details confirming his desire for a divorce emerged, capped by a PFT report that his wish list consisted of the 49ers, Broncos, and Raiders.

It quickly became obvious that Rodgers had a problem not with his teammates or his coaching staff but with the front office. Charles Robinson of Yahoo Sports reported that Rodgers wanted the Packers to fire GM Brian Gutekunst. Rodgers had a chance to refute that and any other report while attending the Kentucky Derby, but he declined to speak on camera with NBC's Mike Tirico. Instead, Tirico and Rodgers spoke off camera—and Tirico later explained that a "fissure" and a "chasm" existed between Rodgers and the Green Bay organization.

Tom Brady's win over the Packers in a game with a Super Bowl berth on the line (despite three second-half interceptions that nearly allowed Green Bay to steal the game) became the explosion of a bomb, the fuse of which had been lit when the Packers drafted Love. Speeding along the process was the juxtaposition of Green Bay's plan to eventually replace Rodgers with Love and a season in which the Buccaneers made everything they did all about Brady. Indeed, later comments from Rodgers to Kenny Mayne of ESPN made it clear that Rodgers believed the team had planned to make the change after the 2020 season but that the "wrench was just kind of thrown into it when I won the MVP and played the way I played last year."

After three months of uncertainty regarding whether Rodgers would show up for the 2021 season, he did. In return, the team wiped out the final year of his contract for 2023, setting the stage for a divorce via trade as early as March 2022 (it may have become official on the day after this book was released) unless Rodgers and the Green Bay front office somehow find a way to mend fences that in recent years have been blown to smithereens.

From Watson to Wilson to Rodgers, the fact that Brady found a team that treated him like more than just a player has caused them to want to play for teams that will do the same. As time passes, more and more quarterbacks will seek similar consideration. As more and more teams capitulate to this quarterback takeover, more and more teams will have to go along or risk having their long-term answer at the most important position in football decide to become a short-timer.

PART IV
COACHES

THE JON GRUDEN TRADE

FOR THEIR FIRST twenty years after joining the NFL, the Tampa Bay Buccaneers stunk. Then came Tony Dungy, and the stinking quickly stopped.

It took a year to eradicate those two decades of mostly foul odor; Dungy's Bucs won only six games in 1996. By the second year, however, things began to fall into place. Dungy's genius-level expertise on the defensive side of the ball, combined with excellent drafting and development of players at every level of the defense, established over time a unit that rivaled all great offense-stifling squads of the past.

The 1997 season featured a 5–0 start and a 10–6 finish, good enough for the team's first playoff appearance in fifteen years as well as only its second postseason victory in franchise history, a wild-card win over the Lions. After a one-year failure to qualify for the postseason (the combined presence of Randy Moss and Brett Favre with the Vikings and Packers, respectively, made it much harder to compete in the NFC Central), the Bucs made it all the way to the NFC Championship game, holding the St. Louis Rams, also known at the time as the Greatest Show(-offs) on Turf, to 11 points, though scoring only 6.

The advancement to the final four in Dungy's fourth season raised expectations that the next two years failed to match. So, after a second straight wild-card loss to the Eagles to cap the 2001 season, the Buccaneers decided to fire Dungy based on concerns that his offense was too conservative.

Firing a coach makes up only half of a fairly important equation for an NFL franchise. If a good team hopes to improve after moving on from its current coach, it needs to find another one at least as good, if not better.

Bill Parcells became Tampa Bay's first choice. The deal seemed to be done, to the point that Jets executive Mike Tannenbaum prepared to become the Buccaneers' GM in anticipation of Parcells's arrival for what would have been his fourth different NFL head-coaching job. (He'd eventually take job number four a year later, in Dallas.) But then Parcells jilted the Bucs, leaving them without a clear-cut candidate to try to take the team Dungy had built to the next level.

The Buccaneers then entered desperation mode, targeting the coaches of both Bay Area teams for a potential trade. In this context, however, "trade" doesn't really apply—no matter how loudly Jon Gruden likes to claim the Raiders "traded" him to the Buccaneers. For Gruden or for Steve Mariucci, who at the time coached the 49ers, the process entailed the Buccaneers working out compensation with the coach's current team if a hire was to be made, followed by an effort to persuade the coach to make the jump to the new team. Unlike players, who (absent a no-trade clause in their contracts) can be moved indiscriminately from team to team, a coach can't be sent to a new franchise unless the coach wants to go.

Gruden undoubtedly wanted to go, even though the Buccaneers negotiated a horrible deal to secure his services. With Gruden entering the final year of his contract with the Raiders, and with Raiders owner Al Davis already souring on Gruden, who was becoming bigger than the team (and, more importantly, than Davis himself), the Buccaneers' interest in Gruden hardly disrupted a long-term arrangement that had been intended to last for another decade or longer. The two sides were already moving toward a divorce, and the Buccaneers paid handsomely to accelerate it.

Tampa Bay sacrificed two first-round picks, two second-round picks, and $8 million in cash for permission to hire Gruden. Despite the steep price, the move paid off immediately. Gruden goosed the offense just enough to complement a defense that remained powerful, thanks to the skills and abilities of Tony Dungy. And with the Bucs facing the Raiders in the Super Bowl, Gruden knew more than enough about the offense he had constructed to help his new defense dismantle it.

Still, the Bucs under Gruden could never duplicate the success of 2002 or even come close to it. Gruden failed to take the team back to the postseason in 2003 and 2004, and he led the team to the playoffs only twice after 2002, engineering one-and-done playoff appearances in 2005 and 2007. After the 2008 season, the Buccaneers abruptly dumped him.

Most would say the Super Bowl win justified the final price tag for a coach the Bucs could have gotten a year later for nothing. Others would look at the full body of Gruden's tenure in Tampa Bay as falling short of what was expected. Regardless, the Buccaneers had found themselves in a tough spot, and they had created a solution that entailed snagging a head coach from another team.

Given the number of desperate teams constantly seeking ways to reverse their fortunes and in light of the significance of a good coach getting the most out of a roster of players, it's surprising that more teams don't try it. Apart from the Chiefs hiring Herm Edwards away from the Jets in 2006 for a fourth-round pick at a time when the Jets were planning to fire Edwards anyway, the tactic hasn't been used. In fact, it's rarely ever even mentioned as a possibility.

Some wonder whether it's part of a gentleman's agreement that teams won't try to intervene in the relationship between another team and its coach since at a minimum, that could give the coach a basis for leveraging his current contract into a better one. Others think it's part of a broader effort by Commissioner Roger Goodell, on whose watch such a move has never happened, to reduce the overall power of coaches. The fact that it happens so rarely and is mentioned so infrequently invites speculation that something deeper is happening, something aimed at keeping it from ever even coming close to happening.

Still, it came incredibly close to happening in 2019. The Cowboys, who had Jason Garrett under contract for another year, wanted to hire Sean Payton from the New Orleans Saints. Payton, at the time, was ready to make the move. As the Cowboys and Saints closed in on a deal regarding the compensation New Orleans would receive from Dallas, something happened. Something completely unrelated to the Cowboys, the Saints, the NFL, or Sean Payton.

Per a source with knowledge of the situation, here's what occurred. New Orleans Pelicans star Anthony Davis made it known in late

January that he wanted out of town. Saints GM Mickey Loomis also served, at the time, as the executive VP of basketball operations for the Pelicans since both teams were held by the same owner. Once Davis made it known that he'd be leaving, Loomis decided he couldn't be the common thread between the bang-bang departures of Davis and Payton from New Orleans.

Instead, the Saints signed Payton to an extension—ending his Dallas dalliance. At least for a few years.

THE ROONEY RULE

FEW THINGS FORCE meaningful change in American business like the credible threat of meritorious litigation. In 2002, the NFL faced just that regarding the league's abysmal record as to the hiring of minority head coaches.

The late Johnnie Cochran, best known for a seven-word mantra first uttered in the closing argument that cemented the acquittal of O. J. Simpson, teamed up with Cyrus Mehri to address the fact that the NFL's teams had hired only five Black head coaches since 1986: Art Shell, Dennis Green, Tony Dungy, Ray Rhodes, and Herman Edwards. Cochran and Mehri's report, titled "Black Coaches in the National Football League: Superior Performance, Inferior Opportunities," served as a clear warning to the league. Change voluntarily, or have change forced upon you through the civil justice system.

The argument was simple: regardless of the processes used to screen and to hire candidates, the results spoke for themselves.

The NFL opted for voluntary change. It came in the form of a simple but groundbreaking requirement that at least one minority candidate be interviewed for every head-coaching vacancy. The measure carried the name of Steelers owner Dan Rooney, a widely respected figure whose attachment to the policy gave it significant and instant credibility.

Critics complained then, and still complain today, that business owners should be able to hire and fire whomever they choose. It's a skewed interpretation of management rights that overlooks the many federal, state, and local protections against decisions that are influenced, consciously or not, by factors that never should be considered, such as race, age, gender, national original, disability, and sexual orientation. The NFL's owners reluctantly agreed to the fairly simple mandate aimed at slowing the process long enough to ensure that at least one minority candidate had been considered, possibly because most realized that at the end of the day, they would still retain the ability to hire and fire without any external scrutiny or oversight.

Some opted for perfunctory compliance, forcing the NFL to enhance and clarify the rule on the fly. When Cowboys owner Jerry Jones hired Bill Parcells in 2003, for example, Jones gave Dennis Green a box-checking interview by telephone. This prompted the NFL to require all minority interviews to happen in person. When Lions GM Matt Millen fired Marty Mornhinweg so that Steve Mariucci could be hired to coach the team (and everyone knew it), minority candidates such as Lions offensive coordinator Sherm Lewis refused to participate in a sham interview. Millen received a $500,000 fine.

The league otherwise has engaged in any and all necessary mental and linguistic gymnastics to avoid building a body of evidence that could and would be used in court, finding ways to excuse violations of the letter and/or spirit of the Rooney Rule. In 2009, for example, when the league's worst-kept secret was that Washington owner Daniel Snyder would fire Jim Zorn and hire Mike Shanahan, Snyder interviewed defensive backs coach Jerry Gray for the job prior to firing Zorn. The league found that this complied with the Rooney Rule, even though the minority candidate was interviewed for the job before it was vacant.

In late 2017, Raiders owner Mark Davis worked out a verbal agreement with former Raiders and Buccaneers coach Jon Gruden to replace Jack Del Rio as head coach, even though Del Rio still had the job (and even though Del Rio was represented by the same agent as Gruden). The league eventually found that the Raiders had complied with the Rooney Rule by interviewing Raiders tight end coach Bobby Johnson and USC offensive coordinator Tee Martin before officially hiring Gruden. The league also found that Gruden's handshake deal that predated both the firing of Del Rio and the interviews of minority candidates wasn't sufficiently final or binding to make the minority interviews meaningless.

Despite the failure of the league to properly enforce the Rooney Rule (or perhaps because of it), the problem of low minority involvement in key roles persists. In 2020, the NFL considered giving teams that hire minority head coaches or GMs (the rule has been expanded to encompass such jobs) extra draft picks as an incentive to do so. Minority coaches balked at the perception that their hiring would come with an asterisk, and Dungy (now enshrined in the Hall of Fame) said that teams shouldn't be rewarded for doing the right thing—that should be its own reward.

Eventually, the NFL crafted a rule that incentivizes the development of minority coaches and executives who leave to become head coaches and GMs elsewhere, offering extra draft picks as compensation for the team that loses a highly qualified minority assistant. While still somewhat problematic in that it offers a perk for teams doing what they should be doing anyway, the current system, where hiring usually happens on a who-you-know or who-you're-related-to basis, needs improvement.

Progress, or lack thereof, won't become apparent for multiple hiring cycles. Through it all, the league needs to remember that if/when true progress doesn't happen, it could find itself precisely where it was in 2002—facing a credible threat of meritorious litigation from a minority assistant coach or executive who believes that advancement has not occurred for reasons unrelated to skills and abilities. Frankly, it may take that kind of threat to finally force truly meaningful change.

THE RANDY RATIO

FROM TIME TO time, a pro football broadcast will proclaim that a team wins a high percentage of its games when its starting running back runs the ball twenty-five or more times on a given day. This hardly means that forcing handoff after handoff until the player gets to twenty-five will trigger victory. It's a retroactive assessment of statistics and trends, an effort to make sense of why and how a team has won.

Sometimes, coaches try to reverse engineer such statistical truths. When they do, it never works.

The most prominent example of the past twenty years came courtesy of Mike Tice, an overmatched head coach of the Vikings who kept a pencil above his ear at all times, possibly to look smart. (It didn't work.) In 2002, Tice's first full season as the team's head coach, he used that ear pencil to scribble out some math.

Tice realized that in the year that he became the interim coach following the firing of Dennis Green, the Vikings won 80 percent of the games in which Hall of Fame receiver Randy Moss had the ball thrown his way at least 40 percent of the time. So Tice had an idea: the Vikings should throw the ball Randy's way at least 40 percent of the time.

Enter the Randy Ratio.

"It's my phrase," Tice said at the time. "I thought it had a little ring to it. If we throw ten balls in a game, four of those balls should be directed to Randy Moss."

For his part, Moss had no complaints. "If we would have been doing this my rookie year, we would have jewelry around here," Moss said when the idea was hatched.

In Week One against the Bears, the Vikings sent 11 of 28 passes (39.2 percent) in the direction of Moss. Minnesota lost. In Week Two against the Bills, 21 of 45 passes (46.6 percent) went to Moss. Minnesota lost again. In Week Three against the Panthers, the Vikings targeted 10 of 30 throws (33.3 percent) to Moss. They lost yet again. In Week Four against the Seahawks, 15 of 53 passes (28.3 percent) went toward Moss. Another loss.

The season improved, but not by much. Minnesota finished 6–10. Moss had 185 targets (with 106 catches) on 558 throws, a full-season percentage of 33.1 percent. So the team failed to achieve the Randy Ratio and, more importantly, failed to contend for a playoff spot, much less earn the "jewelry" to which Moss had referred.

The Randy Ratio failed because everything like it always does. Although certain plays (screen passes, for example) can be designed to put the ball in a specific receiver's hands, an offense works best when the quarterback has license to throw to the open man. Adding the burden of staring down a specific receiver delays the quarterback's progression through the potential pass catchers on a given play, pressures him to throw into coverage, and otherwise keeps the offense from being as efficient as it can be.

Good coaches realize this, constructing an offense with no specific formula or agenda to throw to the best receiver but trusting the quarterback to take what the defense gives him. If the best receiver is blanketed, someone else will be open. Throw it to him without worrying about being second-guessed on the sideline or berated in the huddle for not forcing it to the star player.

With or without a catchy label, teams still fall into that trap. Most recently, the Browns added undue pressure to quarterback Baker Mayfield for all of 2019 and part of 2020 given the presence of receiver Odell Beckham Jr. The constant stress associated with feeding Beckham made it harder for Mayfield to manage the offense. Although Beckham (like Moss) genuinely believed that sending the football his way improved the chances of winning, good defenses know that taking away that great receiver can short-circuit the offense and create chaos, confusion, and complaints, each of which helps set the stage for offensive failure.

The lesson for all other coaches is clear: don't use statistical trends from games that resulted in victory as a template for forcing the ball in a certain direction. Run the whole offense, let nature take its course, and focus on winning. Whether the running back gets the ball twenty-five times or the star receiver has 40 percent of the targets becomes an interesting analysis in hindsight. It never, ever should be regarded as a recipe for football meatloaf.

NICK SABAN

NFL TEAMS FROM time to time develop a fascination with college football coaches. They hope, when hiring someone from the college game, to duplicate the success of the Cowboys of the 1990s, when Jimmy Johnson leapfrogged from the University of Miami to Dallas in 1989 and immediately began crafting a team that would win three Super Bowls in four seasons. The team Johnson put together had enough talent and ability to win its third Super Bowl two years after owner Jerry Jones foolishly fired Johnson and hired Barry Switzer, who was another former college coach but wasn't nearly as skilled as Johnson.

Plenty of other college coaches ended up being not nearly as skilled as Johnson once they became head coaches at the NFL level. Many believed that Nick Saban, a former NFL assistant who became the head coach at Michigan State and then won a national championship at Louisiana State, would be the exception. As the Dolphins learned, Saban wasn't.

After toying for several years with the idea of jumping to the NFL, Saban came to Miami at the behest of Wayne Huizenga, who gave Saban plenty of cash and the keys to the franchise. Accustomed to running the show in East Lansing and Baton Rouge, Saban took the reins in Miami in 2005. He immediately alienated many both inside and outside the organization with his brusque, no-nonsense style, prompting disgruntled team employees and local media members to share details of idiosyncrasies such as blowing his stack when someone put the wrong type of Little Debbie snack cakes in his office (anything other than the Oatmeal Creme Pie was the wrong type) and issuing a terse memo to all employees to not speak to him after someone made the grave mistake of complimenting his haircut.

Saban inherited a bad team in 2005 (good teams typically aren't looking for new coaches), and after an initial 9–7 season, the Dolphins seemed to be moving in the right direction. Saban believed that the franchise was simply a franchise quarterback away from becoming a consistent contender.

He had some options during the 2006 offseason, but not many. Ultimately, it came down to two: free agent Drew Brees, who was leaving the Chargers, and veteran Vikings quarterback Daunte Culpepper, who didn't have a place in the new regime led by coach Brad Childress. Both players had sustained serious injuries. Brees, in the final game of the 2005 regular season, had suffered a shoulder injury that required major surgery. Culpepper had taken a low hit while scrambling during a late-October game against the Panthers and tore multiple knee ligaments.

Brees, despite his eventual run of sustained success in New Orleans, actually wanted to sign with the Dolphins. Saban, as he tells it now, wanted Brees. Saban, as he has told the story multiple times years after the fact, couldn't sign Brees because Miami's doctors wouldn't let him.

After beating around the bush on multiple prior occasions, Saban unloaded in July 2021, claiming that a doctor who "didn't know his ass from a handful of sand" declined to clear Brees medically, preventing the Dolphins from finalizing the contract. Saban also claimed that famed orthopedic surgeon Dr. James Andrews, who had performed the surgery on Brees's shoulder, had said, "It'll be fine."

So much for Saban running the show. Really, if Saban truly were in charge of the team (and he was), he could have overruled Dr. Don't Know My Ass from a Handful of Sand, signing Brees based on the endorsement from Dr. Andrews. Even if the medical staff had the power to trump Saban (it surely didn't), Saban could have taken the matter to Huizenga, explaining the situation and asking the man who holds the equity in the franchise to approve the decision to sign a potential franchise quarterback.

Instead of getting Brees with no compensation to his former team, the Dolphins gave up a second-round pick in a trade for Culpepper, choosing a quarterback with a wrecked knee over a quarterback with a wrecked shoulder. Saban said in 2015 that he'd still possibly be coaching the Dolphins if they'd signed Brees. In 2021, Saban said that he decided after the doctors flunked Brees on his physical, "I'm getting out of here. I'm not staying here."

Neither claim rings true. First, Brees became a Hall of Famer with the Saints due in large part to the skills of coach Sean Payton, an offensive wizard who teamed with Brees to create one of the best coach-quarterback combinations in NFL history. Saban, a defensive specialist, may never have captured that same kind of magic with Brees. Second, Saban rolled the dice with Culpepper and soured on the NFL only after that plan didn't work. Third, Saban (and his wife) badly missed the college game; as the 2006 season unfolded (and after it became clear that the Dolphins wouldn't become contenders) rumors persisted that Saban had become miserable in the NFL and that, after only two years, he'd return to college football.

After Alabama failed to hire Rich Rodriguez from West Virginia, the school came calling for Saban. Chatter of Saban taking over the Crimson Tide grew, culminating in one of the all-time great bald-faced lies in league history. Saban said during a press conference on December 21, 2006, "I'm not going to be the Alabama coach." Fewer than two weeks later, he was.

At Alabama, Saban has become the greatest college football coach of all time, with six national championships (and counting) in Tuscaloosa and teams that contend for a championship even in the years they don't win it. Why, then, does he feel compelled to peddle revisionist history about his time in Miami?

The simplest (and thus likely most accurate) explanation is that Saban knows he failed as an NFL head coach. By pinning the decision not to sign Brees on someone else, Saban plants the seeds for the fairly simple argument that, if the doctors had let him sign Brees, Saban wouldn't have failed. He would have thrived, as he did in Alabama. He would have won multiple NFL championships, as he did in Alabama. And he'd possibly be viewed as the greatest football coach of all time, college or pro.

THE PETER PRINCIPLE,
ON REPEAT

NFL HEAD COACHES come from a handful of finite sources. Teams can hire former head coaches who have resigned or, far more likely, gotten fired. Teams can hire college head coaches. Teams can, but rarely do, try to hire a current head coach from another NFL team. Or, most commonly, teams can hire an offensive or defensive coordinator who never before served as a head coach at any level.

It's the NFL's version of the Peter Principle, a satirical but deadly accurate theory published in 1969 that employees within any business rise to the level of their own incompetence. Within every NFL organization, the first opportunity comes as a "quality control" coach, a fancy title for oftentimes demeaning grunt work. The best of the quality control coaches become position coaches. The best of the position coaches become coordinators. The best of the coordinators (or, more often, the coordinators of the best teams) become head coaches.

Among the various assistant coaches, the job doesn't change dramatically. It's Xs and Os and teaching techniques and plays and concepts and strategies. It's football, and nothing more than football.

For head coaches, different skills come into play. New skills. Skills that someone who has spent years grinding as a pure football strategist may not possess. Head coaches interact with the media. They delegate, or they potentially work themselves into an early grave. They develop a robust pipeline of competent assistants so that when an assistant coach leaves for a promotion elsewhere, the assistant coach can be replaced. They interact directly with the GM and the owner and other executives, who rarely if ever interact with assistant coaches.

Head coaches handle things that most football coaches would rather ignore. Former Buccaneers and Colts coach Tony Dungy tells the story of being asked early in his tenure in Tampa to name the hotel where he'd like the team to stay during a road trip to a specific city.

"Why are you asking me?" Dungy said.

The reply came with a shrug: "Because you're the head coach."

Plenty of coaches immediately thrive in the ultimate coaching job. Plenty don't. Plenty can't make the transition from solely football to all of the other things that go along with football.

Plenty simply can't command the attention and respect of a roomful of grown men. Many fans and media believe that professional athletes find motivation in paychecks and other internal factors, that the days of a raucous "rah-rah" speech or other creative tactics don't matter. They matter. Even the most seasoned, grizzled, and cynical pro football player wants to be inspired, wants to be driven, wants to be led. Coaches who can do that—both when standing before all players and when looking them in the eyes individually—tend to thrive.

Those who can't end up getting fired. It's one of the basic realities of the zero-sum nature of a closed ecosystem with thirty-two teams. For every game won, a game is lost. For every team that succeeds, another fails. And every bad team aspires to become a good team. The easiest and cleanest way to change a team's fortunes quickly, especially given the realities of the salary cap, is not to change the players but to change the coaches.

That dynamic, coupled with fan and media pressure that inevitably builds on teams that languish, causes owners to become impatient, dumping the head coach and searching for another one. The head coach who was dumped sometimes quickly gets another job as an NFL head coach. More often, the head coach who was dumped lands somewhere else as an assistant coach, usually as a coordinator. Sometimes the failed former head coach does so well in his next stint as a coordinator that he eventually becomes a head coach again.

Several coaches have seen this lather-rinse-repeat cycle continuously thrust them into head-coaching jobs for which they simply aren't suited, only to land back in coordinator jobs at which they excel. Norv Turner has become the most prominent example of an offensive coordinator who kept getting hired and fired and hired again. Wade Phillips did the same thing on the defensive side of the ball.

Turner parlayed a stint with the Cowboys in the early 1990s into the head-coaching job in Washington from 1994 into the 2000 season. He then coordinated the offense in San Diego for a year and in Miami for two, performing well enough to attract the attention of Raiders owner Al Davis, who hired Turner to be the head coach. Two years later, the Raiders fired Turner, who stayed in the Bay Area to coordinate the 49ers' offense. A year later, the Chargers made him the head coach, a job he held from 2007 into 2012.

Turner would go back to being an offensive coordinator without ever getting a fourth crack at overcoming the NFL's version of the Peter Principle, but the point was made. Turner routinely did so well as an offensive coordinator that he kept getting chances to do a job he couldn't do well enough, as his career record of 118–126–1 would prove.

Phillips had the same experience, coaching the Broncos in 1993 and 1994, the Bills from 1998 through 2000, and the Cowboys from 2007 into 2010. Including a pair of stints as an interim head coach (Saints and Texans), he finished with a record of 83–69, and he's regarded as one of the best defensive minds of the past fifty years. His defensive acumen kept getting him head-coaching jobs, and his skills as a head coach kept getting him fired.

At least Turner and Phillips kept getting more chances. Most coordinators who become head coaches get one chance to make a good impression. If/when it doesn't work, they go back to being assistants for the rest of their careers, however long or short those careers may be.

THE RESENTMENT
OF BILL BELICHICK

FROM 2001 THROUGH 2019, the New England Patriots had the greatest run of sustained success in NFL history. Nine Super Bowl appearances. Six Super Bowl wins. A division title in every season except 2002 and 2008. It became a generation of mastery, dominance, excellence.

It also spawned widespread resentment.

Unable to compete with the program run masterfully by Bill Belichick, a system premised on working very hard and working very smart and at all times respecting a top-down design in which every person had a role and focused only on that role and nothing else (officially, "Do your job"; unofficially, "Do your fucking job"), other coaches and GMs needed an excuse when pressed by their teams' owners for an explanation of their inability to compete with the so-called Patriot Way.

"We're not good enough" or "We don't work hard enough" didn't fly. And so, inevitably, rivals began to adopt this approach: "If you can't beat 'em, call 'em cheaters."

That was what happened, starting with Spygate I in 2007 (more on that later), Spygate II in 2008 (more on that later), Deflategate (more on that later), and Spygate III in 2019 (you know the drill by now). The Patriots, doing things that others had done in the past and/or were actively still doing, became pursued by those who refused to admit that the Patriots were just better at everything (including the periodic fracturing of the rules). The outcome of the various incidents and allegations has armed fans and media who want to dispute the team's success with the convenient ability to make reckless accusations unsupported by evidence or facts.

In September 2015, after the Steelers lost in New England to open the regular season, Pittsburgh coach Mike Tomlin suggested shenanigans in connection with an issue with the communication system. (Steelers coaches were hearing the New England official radio broadcast instead of each other.) Tomlin made the claim despite having no evidence to support it.

"That's always the case," Tomlin said regarding headset issues when playing at Gillette Stadium in Foxborough. "I said what I said."

The NFL said that Tomlin's contention had no merit, explaining that inclement weather had combined with a power infrastructure issue (whatever that is) to create the problem. The Patriots, in the estimation of the league office, had done nothing wrong.

That doesn't change the fact that fans and media believe that the Patriots are always doing something wrong, that any success comes not from superior preparation and execution but from some form of chicanery. The Ravens, for example, routinely instruct their players when staying in a hotel in the Boston area the night before a game to not put anything relating in any way to game planning or strategy in the trash and to leave nothing in the room that could be found by a housekeeper or maintenance person who may be trying to help out the home team by noticing whatever may be in plain view—or may not.

To some extent, it's human nature to blame failure on foul play, a dynamic that potentially unfolds in any competitive setting. In lieu of admitting that the other side is just better, resort to complaining about corruption, cheating, and fraud. That way, a loss didn't really happen. That way, some will believe that in the absence of cheating, the team that lost would have won.

It's a lazy and irresponsible approach. Yes, the Patriots have aggressively interpreted some rules and quite possibly broken them. Other teams have done the same things and worse, from stealing signals to spying on practices to swiping playbooks to doing anything and everything to gain an edge. Given the high stakes of pro football, the careers that ride on the outcomes of games, and the easy justification based on the reality that everyone does it, well, everyone does it. The Patriots did it, and everything else, too well in the early part of the first decade of the century, making them the inevitable recipient of efforts to apply an asterisk to their accomplishments.

If or when another NFL team has the same kind of sustained success, that team surely will face relentless, and at times wholly baseless, claims of cheating, too. The explanation can never be, after all, that such results are simply the product of sustained excellence.

THE UNREALITY OF THE
NFL'S REALITY SHOW

IT LAUNCHED IN 2001. It peaked in 2010. It still lingers, even though it shouldn't.

Hard Knocks. The NFL's training-camp reality show. Hatched long before 24/7 access allowed fans to know everything there is to know about their favorite team, the NFL Films/HBO joint venture supposedly gives fans a look at what really happens during training camp through the ubiquitous presence of cameras and microphones.

In most respects, it's not real. The team has the ability to veto any and all footage that the producers propose to use. With rare exceptions (more on that in a bit), it creates a skewed depiction that is almost always presented in the light most favorable to the team.

One aspect of *Hard Knocks* that becomes all too real entails the meetings during which players learn that they are being cut or traded. No one wants such a sensitive moment to be recorded and shown to the world. Some coaches (such as Super Bowl LV champion Bruce Arians of the Buccaneers) have insisted that they'd never agree to submit to the show because of that specific aspect of it. Although it humanizes players who when wearing their gear look like robots, it's a little too much humanity.

In 2012, for example, Dolphins GM Jeff Ireland told cornerback Vontae Davis that he'd been traded to the Colts. Davis, shell-shocked by the news, muttered that he needed to call his grandmother. It was objectively heart-wrenching, and it was wrong to let others see Davis in a particularly vulnerable moment.

In 2010, perhaps the best season of the show thanks to the spitfire profanity of Jets coach Rex Ryan, cornerback Antonio Cromartie struggled to rattle off the names of his eight children. The Jets could have insisted that the scene be omitted from the final copy. They didn't. It remains one of the most embarrassing moments in the history of the series.

Concerns regarding a potential double standard when it comes to bad news being communicated have also emerged over the years. In one of the early seasons of *All or Nothing*, an NFL Films/Amazon production that followed teams through the regular season, the Rams fired coach Jeff Fisher with games left to be played. The final product omitted any and all footage from the meeting during which Fisher learned of his fate.

In 2018, the Browns decided to include within *Hard Knocks* certain portions of a meeting that turned awkward when head coach Hue Jackson and offensive coordinator Todd Haley disagreed on whether veteran players should be given rest days in order to keep them healthy. Jackson eventually played the Al Haig card, reminding Haley and the rest of the room that Jackson ran the show. Surprisingly, Jackson later explained that he actually thought the exchange made the coaching staff look good. Unsurprisingly, the Browns fired both Jackson and Haley during the ensuing season.

Other coaches refuse to submit to *Hard Knocks* for completely legitimate strategic reasons. In 2012, Texans defensive end J. J. Watt said that he had picked up Miami's snap count from watching the Dolphins on *Hard Knocks*. Beyond the things that can be gleaned from the scenes that make it to air, coaches such as Bill Belichick have long refused to consider *Hard Knocks* for fear of the ultimate destination of the footage that lands on the cutting-room floor.

The league has created a formula for exempting certain teams from being forced to submit to the show. Only teams that do not have first-year coaches, that have not been to the playoffs in the last two years, and that have done the show within the past decade have an exemption. The rest, in theory, can be compelled to submit.

It has never come to that, fortunately (or maybe unfortunately). Every year, the NFL finds a team that welcomes the intrusion, the hassle, the potential competitive disadvantage. That's because there's always a team that believes five consecutive Tuesday nights on HBO will create a national following for the franchise.

That never happens. It never will. Only consistent winning creates a national following, and teams that win consistently find a way to avoid doing *Hard Knocks*.

Actually, the series would recapture plenty of its cachet if the league ultimately would force a team to do it when the team doesn't want to do it. Coaches would give dirty looks and/or middle fingers to the camera. Scenes could include spirited negotiations and disagreements regarding the limits of the show's access. The tension coming from those who have no desire to be recorded would make the series come far closer to capturing reality than it ever has or ever will.

JIM HARBAUGH VS. JIM SCHWARTZ

IN THE EARLY portions of the past decade, John and Jim Harbaugh became two of the most accomplished coaches in the NFL. Both have reputations for being fiercely intense and competitive. In 2011, that intensity and competition led one of them to cause a minor melee in Michigan.

Those who know both men—Jim coached the 49ers from 2011 through 2014, and John has coached the Ravens since 2008—claim that they possess equal fire but that John usually does a better job of keeping it under wraps (except, for example, when the lights went out in the second half of Super Bowl XLVII, which pitted brothers against each other for the first time ever in the league's championship game). Jim, on the other hand, typically wears his heart, mind, ego, and temper on his sleeve.

It came to a head in Jim's sixth game as coach of the 49ers. And it had its roots in a dinner with the coach of his opponent that day. At the NFL's annual meeting in March, not long after a lockout that would wipe out the offseason program had commenced, Lions coach Jim Schwartz lectured Jim Harbaugh on the challenges of being competitive in his first season on the job given the lack of opportunities to practice from April into June.

"We were having dinner the other night, and Jim Schwartz told [Jim] basically there's no way you're going to be able to get it done [if the lockout lasts into the summer]," John Harbaugh said at the time. "[Schwartz] told him there's no way you're going to be able to accomplish what you need to accomplish in two weeks if this thing lasts a while. Jim [Harbaugh] just kind of bit his tongue, which is what you've got to do in this situation. Because there's nothing you can do about it."

Jim Harbaugh had a chance to do something about it when the 49ers visited the Lions on October 16, 2011. Detroit had started 5–0 for the first time since 1956. The 49ers unexpectedly had won four of five games to start the year but were 4.5-point underdogs.

Regardless of whether Jim Harbaugh still had the offseason condescension from Schwartz in mind (and surely Harbaugh did), another incident laid the foundation for what was eventually to come. After Lions quarterback Matthew Stafford connected with tight end Brandon Pettigrew on a 16-yard touchdown pass, Jim Harbaugh threw the red challenge flag. That year, however, the league had passed a rule making all scoring plays automatically reviewable. Harbaugh drew a 15-yard penalty for challenging a play that coaches no longer could challenge. On the other sideline, Schwartz taunted Harbaugh, strutting and preening and shouting "Know the rules" at Harbaugh, whose expression suggested that he was more dumbfounded by the development than disrespected by Schwartz.

The touchdown plus the extra point had given the Lions a 10–0 lead. The 49ers, however, managed to erase the deficit, to take the lead, and to hold the lead, winning the game 25–19 and dropping Detroit to 5–1. That was when things became interesting.

Harbaugh got excited. The TV copy shows him pulling up his shirt to reveal a ghostly white midsection. But Harbaugh wasn't trying to show off his incipient dad bod; the gesture came from a gimmick Harbaugh had hatched to inspire a blue-collar work ethic in his players.

After the initial rosters for the season had become set, Harbaugh had had work shirts made for all players and coaches. Dark blue, short sleeved, with a name plate stitched over a pocket. Harbaugh had explained that the 49ers would be a rough-and-tough team that earned each day's pay. And, like blue-collar workers, they'd come home, kiss the wife and kids, grab a beer, sit in a favorite chair, untuck the work shirt, and watch TV.

Harbaugh, in his excitement, untucked his shirt as a nod to the hard day of work that had led to an upset win in Detroit. The excitement continued into a hard postgame handshake with Schwartz, followed by a slap on Schwartz's back. Schwartz called out to Harbaugh, Harbaugh said something back to Schwartz, and Schwartz then followed Harbaugh, chasing him in order to confront him (or, at a minimum, to create the impression that he was *trying* to confront Harbaugh).

Officials and players and photographers and even 49ers PR director Bob Lange (in full suit and tie) scurried to keep Schwartz from getting too close to Harbaugh. The teams congregated at the lone tunnel to the locker rooms, and cooler heads eventually prevailed.

Not everyone wanted things to quiet down so easily. When 49ers linebacker NaVorro Bowman realized what was about to happen, a team official cautioned him, "Be smart." So Bowman put his helmet on and buckled his chinstrap before running to the middle of the action.

Ultimately, there was not much action. The incident, however, is one of the biggest examples from the past twenty years of the manner in which competitive drive mixed with toughness, real or contrived, can spill beyond the players to the coaches, causing one to be perhaps a little too exuberant and forcing the other to try (or at least to seem to try) to confront his foe with physical force.

For Schwartz, it was good that his effort was unsuccessful, or at least inauthentic. Harbaugh, a first-round draft pick of the Bears and long-time NFL quarterback, likely would have made quick work of Schwartz, a Division III linebacker at Georgetown who never played a down of football beyond college.

THE NEAR TRADE OF JIM HARBAUGH

FORMER 49ERS COACH Jim Harbaugh has a habit of wearing out his welcome. It dates back to his childhood.

Jack Harbaugh, like his sons Jim and John, coached football. As a result, the family frequently relocated. In *My First Coach*, Jim told Gary Myers that on one of Jack's coaching stops, Jim was ready to go before his father's next job became available.

"Today I lost my last friend," Jim told Jack. "It's time for us to move again."

Before becoming the head coach at Michigan in 2015, Jim moved again after every four years of his coaching career, from the Raiders, where he was a low-level assistant, to a trio of head-coaching jobs at the University of San Diego, Stanford, and the 49ers. Even though the 49ers made it to the Super Bowl in only Harbaugh's second season, he was already coming close to losing his last friend.

Harbaugh, who once admitted in an HBO profile that he has a habit of losing favor over time, battled nearly from the get-go with 49ers GM Trent Baalke. The relationship grew frayed to the point of awkwardness and then to the point of hostility. Once, at a league meeting, the two men ended up in the same elevator car, and the other passengers sensed the dysfunction flowing from their complete and total lack of interaction or acknowledgment of each other.

The 49ers qualified for the postseason in each of Harbaugh's first three seasons with the team. The relationship nevertheless became so frayed that another team decided to make a run at luring Harbaugh to a new NFL city.

The Browns wanted to bring Harbaugh to Cleveland. The move would have put him in the same division as his brother, Ravens coach John Harbaugh, setting up two games per year between them. The Browns definitely could have used Jim; the franchise had already ripped through seven coaches since reconstituting in 1999. Jimmy Haslam had purchased the team in 2012, and the Browns had already fired Pat Shurmur after only his second season and Rob Chudzinski after only one.

After the Browns hired Mike Pettine, word emerged that they had worked out the first part of a potential acquisition of Jim Harbaugh, striking a deal with the 49ers on compensation. All that remained was to get him to agree to take the job. Harbaugh ultimately declined.

At the time, the 49ers and Harbaugh denied it vehemently. The Browns, however, didn't. Their official statement acknowledged only that the team had conducted "an extensive coaching search" and had "explored several options" before landing on Pettine.

In hindsight, the 49ers surely wished that Harbaugh had said yes. After one more season, rife with even more turbulence than any of the first three combined, the 49ers fired Harbaugh. In one final act of dysfunction, the team claimed that the decision was mutual. Harbaugh said that it most definitely was not.

The 49ers then set up a revolving door, hiring Jim Tomsula and firing him after one season before hiring Chip Kelly and firing him after one season. Things calmed down dramatically when Kyle Shanahan took the job, and in his third season, Shanahan took the 49ers back to the Super Bowl.

Harbaugh, for his part, ended up back at Michigan, his alma mater. His shadow loomed over the NFL for several seasons, but as he resisted potential professional interest and as his Wolverines struggled, he slid from the A-list. It could be that his lack of interest in essentially being traded to the Browns will cap his NFL head-coaching experience at four years with only one team.

Which was more than long enough to wear out his welcome and ended just as he lost his last friend in San Francisco.

ANOTHER GENERATION
OF BELICHICKS

IN MOST AMERICAN businesses, nepotism has become a no-no. In the NFL, hiring relatives continues to be as typical as a play-action pass.

It's unclear why the NFL tolerates something that so few other industries allow. The easiest explanation comes from the reality that most franchises operate as family businesses. When the primary owner, usually someone who made enough money in another line of work to buy an NFL team, can no longer continue, he or she either sells the team or passes the equity to one or more children. Obviously, one of them must then run the business.

For that reason, most owners involve their children in the business before the owner no longer owns the team. This prepares the children for the obligation that one of them will eventually inherit the franchise, serving as what the league calls the "controlling owner" of the team.

It therefore feels hypocritical for owners who routinely dabble in nepotism to slam the door on other hiring decisions based on lineage. If the head coach wants to hire his son to serve as an assistant coach, how can the owner who has hired his or her son or daughter to serve as a front-office executive say no? As a result, very few NFL ownership groups ever adopt the same type of nepotism policy that so many other businesses routinely promulgate.

For coaches who hire relatives, several different reasons motivate such moves. First, trust is critical among a coaching staff. A head coach can trust his children more than he can trust anyone else. Second, coaches are typically absentee parents during their children's formative years. After the parent has not been around much for eighteen years, hiring a child to serve as a coach guarantees that parent and child will be working closely together, hour after hour, day after day, week after week, month after month. Year after year. Third, children of coaches grow up with the game. It's not too big for them. They understand how it looks, how it feels, how it works. 49ers coach Kyle Shanahan, for example, wouldn't have become the great coach that he is if he hadn't had so much exposure to the game through his father, two-time Super Bowl winner Mike Shanahan.

The practice still creates problems. With most coaching jobs over the years going to white men, valuable spots in the pipeline of training and experience that go to the children of coaches also go to other white men. Jobs are filled based on factors other than merit, and candidates with perhaps less ability and potential get opportunities to learn and grow for which others are perhaps objectively more qualified.

In New England, for example, one of the greatest coaches of all time in any sport has employed two of his sons. Steve and Brian Belichick have worked, they've learned, they've grown, they've taken on increased responsibilities, and they've been groomed to become a living, breathing enhancement of the legacy of Bill Belichick. If the NFL prevented nepotism among its various teams, the two spots that Belichick's sons have occupied would have gone to someone else.

Of course, a team-by-team nepotism rule would quite likely spawn a series of quid pro quos, with one coach hiring another coach's child and vice versa. A league-wide rule prohibiting Belichick's sons from working for any team for as long as their father serves as a head coach would likely be far too broad and quite possibly would violate antitrust laws.

For that reason and others, it remains unlikely that a team- or league-based ban on nepotism will ever materialize. Unless any such rule also applied to the hiring of the children of owners, the double standard would make it even more awkward for an owner to do with his or her own children what the coach would be prevented from doing with his.

MATT RHULE BLOWS THE SALARY CURVE (AND IT DOESN'T MATTER)

WHEN THE MEN who founded the NFL gathered at a Canton, Ohio, Hupmobile dealership in September 1920, they would have benefited from better legal advice.

In hindsight, those who started the league should have structured it as a single business entity, with the various owners of the teams acquiring shares of the broader business. That would have avoided any and all possible claims of collusion or antitrust violations arising from the efforts of multiple independent businesses to make coordinated decisions.

Of course, that hasn't stopped the league from engaging in collusive activity. With players, federal labor laws permit it (to an extent, as the Colin Kaepernick case revealed). With everyone else, the various franchises make collective decisions even as a risk of litigation lingers in the nooks and crannies of every move made.

Some believe that NFL owners for years have had a wink-nod agreement regarding the money paid to head coaches. Even as player pay skyrockets (thanks to a salary cap tied to revenue), coaching pay hasn't kept pace. Coaches, for the most part, simply don't make as much as they're worth.

That began to change when owner David Tepper, one of the newest members of Club Multibillionaire, decided to blow the curve in order to hire Matt Rhule to coach the Panthers. Tepper gave Rhule a seven-year, $62 million contract, an unprecedented salary of nearly $9 million for a first-time NFL head coach. The move raised eyebrows throughout the league, and it rankled owners who prefer to keep the coaching budget under control.

The premium paid by the Panthers kept Rhule from interviewing with the Giants (New York co-owner John Mara had a chance to offer a similar contract but flatly declined). While it prompted some other coaches to wonder whether their contracts would be adjusted accordingly, most owners brushed off Rhule's contract as an aberration—and most coaches and their agents went along with that.

When the 2021 coaching carousel spun to a stop, $8.85 million per year hadn't become the floor for entry-level coaches. And it still remained the ceiling.

Regarding more established coaches, few know what the ceiling is. As multiple sources have explained it over the years, teams find a way to funnel extra compensation to coaches so that the "official" numbers reported to the league don't violate the unspoken gentleman's agreement regarding coaching pay. From Patriots coach Bill Belichick to Seahawks coach Pete Carroll to Saints coach Sean Payton and others, the actual earnings are dramatically higher than the numbers that are bandied about by agents and media. Belichick, for example, is believed to be making more than $20 million per year.

He's worth it. He's proven that again and again. A great coach has as much or more value than a great player, and the best coaches should make as much as the best players. The league, however, has done a great job of holding those numbers down in order to keep the rising tide from lifting lesser boats.

Technically, this habit potentially violates federal antitrust laws. As a practical matter, it won't make a difference. For the same reasons that the league has avoided a racial discrimination lawsuit arising from poor hiring practices when it comes to minorities, it won't face an antitrust claim or any other type of lawsuit for attempting (and succeeding) to keep the market for coaching pay from growing at a more robust rate.

Who will give up his career to sue the league over a subtle understanding regarding the money paid to head coaches? The coach who files the lawsuit would fear being ostracized, and his fears would be justified. Even though that would expand the potential liability of the league, it wouldn't put the coach in a job. And that's ultimately what the coach wants.

Should the money for all head coaches be better? Yes. Is it good enough to ensure that no coach will bite the hand that feeds him more than he can eat, even if it's less than he should get? Absolutely.

When it comes to their careers, coaches are very conservative. Few ever position themselves for free agency, even though the best of them could name their price with a new team. They prefer the bird in the hand, they realize they're being paid handsomely, and they know that they'd do exactly what they're doing for a lot less money, or possibly none at all, if they had to.

It all adds up to more money staying in the coffers of the billionaires and less money flowing to the millionaires who directly influence the fate of a given team. It's yet another reason why owning an NFL team continues to be one of the best investments anyone with the means to buy one can make.

PART V
OWNERS

THE HIRING OF MATT MILLEN

NFL OWNERS NOTORIOUSLY don't know what to do in order to make their teams better. The best example of this reality comes from the Lions' misguided decision to put Matt Millen in charge of the team's football operation.

It happened after the 2000 season. The organization had completed a fairly successful (by its own relaxed standards) decade with a seventh nonlosing season in ten years. But the Lions seemed to lose their way following the abrupt retirement of Hall of Fame running back Barry Sanders in 1999. The Lions had believed that Sanders would eventually take Detroit to the proverbial next level, but he never did, and now longtime owner William Clay Ford wanted to make a bold, brave move.

The line between courage and kookiness continues to be a thin one, however, and the Lions went full fuckin' nutty when Ford gave the keys to his football Edsel not to an established evaluator of talent or a proven builder of successful organizations but to a former player turned broadcaster. Millen, a previously popular figure who had climbed to No. 2 in the Fox analyst pecking order, behind only John Madden, had carved out a respectable niche. Millen did the job well. As it turned out, he did the job *too* well.

Millen had a habit during broadcast production meetings and elsewhere of telling bad teams how to get better. Some, such as Saints coach Jim Haslett, wanted to knock Millen's block off. Others, like the Lions, became smitten with Millen's blunt, plainspoken, here's-what-you-need-to-do routine.

So the Lions, who first tried to hire him in the spring of 2000, decided to make Millen the team's GM. He got the job despite never having worked as a scout, the normal and accepted path to becoming, essentially, the top scout in the organization. Those who grind through the scouting life, traveling to obscure places, obsessively studying film, and gathering every shred of evidence in a usually fruitless effort to bend the crapshoot that is the NFL draft in their teams' favor, resent this kind of dramatic departure from the usual progression.

Most if not all young scouts put in the hours and the effort in the vague hope that maybe, someday, they'll ascend to the top of a front office. By plucking from the broadcast booth a meatheaded former linebacker with zero experience in evaluating football for a living, with their livelihood riding on his ability to do it well, the Lions were asking for trouble.

Millen exacerbated the problem by not making up for his lack of credentials with fresh calluses; rather, he didn't work nearly hard enough. He commuted back and forth to Detroit from Pennsylvania. He admitted to *Sports Illustrated* in 2013 that he hadn't traveled to enough college games and that he hadn't done enough scouting until the draft approached.

Millen's lack of experience, skill, and work ethic showed. Quickly. A 9–7 record in 2000, the last season before he arrived, disintegrated to 2–14 in 2001. Then 3–13. Then 5–11, 6–10, 5–11, and 3–13.

The team showed promise in 2007, winning seven games for the first time in Millen's tenure. But that was when the bottom dropped out. In 2008, the Lions become the first team in NFL history to lose sixteen games and win none.

Along the way, Millen developed a reputation for burning first-round picks on receivers who never panned out, such as Charles Rogers, Mike Williams, and Roy Williams. To Millen's credit, he wisely didn't pass on Calvin Johnson with the second pick in 2007 after the Raiders foolishly opted for quarterback JaMarcus Russell over one of the best receivers of his or any generation.

Millen also became the only person fined by the NFL for violating the Rooney Rule, which mandates that at least one minority be interviewed for every head-coaching job. Millen didn't do enough to mask his intention to hire former 49ers coach Steve Mariucci and wasn't able or willing to persuade a minority candidate, including Lions offensive coordinator Sherm Lewis, to sit for the job. In response, the league hit Millen with a $500,000 penalty, a bill that some believe ultimately, and secretly, was paid by the team.

The team eventually paid for the decision to hire Millen and then to not fire him once it became obvious that he lacked the natural ability for the job or the desire to develop the appropriate skills on the fly. It's hard to fault him for accepting the money and the power and influence that went with the position, but he should have known that he needed to move to Detroit, bust his butt every day, and do all the things that a good GM needs to do in order to be something other than a perpetual loser.

If only Matt Millen had had a Matt Millen to tell him what to do, maybe it all would have worked out.

THE COMMISSIONER

DURING THE LOCKOUT of 2011, when the league office hoped to sway public opinion in the direction of the billionaires who had frozen out the players in order to get them to cry uncle, the NFL floated the notion that the commissioner represents not only the league's owners but also the entire sport. The truth was, and still is, that the commissioner represents the league's owners, period.

He's their face, their voice. He's their liaison to the football-following world. He's paid (and paid obscenely well) to serve as the public pin cushion for any and all unpopular policies and practices of those who own the teams. Those who pick the commissioner. Those who pay the commissioner. Those who could easily fire the commissioner and hire a new one.

Players don't determine the commissioner. Fans don't determine the commissioner. The media doesn't determine the commissioner. The thirty-two owners do. The owners represent his sole constituency.

If they remain happy, he remains employed. If they remain very happy, he earns more and more money.

At this point, no one knows how much the commissioner makes. That development became an unintended consequence of the disingenuous suggestion, advanced aggressively by the NFLPA during and before the work stoppage that wiped out the 2011 offseason, that because the NFL operates as a tax-exempt trade association, the league and its teams don't pay taxes. The teams most definitely do pay, and always have paid, taxes. The league, which passes money through to the teams, previously did not.

Although the arrangement had a tangible benefit for the league, it became outweighed by the false perception that the league somehow doesn't pay its fair share. And when the league altered its tax status in 2015, it avoided the requirement to file an annual form disclosing the compensation paid to the commissioner and other high-level executives.

As a result, no one knows how much the commissioner actually makes, and no one will know that number with any real certainty unless and until the league resurrects its tax-exempt structure. It's generally believed that the commissioner receives $40 million per year. Whether that amount is too high, too low, or just right, that's the perception.

The reality is that as the league has grown, the job has become much more complicated. Some have speculated that the commissioner will eventually come not from the world of football but from the broader ranks of corporate CEOs, where top executives bounce from business type to business type, often with no prior experience in whatever widget the company makes or service it provides. CEOs require skills that sweep far beyond a lifelong knowledge of the product. Their gigantic salaries and bonuses are justified by a broad and expansive vision for the organization, an uncanny ability to delegate, and the interpersonal attributes necessary to quickly understand and navigate the many relationships that ultimately determine failure or success.

For the commissioner, thirty-two specific relationships matter most. Some require more care and feeding than others. Some become more important than others, given that only a handful of owners truly run the league. Regardless, the commissioner's political realities are fairly narrow and finite. It doesn't take much to make everyone happy or to keep everyone happy. Especially as the money keeps flowing and flowing.

It's nevertheless important for the commissioner to be surrounded by executives who can be trusted to provide appropriate advice and to otherwise handle their areas of responsibility effectively and independently. For years, insiders have questioned whether the league's current commissioner, Roger Goodell, has the best available help at his disposal. Some wonder whether Goodell wants to protect himself against any in-house threats by having no one on the payroll who could sufficiently impress the owners that they would eventually start kicking around the idea of whether one of the lieutenants should become the general.

Although it's human nature to have those concerns, the challenge for the commissioner is developing the confidence and security to realize that constructing a deep and talented cabinet serves the best interests of the game. Indeed, many of the challenges the league has faced since Goodell became commissioner have come from the fact that the people working for Goodell keep dropping the ball.

It doesn't help that Goodell has, in some respects, created an atmosphere that favors those who tell him what he wants to hear rather than what he needs to hear. For those in a position to advise Goodell, survival means giving him what he wants along with not standing out as someone who could succeed him.

When Goodell spent a couple of weeks in 2014 genuinely concerned that the Ray Rice domestic violence fiasco would possibly end his tenure as commissioner, a common question emerged: how much less could the NFL pay its commissioner given the number of people who could steer a billion-dollar business through largely blue, mostly calm, and always open waters? That question never achieved much traction before the scandal subsided and Goodell settled into a tenure that lasted through the rest of the decade and beyond as the commissioner not for the entire game but for the thirty-two people with the power to decide whose signature will appear on each and every official football.

DANIEL SNYDER

FEW NFL NAMES spark more immediate derision than Daniel Snyder. The words, for many fans, don't roll off the tongue but ooze from the papillae. His name has become synonymous with dysfunction during his twenty-plus years as owner of the Washington Football Team, a label that he abruptly instituted under mounting pressure after years of belligerent, all-caps "NEVER" intransigence regarding the prior moniker, a dictionary-defined racial slur.

The above paragraph contains statements of opinion, not fact. In fact, all statements contained in this chapter reflect opinion, not fact. Because the fact of the matter is that Snyder will, in my opinion, potentially weaponize the legal system to quiet those who dare to criticize him.

Then again, if Snyder were to sue everyone who criticized him, he'd spend all of his time in court.

It's unclear why anyone with the money to buy a football team would want to own a football team. Some in the sport compare the endeavor to politics, calling it Hollywood for the ugly. Others who understand the scrutiny directed at those who previously thrived in anonymity have come to the conclusion that the only thing better than being rich and famous is being rich.

Early in his tenure, Snyder seemed to be headed for the good kind of fame. His franchise was apparently on a path to consistent relevance and contention. In 1999, the year Snyder purchased the team for which he had cheered as a boy, Washington returned to the postseason for the first time since 1992, Hall of Fame coach Joe Gibbs's final year with the franchise. Then, in 2000, Snyder and company tried to buy a championship team, adding a pair of future Hall of Famers (defensive end Bruce Smith and cornerback Deion Sanders) in free agency and securing tackle Chris Samuels and linebacker LaVar Arrington with the second and third overall picks in the draft.

Expectations skyrocketed. Fans of other teams began to accept that, as it had in 1991, Washington would engage in domination on the road to eventual coronation. Neither happened. The team lost six of its first thirteen games, triggering the firing of coach Norv Turner. Washington finished 8–8, missing the playoffs entirely.

The team's only accomplishment of significance in the 2000 season? It became the answer to a trivia question as the last franchise to lose in Pittsburgh's storied Three Rivers Stadium. (The Steelers christened Heinz Field in 2001.)

The nonwinning seasons continued for Washington beyond 2000, with a total of sixteen of them through 2020. (Then again, a 7–9 record in 2020 was good enough for a division championship.) Fans lost interest in attending games at a stadium that opened in 1997 but looks and feels as if it has been around since 1897. A season-ticket waiting list evaporated, and the team, after years of pretending it still existed, eventually admitted that it no longer did.

The sluggishness of the squad and the staleness of its home venue tell only part of the story. The franchise under Snyder has had a rocky ride, with a cancerous culture that ultimately forced Snyder to make major changes in 2020, at about the same time that he finally dumped the long-standing team name.

Part *Animal House* and part *Mad Men* (based on claims made in news accounts and elsewhere), the organization over which Snyder presided allegedly objectified females, particularly the cheerleaders. In a flurry of stories that emerged prior to the start of the 2020 season, the *Washington Post* painted a troubling picture—and in turn exposed the shocking practice of (allegedly) cobbling together certain outtakes from cheerleader video shoots and creating a montage for the entertainment of (allegedly—again, I'm trying hard not to get sued here) Snyder and other executives. The situation prompted Snyder to hire an outside lawyer to conduct an "independent" investigation (of course, there's nothing independent about an investigation conducted by a lawyer who has been hired to do the investigation by the company the lawyer is investigating). The league eventually assumed control of the probe once the allegations of the cheerleading outtakes video surfaced, necessarily making the investigation slightly more independent.

In July 2021, the league imposed a $10 million fine on the team for the misbehavior, and Snyder "voluntarily" decided to step aside from the day-to-day management of the team, giving the reins to his wife. The commissioner requested no written report from the lawyer who performed the investigation, eliminating any chance of the written report being published and in turn preventing any specific findings from creating a fan and/or media uprising that would force Snyder to sell the team.

On top of that, Snyder spent most of 2020 and the early part of 2021 squabbling with a trio of limited partners who had been trying to sell their stake in the team for years. From arbitration and litigation filed by them to a litany of legal proceedings sparked by Snyder in an effort to prove that one or more of his limited partners tried to falsely link him to notorious alleged sex offender Jeffrey Epstein, Snyder played defense and offense at the same time, all with only one overriding objective in mind. As one source explained to PFT, Snyder hoped to avoid having to sell the team because he plans to keep it and, in time, to have his children own and run it. Washington fans can only hope, if this happens, that the Snyder children have learned how not to run the business by watching their father and then doing the opposite.

In my opinion.

THE LOCKOUT

IN 2006, AT a time when former commissioner Paul Tagliabue wanted to retire, the league and the union rushed to work out a new labor deal. Not long after the ink dried on the revised agreement, the owners wanted it undone.

The CBA included a provision allowing either side to opt out early, cutting the contract short after the 2010 season. When the window opened on an opt-out, the owners moved immediately to pull the plug. They despised the 2006 CBA, believing that it threw the balance of power out of whack in many ways, most importantly monetarily.

Almost from the moment that the league flipped the switch, the owners sent clear signals that they intended to lock out the players and force them to eventually accept the league's terms, even if it meant wiping out a full season of football. Most fans ignored the situation, giving little or no thought or concern to the squabbles of the rich and famous and deciding to worry about the situation only if/when there was no football.

Twice before since the AFL-NFL merger, regular-season football games had disappeared from the calendar. In 1982, a player strike canceled seven weeks of the regular season and forced the league to use an unprecedented sixteen-team postseason tournament to crown a champion. (Washington won it.) In 1987, another strike scrapped a week of games and resulted in three weeks of replacement players. (Washington won the Super Bowl again.) The manner in which the players caved in 1987 made the owners confident that once again, they'd get their way.

They had good reason for optimism. Football players want to play football. They want to be paid to play football. Each week of lost games disappears forever with no opportunity to catch up on backlogged orders via overtime, as might happen in a normal unionized shop. Since the owners (especially those who have other business interests) have plenty of money, those who hold equity in the franchises are much more willing to cancel games than the men who suit up and play. Until that changes, players won't have at their disposal the ultimate weapon for winning a labor fight: the willingness to strike or the inclination to absorb a lockout.

Without the same kind of alternative that the owners have at their disposal (i.e., the ability to hire so-called scabs to play the games), the players can never fight fire with a flamethrower. In theory, they could set up their own games. They could start their own league, staging contests with the world's best players playing in different uniforms and different colors under different coaches. The broader logistical challenges would become daunting, from securing stadiums to selling tickets to setting up football operations to finding partners to televise the games, especially when it would all potentially be part of an elaborate bluff. Unlike the owners, who have the infrastructure in place and will use it with or without the current unionized workforce, the players would be spending a lot of time and money setting up an alternative league that, ideally, would never open its doors to customers.

The owners knew this, and the owners took full advantage of it. They locked the players out on March 11, 2011, killing a robust cycle of free-agency comings and goings and shuttering the offseason workout program, which always generates plenty of news and interest in the season to come. The draft still happened, creating for teams the unusual occasion of adding incoming rookies before the annual wave of veteran players coming, going, and/or staying. (Some coaches think it should be that way every year, as it normally is in the NBA.)

Ultimately, after the predictable (and potentially effective) decertification of the union followed by antitrust litigation challenging the lockout as illegal (if there's no union, there's no antirust exemption for the thirty-two teams and no legal ability for them to come together and freeze out workers) and various skirmishes and appeals and posturing and preening and threats and promises and PR battles and everything else that goes into a high-profile work stoppage, the two sides came together and crafted a deal without sacrificing any football games. Well, they gave up one. The annual Hall of Fame game, the sixty-fifth preseason contest, didn't happen. Commissioner Roger Goodell and NFLPA Executive Director DeMaurice Smith instead used the occasion of the Hall of Fame enshrinement celebration to sign the new labor deal, a ten-year, eleven-season contract that brought long-term labor peace.

The agreement triggered complaints from both sides, which likely means it was a good deal. The owners agreed to dramatic reductions in offseason practice and padded sessions during training camp and the regular season. As one extra-salty team official said at the time, "The players secured everything but the ability to have someone else play the games for them." The owners, realizing that less work wouldn't cost them more money (in fact, they saved money with fewer work days), had no qualms about agreeing to the terms in order to persuade the players to accept the financial aspects of the deal.

Agents and those in the media with an antiunion bias (and there are plenty whose feet fit that specific shoe) began to complain that the deal hurt players financially, rattling off various concerns that ignore one very important reality: when the time came to miss games and game checks, the players weren't going to miss games and game checks. They just weren't. As a result, the NFLPA had to strike the best deal that it could, fully aware of the fact that when push came to shove, the players would accept whatever terms they had to accept to get back to work.

Whether that ever changes remains to be seen. In early 2020, the players agreed to another ten-year, eleven-season deal via a close vote that, but for the declaration of a pandemic during the voting window, might have gone the other way. By 2030, things could be very different. But one thing will remain the same: players, with a finite number of years for playing football, won't want to lose games and game checks, and owners who own teams for decades and longer will always be willing to give up a season of football if it means keeping the players from getting too much.

THE MISADVENTURES OF
JIMMY HASLAM

"BEHIND EVERY GREAT fortune there is a crime."

That quotation, attributed to Honoré de Balzac, appears as the epigraph to Mario Puzo's *The Godfather*. And while a crime may not be behind the fortune that allowed Jimmy Haslam to buy the Cleveland Browns, a crime definitely fueled (pun definitely intended) his accumulation of cash via the truck-stop business from which he and his family made their millions upon millions.

The situation first emerged on Tax Day in 2013, less than a year after Haslam had used a chunk of his family fortune to buy the Browns. FBI agents, after nearly two years of secretly compiling evidence thanks to an employee who served as a whistleblower, swarmed the Knoxville, Tennessee, headquarters of Pilot Flying J. Haslam initially proclaimed that everything would work out in favor of the company. It most definitely would not.

Pilot Flying J had engaged in blatant fraud against its customers. Specifically, the company had promised rebates that it never delivered, assuming that small, unsophisticated trucking companies would never put two and two together and realize that they had been shorted. They didn't, but the federal government did, indicting multiple employees and executives and seemingly working its way up the ladder to Haslam, the CEO.

Multiple layers and levels of employees flipped, allowing prosecutors to climb rung after rung, higher and higher, until they presumably had enough evidence to indict Haslam. They never did. Despite indications that Haslam knew about the scam, he was never charged with any crime.

Haslam was never charged with any crime even though former Pilot Flying J president Mark Hazelwood received a twelve-and-a-half-year prison sentence. (The conviction was overturned in July 2021 by an appeals court based on the trial judge's decision to let the jury hear tape recordings of Hazelwood making racist and sexist remarks.) Haslam was never charged with any crime even though his company eventually paid a $92 million fine to resolve its own liability. Haslam was never charged with any crime even though more than a dozen other executives pleaded guilty.

Haslam either knew exactly what had transpired or played to perfection the role of Mr. Magoo, oblivious to the widespread fraud happening right under his nose. Neither look is a good one for a billionaire and supposed captain of industry.

Through it all, the NFL did nothing. Despite a newfound willingness (thanks to the Ray Rice debacle in 2014) to disregard the often incomplete and failed efforts of the criminal justice system and launch its own investigation, the NFL never, as far as anyone beyond the league's headquarters knows, explored whether Haslam bore any responsibility for the crimes of his company and his key employees. The NFL never placed Haslam in any sort of jeopardy or under any sort of scrutiny, even after a jury convicted Hazelwood in 2018.

Despite the periodic claim that the NFL holds nonplayers to an even higher standard than players, the league never took action of any kind against Haslam. It simply doesn't add up. Common sense suggests that Haslam isn't Mr. Magoo—that he isn't, and wasn't, clueless as to the things his executives had done.

Haslam established the culture that caused so many executives to be involved in such a toxic and poisonous effort to prey on customers. Surely he said or did something at some point that caused so many of his employees to believe that such behavior was not only tolerated but also expected.

The NFL nevertheless looked the other way. The NFL looked the other way because it could. The NFL looked the other way because Haslam never faced any criminal charges, even though it seemed that he would, or at a minimum that he should.

Although, technically, the misconduct had nothing to do with Haslam's ownership of the Browns, the widespread fraud visited upon the customers of Haslam's company cried out for more than, well, nothing at all. It was odd. It was confusing. It simply wasn't the kind of thing that the NFL ignores when players do things unrelated to their jobs as NFL players.

The difference could lie in the basic reality that when players do things they shouldn't do away from work, the crimes aren't financial or fraudulent. Players who get in trouble away from work typically engage in violent or dangerous acts that create a far more conspicuous PR problem for the league because they involve victims who have suffered far greater tangible and immediate damage than financial losses.

Regardless, crimes are crimes. Misconduct is misconduct. If the league truly intends to secure the ability to punish all of its employees or representatives, players and nonplayers alike, for violations of the law unrelated to their official duties, it should have done something—anything—to explore whether and to what extent Haslam violated the same Personal Conduct Policy that it so often utilizes against players who run afoul of its terms.

The inescapable conclusion is that the league applies two standards, two sets of rules. One results in players routinely and aggressively facing consequences for doing things they shouldn't have done, while the other conveniently and/or strategically ignores the league's owners doing things they shouldn't have done.

It's no surprise. The commissioner is employed and paid by the owners, not by the players. When the time comes to hold one of the persons who employ and pay the commissioner accountable, a dramatically different posture is assumed. It's a posture of tolerance, of patience, of understanding—the very things the league rarely shows to the parade of interchangeable parts of the broader NFL machine, pieces of the puzzle that routinely can be cast aside because they eventually will be anyway.

THE SUSPENSION OF JIM IRSAY

THE NFL LIKES to say that it holds nonplayers to a higher standard than players. It sounds good—until it's time to actually hold an owner to a higher standard.

Sometimes, as in the case of Browns owner Jimmy Haslam, the league can justify (if only to itself) looking the other way. In the case of Colts owner Jim Irsay, the circumstances left the league with no alternative.

Arrested for driving under the influence of medication in March 2014, Irsay had multiple bottles of prescription drugs and more than $29,000 in cash in his Toyota Highlander. Asked to recite the alphabet from "C" to "N," Irsay complied. Then he started again from "A" and took it all the way through "Z"—and capped it off with a flourish, adding an "I," an "N," and a "G" for good measure.

Irsay eventually reached a plea deal, resolving what started as multiple felony charges but became a pair of misdemeanor counts. Prosecutors claimed that Irsay had oxycodone and hydrocodone in his system.

The league eventually took action, and the punishment was indeed more severe than it would have been for a player. At the time, the NFL's labor deal called for a two-game suspension for a player found responsible for a DUI. The league hit Irsay with triple the banishment—six games—along with a whopping $500,000 fine.

It seemed harsh on the surface. Some thought it was too harsh. On closer inspection, it could be argued that the punishment wasn't nearly harsh enough.

The financial penalty failed to mirror the punishment that a player experiences in similar situations. Beyond the $500,000, Irsay suffered no other monetary consequence. Thus, during his six-game suspension, he and his franchise still got all of their revenue from tickets sales and TV rights.

Players who are suspended lose *all* the compensation they would have earned during the missed games, and they forfeit (where applicable) a corresponding chunk of their signing bonuses. The numbers climb quickly, and for many players, the amount easily exceeds $500,000.

While suspending an owner generated a clear and potent headline, Irsay lost nothing close to the millions in revenue that continued to flow into the team's coffers as he watched the games from his mansion instead of viewing them from his luxury suite. For each and every one of the six games for which he was suspended, the team continued to generate enormous profits that he continued to be able to do with as he pleased.

A suspension of an owner doesn't become a real suspension unless and until it comes without pay. The NFL suspended Irsay for six games with pay, fining him an amount that pales in comparison to the profits he continued to realize from the games from which he was otherwise banished.

Commissioner Roger Goodell defended the decision, explaining that the rules prevented him from taking more from Irsay than $500,000. That rule, conveniently, came from the very people who were insulated from facing consequences for their own behavior commensurate with the consequences players face for theirs.

Goodell could push to change those rules, but why would he? With a constituency of thirty-two to determine his ongoing employment and the financial terms of it, why would he lobby for a revision to the rules for which none of those thirty-two would ever clamor?

Former Colts defensive end Jerry Hughes immediately saw through the end result of Irsay's punishment. "It's kind of like a slap on the wrist," Hughes told ESPN at the time. "But it is what it is. It's the business. . . . I'll just let the numbers speak for themselves. I mean, he's a billionaire, so I'm pretty sure [$500,000] won't hurt too badly."

Most billionaires would claim that $500,000 is still $500,000, and most billionaires don't become or stay billionaires by treating $500,000 like pocket change. Still, in comparison to players and others who, when suspended, lose every penny they would have earned during the time of their suspension, $500,000 for an owner who otherwise faced losing more than 35 percent of his annual profits definitely becomes the coins not worth fishing out of the couch.

JERRY JONES VS. ROGER GOODELL

THE COMMISSIONER WORKS for thirty-two people. This makes his overriding objective clear: keep as many of those thirty-two as happy as possible. Most importantly, Roger Goodell needs to keep the most powerful of those thirty-two owners as happy as they need to be.

In 2017, Goodell made one of the most important owners unhappy. And it sparked a protracted power struggle between America's commissioner and the owner of America's team.

As Goodell negotiated his first new employment contract since the Ray Rice fiasco had threatened to end his tenure prematurely, Jones pulled with both hands on the thread that had begun fraying in September 2014, when the Ray Rice elevator video had become public. The owners could pay Goodell a lot less than they pay him, or they could find someone else to do the job for a lot less than Goodell makes.

Jones's specific frustrations with Goodell flowed not from the Rice incident but from Goodell's handling of the lingering controversy regarding players protesting during the national anthem, which started in August 2016 and had a silo full of jet fuel thrown onto it by President Donald Trump in September 2017 at an Alabama rally that included a demand that the league's owners should, in regard to any protesting player, "get that son of a bitch off the field." Jones staunchly supported forcing players to stand for the anthem, recognizing the financial risk to the league and its various teams from fans being alienated by the perception that such protests disrespect the flag, the country, and/or the military.

As Jones insinuated himself into Goodell's contract negotiation, Jones recruited (as multiple owners firmly believe) John Schnatter, the founder of the Papa John's pizza conglomerate, to join in the anti-Goodell movement. In November 2017, Schnatter took aim at Goodell in a quarterly earnings call.

"Good or bad, leadership starts at the top, and this is an example of bad leadership," Schnatter said in prepared remarks regarding the anthem issue. "This should have been nipped in the bud a year and a half ago." Schnatter also blamed reduced corporate earnings on the Stars-and-Stripes skirmish. "The [NFL] controversy is polarizing the customer, polarizing the country," he said at the time.

The controversy stoked by Jones, who only two days after Schnatter's comments publicly dubbed him "a great American," polarized NFL ownership. For Jones, the problem was that he had only one primary supporter on his end of the spectrum: Washington owner Daniel Snyder. The rest of the owners aligned either with those who wanted to keep Goodell and extend his deal or those who remained neutral.

Jones refused to back down. At one point, he threatened to sue over the extension of Goodell's contract. This prompted some owners to consider the possibility of invoking a little-known provision in the NFL's Constitution and Bylaws that could have compelled Jones to forfeit his franchise. In lieu of launching the nuclear option, the owners ordered Jones to cease and desist in his efforts to block Goodell's contract, warning him that his behavior could be regarded as "conduct detrimental" to the league.

Jones eventually backed down, and Goodell got his fat new contract. Goodell then ordered Jones to reimburse the league for $2 million in legal fees incurred as a result of his threat to sue. Jones, a multibillionaire who soon would purchase a $250 million yacht, shrugged at the punishment.

"When you get pretty supportive, then you run or get a chance to pay the fiddler," Jones told ESPN at the time, rattling on as he often does in a way that perhaps he alone fully comprehends. "I have understood that. The commissioner has that power."

Indeed he does. And the commissioner emerged from the attack on his authority with even more power, along with a guaranteed commitment worth up to $200 million over five years. The commissioner had so much power that when league spokesman Joe Lockhart characterized the contract as the commissioner's final one, the commissioner promptly disputed that claim. Not long after making those remarks, Lockhart was gone.

That move may have helped Goodell and Jones find a thin slice of common ground. Jones said that he was "proud" to see Lockhart go, a confusing claim that quite possibly spoke to the political and philosophical divide between the left-leaning Lockhart and the right-leaning ownership structure, which largely supported Donald Trump and wanted to appease those who, like Trump, believed NFL players should stand for the anthem at all times.

Regardless, Goodell won, Jones lost, and the commissioner secured the ability to remain on the job through 2024 and possibly longer. The issue quickly became forgotten as all involved got back to the business of making a shitload of money on a regular basis.

ROBERT KRAFT WINS
ONE FOR THE LITTLE GUY

ON AN OTHERWISE quiet February Friday morning in late 2019, a stunning item of NFL news emerged out of nowhere: authorities in Florida had charged Patriots owner Robert Kraft with receiving something other than a massage at a massage parlor.

Over the course of three separate days, two local sheriffs and a state prosecutor consistently declared that the broader operation involved victims of human trafficking. It did not, and they soon abandoned that claim. That blatant and craven item of embellishment became the first sign that something was seriously amiss.

In many such cases, when a grown man (often married) ends up in a massage parlor on the receiving end of something more than a massage, the situation is resolved quickly and quietly. A protracted fight serves only to make things worse for someone who would otherwise plead guilty, pay a fine, deal with the public and private consequences, and move on—before the video evidence of the encounter can be released.

On the surface, Kraft, a widower who has given millions to support reforms in the criminal justice system, had nothing to lose and more than enough money to win. In reality, he had something to lose. The league would have disciplined him, likely via a suspension, if he'd ultimately pleaded guilty to or been convicted of solicitation charges. More importantly, Kraft strongly believed that he had violated no laws and done nothing wrong.

Kraft hired a team of lawyers to fight the charges aggressively, attacking the broader surveillance program as a violation of the rights of anyone and everyone who received a nonmassage "massage." The fabricated premise of human trafficking made it easier for the authorities to obtain a "sneak-and-peek" warrant, allowing a hidden camera to be placed in the Orchids of Asia massage parlor, where it recorded much more than alleged sexual activity between employees and customers. That became the key to beating back the prosecution.

The fight launched by Kraft exposed enough evidence of the broader effort to result in civil litigation, filed on behalf of multiple local citizens by attorney Joe Tacopina. "It's a nightmare," Tacopina said at the time in an appearance on CNN. "It's as if they put a camera in a bathroom and recorded people going to the bathroom. I mean, these people ranging from forty-year-old males to seventy-five-year-old females in a state of undress getting massages. Nothing more. Legitimate massages. And wound up on a videotape that is perilously close to being put out in the public domain."

The video nearly entered the public domain due to a broad Florida law that makes all documents and evidence generated by law-enforcement officials subject to disclosure on request. Kraft's efforts prevented that from happening.

"If this was not pushed and exposed, and if it was Robert Smith, not Robert Kraft, we would have never known what happened here, and there were some serious invasions of privacy rights of citizens of Jupiter, Florida, and serious violations of the law by law enforcement," Tacopina said at the time. "Robert Kraft, who I don't represent, has done some very good things for this community."

Kraft kept fighting. He won. And he kept winning. When a Florida appeals court ruled that the authorities had indeed violated the rights of Kraft and others through the broad and indiscriminate use of secretly installed video cameras, prosecutors chose to drop the case instead of taking a losing argument to the Florida Supreme Court.

Prosecutors opted not to appeal the ruling to the highest court in the state because a loss could have had "broader, negative implications" for future investigations. In other words, prosecutors feared that the Florida

Supreme Court would react to a clear and obvious violation of individual privacy rights by creating a standard that would have made it much harder to violate individual privacy rights in the future.

The saga ended in a resounding victory for Kraft. Although no win in court could unring the bell, the bell could have clanged a lot longer and harder if Kraft had lost in court and if the video had dropped into the hands of the media. (It eventually was destroyed, by court order.)

Given the result, the league took no action against Kraft. How could it? The charges had been abandoned, and in the eyes of the law, he'd done nothing wrong. Despite lingering concerns about a double standard, no player caught in a similar predicament would ever have suffered discipline from the league if, at the end of the day, the solicitation charges had been dropped.

Few if any players would have fought the way Kraft did. Even though he surely did it to help himself, his efforts led to a significant incidental benefit for plenty of others whose rights had been blatantly violated by such abusive law enforcement tactics. The national attention that the case received potentially will influence authorities in other states to think twice before launching a quick-and-easy sting operation that aims to catch in the act people who get a massage with benefits but that also grossly invades the privacy rights of those who simply want, and merely get, a massage.

THE GREEN BAY DYNAMIC

IN 1923, THE Green Bay Packers needed money. Specifically, they needed $5,000. The Packers raised that money by selling stock. And thus was born the first, and only, publicly owned franchise in NFL history.

No other team did it at the time, and the league has since forbidden other teams to adopt a corporate structure. With four additional stock offerings since the initial one, whether to scrounge $15,000 to get the team out of receivership in 1935 or to fend off competition from the All-American Football Conference in 1950 or to raise $24 million for Lambeau Field enhancements in 1997 or to generate $143 million for an expansion of the venue in 2011, the Packers' status as a team without a traditional owner has permanently become part of the fabric of the league.

It creates a unique dynamic that none of the other thirty-one teams experiences. The NFL requires that one person must have ultimate control of the team for the purposes of voting on league matters. For most franchises, with that absolute power comes the ever-present ability to make major decisions about the direction of the team at any given time.

For the thirty-one teams that are not the Packers, the controlling owner can roll out of bed on any given morning and fire the coach. Or the GM. Or both. Or anyone. Or everyone. While those decisions can become expensive in light of contractual buyouts (and the fact that the replacement will command a significant compensation package), NFL franchises print money. Besides, buyouts become write-offs, a cost of doing business, a detail that doesn't, or at least shouldn't, make a multi-billionaire flinch.

Given some of the bad decisions made by traditional owners over the years, there's something to be said for the Packers lacking one specific person who could catch a wild hare and start running off high-quality personnel. However, the lack of someone who can exercise swift, sudden, and final justice at any given moment invites the potential for complacency.

The Packers, like every other NFL team, generate a significant profit every year (with the exception of 2020, due to the pandemic). Unlike every other NFL team, the Packers must make their financial affairs public. The annual report, released every July, provides a snapshot of the broader fiscal status of the league. And regardless of any other maladies that may periodically plague pro football, the NFL always maintains its financial health.

The mission of any corporation is to make as much money as possible. In that regard, the Packers succeed every year. Throw in the fact that their season-ticket waiting list stretches for decades, and it's clear that the game-day revenue has little relevance to winning and losing. Thus, winning and losing may not mean as much for a corporation as it does for an individual who covets the Lombardi Trophy as a sign of individual achievement and inherent worth, making an owner more likely to spend more money on free agents or to happily pay buyouts and to procure replacements of coaches and GMs who aren't getting it done.

For a corporate-owned sports franchise, success arguably means being good enough. Indeed, the chase of greatness may trigger the law of diminishing returns, where the extra money spent in the quest to add to the haul of championships easily becomes wasted when the annual king of the NFL mountain gets there as much through the timely bounce of the ball or a fluke of Mother Nature or an instance of officiating incompetence that, while definitely hurting one team, definitely helps the other.

Of course, the Packers can't say they're content to be good enough. All teams must tell their fans that the goal every year is to win a Super Bowl. Privately, however, no team in its right mind can use securing a championship as the annual determining factor in the most basic pass/fail formula in sports. If so, even the Patriots, who won six Super Bowls from 2001 through 2018, will have failed 66.7 percent of the time.

Vanity, ego, and pride can get in the way of these basic financial realities, compelling some owners to write bigger checks in order to convince (fool) themselves into thinking that the extra money will enhance the chance of success. A corporation, by definition, doesn't think that way. A corporation, in theory, operates above the personalities or insecurities or frailties of any one person. A corporation, in many respects, has a greater sense of self-awareness than any individual when it comes to understanding the definition of success and the path that leads to it.

That's not to say the Packers management doesn't *want* to win the Super Bowl. The point is that the Packers succeed regardless of *whether* they win the Super Bowl. That results in less pressure being placed on the coaching staff and the front office to win the Super Bowl. And that potentially results in the football operation concluding that being good enough to contend is good enough to remain employed.

Frankly, that may be the better approach. Instead of rushing to kick in the door and tripping on the sidewalk, the Packers tend to perpetually hang around the porch. From time to time, they'll find their way inside. Through it all, they'll satisfy their overriding corporate mission of making as much money as they possibly can.

THE RISE OF ANALYTICS

ONCE UPON A time in the NFL, the quarterbacks called the plays. The coaches eventually and systematically took that power from the quarterbacks. Currently, owners eventually and systematically are taking the power to call plays from coaches.

It's happening under the umbrella of analytics. Owners have begun to hire experts in probabilities and statistics and variables and other data-driven processes, and those employees, lacking the accountability that applies to coaches, spit out a flow chart that supplements (or replaces) in-the-moment coaching judgment based on all available factors steered ultimately by a gut feeling resulting from years and/or decades of experience.

The algorithms constantly evolve and improve, taking into account the various what-about factors that coaches have identified as missing from past formulas. The skills of the various players on the field, the weather, the wind, the playing surface, anything and everything that drives subjective decision-making and converts to something objective. If the coach ignores the recommendations arising from the numbers, the coach risks stepping onto the ultimate told-you-so rake. If the numbers say to go for it or not go for it on fourth down or to go for two or to not go for two after scoring a touchdown or to do whatever the coach's instincts tell him not to do and the coach's decision fails, the analytics specialist is vindicated. Conversely, if the coach does what the numbers dictate and it doesn't work, the coach can shrug and say he simply did what the numbers required.

Although coaches and owners and others in football organizations don't always talk openly about it, these decisions flowing from X percentage of this and Y percentage of that have prompted coaches to subtly but clearly shift from a mindset that not long ago saw coaches opt for the conventional move over the unconventional because failing at the unconventional can spark the kind of criticism that can get the owner to start thinking about whether the coach should go. Now, coaches increasingly embrace the unconventional because the analytics experts call for the unconventional to be done—and coaches who don't want to answer to the owners who have invested in an analytics department are doing the unconventional, ignoring media scrutiny because external noise and criticism have become irrelevant to internal processes and opinions.

Some coaches have accomplished enough to ignore the analytics opinions or, even better (from their perspective), to influence owners to refrain from developing and/or relying upon analytics departments that serve to constantly peer over the shoulder of the coach, nudging him to make decisions in the moment that may contradict the decisions the coach would otherwise make. If the coach ultimately will be the one to be fired if/when the team has an unacceptable number of unsatisfactory seasons, the coach should be the one making the decisions.

That's the fundamental problem with analytics. At the risk of raising the ire of a fairly loud and robust online analytics mafia (then again, they probably won't buy this book anyway), the percentages that drive these decisions arise from years and years of actual game scenarios, game after game and month after month and season after season. Over and over and over again. The numbers may support going for it on fourth down every time a given set of circumstances is encountered. But coaches don't have the benefit of playing the percentages game after game, month after month, season after season. One bad decision in one big spot can get a coach fired.

Sure, a long-term, big-picture approach would entail picking a specific path in one specific moment. But a coach's career inevitably consists of far fewer moments than the many iterations that gave rise to the percentages driving the decisions made at any given time.

Good luck getting an owner who has gone all in on analytics to see it that way. The owner hires the math whiz. The owner needs to justify the investment in the math whiz. The owner often has the math whiz in the owner's suite during games, far above the crucible in which the coach makes decisions based on the math whiz's calculations—or not. And the coach knows what's going on, knows that the math whiz has created a chart that should always be followed, knows what the math whiz will say if/when the coach doesn't do what the chart says.

The chart. The chart. The chart. It started in 1994 as a simple matrix for deciding when to go for two (that's the year the NFL embraced the college alternative to the one-point try) and grew into something that covers scores of decisions and areas of discretion to the point that some of the most fundamental game-day responsibilities of a coach—knowing when to go for it on fourth down, when to go for two, when to call a timeout, when to attempt an onside kick, etc.—have essentially become automated. The coach follows that chart unless the coach wants to risk ignoring it, thus giving the owner a more tangible basis for concluding that the coach who won't listen to the math whiz should simply be replaced by one who will.

PART VI
HEALTH AND SAFETY

THE DEATH OF KOREY STRINGER

YEARS BEFORE THE NFL underwent an epiphany regarding head trauma, the league experienced a reckoning regarding the practice of practicing in oppressive heat and high humidity. And it happened because a twenty-seven-year-old husband and father paid the ultimate price.

July 31, 2001. Korey Stringer, a first-round pick of the Vikings in 1995 when he was only twenty years old and a Pro Bowler in his final NFL season, hadn't been able to finish a morning practice one day earlier due to exhaustion, and he sat out the afternoon session. Determined to put in his work the next day, a morning that saw the heat index in Mankato, Minnesota, spike to 99, Stringer vomited three times but completed a two-and-a-half-hour practice. He grew weak and dizzy after it ended.

When Stringer later arrived at a local hospital, his body temperature had skyrocketed to 108 degrees. He died in the early hours of August 1 due to organ failure resulting from heatstroke.

Just like that. A professional athlete felled in the blink of an eye by the combination of high external temperatures, a large body (a requirement of his job), and pounds and pounds of football pads. Chatter emerged about supplement use as the Vikings circled the legal wagons, but the autopsy showed that Stringer had neither ephedra nor any other supplement in his body at the time of his death.

The sudden passing of Korey Stringer threw a lightning bolt throughout all of football, forcing pro, college, and high school teams to immediately reconsider padded practices in stifling heat a badge of honor. Although the *Junction Boys* days of practicing in sweltering conditions with at most a mouthful of warm water from a dusty jug had long since evaporated like the liquid the players were instructed to swish in their mouths and expectorate on the dirt, football players continued to practice in high heat and humidity. It continued to be part of the price paid for the privilege of getting "in shape" and more importantly to prove dedication to the team by fighting through extreme forms of physical adversity.

Today, a similar incident at the NFL level would surely trigger a league-wide shutdown of training camps for a full assessment of the situation, a sign of the significant progress the league has made when it comes to caring about player health and safety. In 2001, however, the game barely missed a beat.

Yes, changes were made as a result of Korey Stringer's death. Teams practiced later in the day, after temperatures had dropped. At lower levels of the sport, deaths and serious illnesses that happened, but that generated far less attention, became more of a rarity. And that's an enduring benefit arising from the untimely passing of a young man who should still be alive, more than twenty years later.

The incident inevitably, and justifiably, sparked high-stakes litigation against both the NFL and Riddell, manufacturer of the helmet and shoulder pads Stringer wore. Stringer's widow, Kelci, settled with the league eight years after Korey's passing. The resolution included the establishment of a heat-illness prevention program. Two years after that, Stringer's widow settled with Riddell.

The death of Korey Stringer created other consequences for the Vikings. Before the 2001 season ended, owner Red McCombs fired longtime head coach Dennis Green, who had taken the team to the NFC Championship in 1998 and 2000. Hall of Fame receiver Cris Carter later theorized in his book, *Going Deep*, that the incident affected the manner in which Hall of Fame receiver Randy Moss viewed management, laying the foundation for an eventual divorce after the 2004 season.

"He started to put up a wall at that point," Carter wrote. "Korey was Randy's best friend on the team and a lot of things were said after he passed. It was alleged that the Vikings could've done better when [Stringer] started complaining about his [health] problems, and I know his wife wasn't happy about how the team responded after his death. Randy wound up in that camp as far as fighting the team."

The death of a player would cause far more problems and consequences for an NFL team today, now that so much more is known about the physical risks that players take and the various methods available for avoiding having a player give his life for the game he loves. In 2009, the same year that Kelci Stringer settled with the NFL, Bengals quarterback Carson Palmer predicted in a roundtable discussion conducted by Peter King of *Sports Illustrated* that another fatality was inevitable.

"The truth of the matter is . . . somebody is going to die here in the NFL," Palmer said at the time. "It's going to happen."

The mere suggestion by Palmer of death on a professional football field created a major stir, and to date, Palmer's prediction has not come to fruition. If/when it ever happens again, some believe it would become a tipping point that would wreak far more havoc on the status of the sport than any of the political huffing and puffing of recent years. Although Stringer's death happened in a far different context than the application of a devastating blow absorbed while playing the game, legitimate fear of another instance of the worst-case scenario has contributed to unprecedented league sensitivity to the possibility of a player losing his life.

As a result, the game has become much safer in every way. Some bemoan the fact that football isn't the game it used to be, when devastating hits that left players lying motionless were celebrated actively rather than disciplined aggressively. Still, those who run the sport have realized that its survival hinges in many respects on the survival of its participants.

Although the financial interests of those who own NFL teams have contributed significantly to their commitment to doing the right thing by all current and future players, those concerns have nevertheless compelled the league to do the right thing by all who play the game. The realization came too late to save the life of Korey Stringer, but it undoubtedly has saved the lives of others at every level of the sport.

THE ROY WILLIAMS RULE

IN 2002, A defensive back entered the NFL with a high degree of skill and a specific tackling technique that would force the NFL to eventually revise its rule book. Roy Williams, an Oklahoma safety taken by the Cowboys with the eighth overall pick in the draft, became widely known for a maneuver that entailed dragging the ball carrier down from behind by inserting his hand into the back of the shirt collar and pulling.

He did it in college. He did it in the NFL. He did it well. He did it too well.

The so-called horse-collar tackle caused plenty of lower-body injuries. The abrupt yanking of the jersey, a tactic for which there is no effective defense, dramatically hurls the offensive player to the ground, collapsing him backward onto his legs, twisting his body into an awkward and vulnerable pretzel, and considerably increasing the possibly that something will snap.

Most notably, Williams broke the leg of Eagles receiver Terrell Owens by using the horse-collar tackle in late December 2004. That injury, and other incidents related to the technique, resulted in the league doing something that it had rarely done before: changing the rules specifically to promote the safety of the players.

Gone in an instant was the horse-collar tackle, a measure known initially as the Roy Williams Rule. In May 2005, twenty-seven of the NFL's thirty-two teams voted to banish the practice. Unsurprisingly, the Cowboys opposed the measure. (The Lions, Patriots, Saints, and 49ers also voted against it.)

It has evolved over the years to expand the protection afforded to offensive players. In 2006, the requirement that the hand of the defensive player actually be inside the shoulder pads broadened to include any tackles involving the top of the jersey. A decade later, the league stretched the danger zone down to the name plate.

Horse-collar tackles still happen from time to time. Violations are much easier to spot than other infractions given the awkward, rapid movement of the offensive player's upper body toward the ground. More than fifteen years later, players moving at full speed inadvertently get their hands in or near the back of the collar in the same way that they accidentally grab and pull face masks.

Flags fly as quickly for horse-collar tackles as for face masks. The league office also levies fines and, if necessary, suspensions to get defensive players to stop engaging in the illegal and unsafe act.

In 2007, the league actually suspended for one game the man for whom the rule was named. Williams had committed three illegal horse-collar tackles during the season, and his third infraction, involving Eagles quarterback Donovan McNabb, sidelined Williams for a week.

Wade Phillips, who coached the Cowboys at the time, had a pragmatic assessment of the situation. "It wasn't against the rules until a couple years ago," Phillips said. "But that's the rule, and we need to abide by it. He's just going to have to learn to do it different. And he passed it up a couple times in that game."

Despite the extra protections that apply to quarterbacks, the horse-collar rule does not apply in one specific situation: quarterbacks who are in the pocket. The Steelers proposed expanding the rule to include quarterbacks in the pocket in 2012, an obvious effort to protect their mobile (and injury-prone) quarterback, Ben Roethlisbeger, from being injured if/when suddenly pulled down from behind. The league didn't adopt it; Falcons president Rich McKay, who also served as the chairman of the Competition Committee (the group that officially proposes rule changes), said that the league "didn't see the injury risk" for a quarterback who isn't moving.

That's the key: movement. A player moving forward incurs an enhanced risk of injury if suddenly dragged down from behind. Roy

Williams made such a career of it that the league had to do something about it.

This change became a major step in the direction of promoting and protecting player health and safety. Although far bigger changes would come several years later, the league's willingness to outlaw a technique that inflicted injury on players showed that it would, under certain circumstances, choose health and safety over the otherwise all's-fair approach to the game of football.

CHRIS SIMMS NEARLY
DIES ON THE FIELD

CHRIS SIMMS, THE son of Super Bowl XXI MVP Phil Simms, was arguably best known before 2006 for absorbing misguided criticism from Super Bowl XXIX MVP Steve Young for a supposed "laissez-faire" (incorrect use of the term, by the way) upbringing that had left Chris unprepared for the cold, hard reality of a high-accountability life in the NFL. As Chris tried to prove that he had earned a football career based on his own skills and abilities and not his name, he nearly gave his life in the process.

It happened on September 24, 2006. On a very hot day in Tampa, the game pitted the Buccaneers against a solid Panthers team that had a suffocating defensive line. Hit repeatedly by the likes of Carolina linebacker Thomas Davis, defensive end Mike Rucker, and defensive end Julius Peppers, at some point during the game, Chris, Tampa Bay's starting quarterback, suffered a ruptured spleen. In an effort to prove that he was indeed tough enough for the NFL despite having grown up amid relative privilege (which Steve Young did, too, by the way), Chris decided to keep playing, no matter what.

Near the end of the third quarter, the fourth-year quarterback's struggles became obvious. After a false start from an offensive lineman that happened as, according to Simms, the "curtains were coming down," he moved toward the sideline, dropped to a knee, and ended up briefly in the locker room for an evaluation that nevertheless had him back in the game after missing just a couple of snaps.

As Simms explained it, he received an IV. They pushed around on his torso a bit. He said he was good to go.

"I was desperate," Simms told me. "We were 0–2. . . . But I was dying slowly."

Still struggling in the fourth quarter, Simms helped the Bucs take a late lead. As he tells it now, he realized that he was bleeding internally.

The Panthers ultimately won the game on a 46-yard field goal with two seconds left. When the game ended, Simms engaged in the customary midfield meet-and-greet with Panthers quarterback Jake Delhomme. Delhomme said to Simms, whose face by that point had gone the color of the road jerseys that Tampa Bay chose to wear on a sun-drenched day, "You don't look so good."

He didn't look so good for good reason. Doctors realized that Simms was indeed suffering from internal bleeding. An ambulance took him to a local hospital, where he underwent emergency surgery that removed his spleen and saved his life.

Simms, who would go on to become a very good broadcaster (as well as the on-air partner and close friend of the person whose name appears on this book), applied his usual loose (but not laissez-faire) attitude to the situation not long after it happened. Asked during his first postsurgery press conference whether he'd continue his career, Simms laughed and said, "Why not play? I can't hurt my spleen again."

He'd eventually realize that the removal of the spleen diminished his proprioception, making it very difficult for him to control his movements and, most importantly, to throw a football. He worked and fought and pressed and eventually got back to the NFL as a backup, but he never had the career he could have had but for the injury.

That he didn't die on the field or in the locker room or in the ambulance or on the operating table was great for Simms but also very good for the NFL, which would have had another Korey Stringer–style problem arising not from practice on a hot and humid day but from the playing of a game during which Simms suffered a ruptured spleen and no one bothered to notice.

In today's NFL, that wouldn't happen. Although spotters and trainers and doctors currently scan the field constantly for signs of potential head trauma, the sensitivity to health and safety sparked by concussions under modern standards surely would have resulted in a more exacting examination during Simms's third-quarter visit to the locker room and, inevitably, a decision to let rookie Bruce Gradkowski finish the game. That's a clear and tangible benefit flowing from the league's realization that the long-standing practice of saying "How many fingers?" (the correct answer is always "Two") and brushing off a brain injury as a bell-ringer had to end.

It marked, to borrow Steve Young's term, the cessation of the league's laissez-faire approach to injuries of all kinds, forcing the NFL and its teams to place the single-minded desire of coaches to get players back on the field behind the short- and long-term interests of the players. Regardless of how the NFL got there, get there it did. Fortunately, it happened without Simms or anyone else having to lose his life during or immediately after a game.

THE CONCUSSION EPIPHANY

ANYONE WHO EVER played tackle football at any level knew it. Anyone who ever watched an endless stream of boxers become "punch-drunk" knew it, too. Even with a helmet (and for years, the prevailing helmet technologies didn't do much to insulate the cranium from the various forces applied to it), football players suffered concussions and subconcussive blows to the head that only got worse as boys became adolescents and then full-grown men. The simple realities of Newtonian physics confirmed for anyone with a basic degree of common sense that, for the same reasons that people instinctively knew in the years before a large-font surgeon general's warning became attached to every pack of cigarettes that sucking the smoke of tobacco leaves into their lungs isn't good for them, football can potentially be hazardous to the health of a football player.

The NFL managed to kick the can for decades when it came to repeated blows to the head. In 1994, the league formed the so-called Mild Traumatic Brain Injury Committee, which was led by former commissioner Paul Tagliabue's personal rheumatologist and spent much more time downplaying the risks than fully and completely understanding them. The inevitable reckoning was successfully delayed for a decade and a half. As always, however, the reckoning eventually arrived.

When Congress becomes involved in matters of otherwise private enterprises, the stewards of such enterprises and those with a vested interest in them ask loudly, "Doesn't Congress have better things to do?" The reality remains that certain private enterprises sufficiently affect the public interest to justify the interest and potential intervention of the federal lawmaking bodies. That was what happened in October 2009, when the House Judiciary Committee summoned Commissioner Roger Goodell and NFLPA Executive Director DeMaurice Smith to testify regarding the issue of head trauma. The House Judiciary Committee's message was clear: You have a problem. Clean it up on your own, or we'll clean it up for you, and you won't like how we do it.

With overt threats against the league's broadcast antitrust exemption, an extremely valuable legislative creation that allows the league to sell all TV rights to the various networks in a block rather than team by team, the NFL moved quickly to address the problem. Barely more than a month after Goodell and Smith answered tough and pointed questions about the issue of concussions, the league passed unprecedented and sweeping guidelines regulating the ability of players who have suffered concussions to return to practices and to games.

Responsibility for the problem undoubtedly attached to both the league and the union. Although the seminal book on the topic, *League of Denial*, takes aim exclusively at the league, the NFLPA—the legally recognized organization responsible for the health and safety and all other rights of NFL players—had a seat at the table throughout the full existence of the Mild Traumatic Brain Injury Committee, and the union had quite frankly failed its members every bit as badly as the league had failed its employees. As Smith, who'd been running the NFLPA for less than a year, admitted to Congress, the union "has not done its best in this area," and it "will do better."

Starting in late 2009, the league and the union began to do better. They had no choice. The long-overdue reckoning had arrived. Football would change or suffer, possibly die. Now, with the benefit of more than a decade of hindsight, it's clear that forcing Goodell and Smith to confront the issue under the threat of external change sparked internal change that dramatically transformed the game.

The NFL hoped that its efforts to increase sensitivity to concussions would trickle down to lower levels of the sport. Unfortunately, lower levels of the sport (particularly the high school level) lacked the medical expertise to properly ensure that concussed players would be spotted, removed, and kept from playing until fully healed. The league, intent on ensuring that the pipeline of future football players wouldn't diminish (it nevertheless did), worked to lobby all states to adopt a version of the Lystedt Law, a measure first passed in Washington after Zachary Lystedt returned to football activities with a concussion and suffered serious brain damage.

Beyond changes to the law, the NFL tried to spark a change to the culture of football, a culture that otherwise rewarded a willingness and resolve to play through any and all injuries. For brain injuries, the challenge became persuading players to behave counterintuitively, tapping out when suffering a potential concussion in lieu of fighting through it. Even now, this approach has significant flaws. Although Steelers quarterback Ben Roethlisberger received widespread praise for self-reporting concussion symptoms and exiting late in a 2015 game that the Steelers would lose to the Seahawks, most saw that as the exception rather than the rule.

It's one thing for a franchise quarterback with no fear of losing his starting job to raise his hand and report a potential concussion. It's quite another for a veteran player who wants to preserve his place on the first string, his roster spot, and/or his salary to voluntarily exit the fray and give his replacement a chance to shine and potentially take his job.

Even those with job security routinely find ways to keep playing after absorbing a head injury. Steelers receiver Hines Ward has admitted that after suffering a concussion on a hit from Ravens linebacker Ray Lewis, Ward grabbed his ankle in an effort to fool trainers and doctors. (It didn't work.) Hall of Fame quarterback Peyton Manning said in 2011 that he'd deliberately tank the baseline cognitive test conducted in the preseason in order to more easily pass the test if/when he had to take it again in the wake of suffering a head injury.

"They have these new [brain] tests we have to take," Manning said at the time. "Before the season, you have to look at 20 pictures and turn the paper over and then try to draw those 20 pictures. And they do it with words, too. Twenty words, you flip it over and try to write those 20 words. Then, after a concussion, you take the same test, and if you do worse than you did on the first test, you can't play. So I just try to do badly on the first test."

After Manning's comments created a stir, he tried to say he was joking. Few believed it because most understand that the effort to get football players to willingly not play football simply isn't practical. Still, the long-term viability of the sport isn't practical if the NFL doesn't try its damnedest to protect players from each other, and ultimately from themselves. Starting in 2009, the NFL finally realized that the long-term health of the sport demanded an effort to make meaningful changes to the way everyone treats and regards head trauma.

DEFENSELESS RECEIVERS

OCTOBER 17, 2010. It happened in roughly fifteen minutes of real time, maybe less. Three different games. Three different helmet-to-helmet hits delivered to players who had just caught passes. Three different collective shudders throughout the NFL.

From Falcons cornerback Dunta Robinson blasting Eagles receiver DeSean Jackson to Patriots safety Brandon Meriweather popping Ravens tight end Todd Heap to Steelers linebacker James Harrison waylaying Browns receiver Mohamed Massaquoi, the league's concussion epiphany from nearly twelve months earlier suddenly faced its biggest practical test.

The league promptly levied fines, but as NBC's Rodney Harrison explained that same evening on *Football Night in America*, players accept that they'll absorb monetary punishment for playing the way they think they need to play. Behavior ultimately changes only if the NFL removes players from the field.

Beyond the financial penalties, the NFL made an on-the-fly adjustment to the rules without technically changing the rules. The actual rule change had come in the 2010 offseason, with the league banning blows to the head and neck area of receivers in the act of catching a pass and other players in a defenseless posture. The midseason bang-bang-bang of bang-bang plays nudged the league toward instructing officials to be even more vigilant in protecting defenseless receivers, instructing the officials to err for a time on the side of throwing the flag.

The term "err" eventually faded because it implied a willingness to accept mistakes by the officials (and to reward 15 yards of field position) in the name of health and safety. The approach generated fouls when fouls, on closer examination of various specific plays, hadn't happened. The league has resisted making these fouls subject to replay review, forcing officials to determine with the naked eye and at full speed whether, for example, a receiver's head jerked violently because he'd suffered a forbidden blow to the helmet or because a clean, legal hit had quickly and abruptly moved his torso in the direction that his body (and his head) hadn't been going.

Fans became aggressively dissatisfied with the sudden illegality of hits that for decades had represented the essence of football—elite athletes colliding in ways that generated loud noises from the gridiron, evoked oohs and aahs from the audience, and sold thousands of videotapes with titles such as *Crunch Course* and *NFL's Greatest Hits* and *Big Blocks and King Size Hits*. At one point, ESPN regularly showcased devastating blows in a feature dubbed *Jacked Up!* The league briefly even sold photos of the Harrison hit on Massaquoi before abruptly realizing that the glorification of such moments didn't mesh with the efforts to eliminate them.

Fan resistance was fueled by the complaints of people such as Jon Gruden, the Super Bowl–winning coach who at the time served as the high-profile and highly compensated analyst on ESPN's *Monday Night Football*. His snarling public complaints regarding the application of the rule prohibiting helmet-to-helmet hits on defenseless receivers forced the league to clarify the provision in an effort to secure buy-in from the public and from the players and coaches.

Indeed, the problem went well beyond those who broadcast NFL games. In November 2011, Steelers safety Ryan Clark disclosed that he had received a $40,000 fine for a hit that Steelers coach Mike Tomlin had praised in the film room. Clark, who continued to insist that he had done nothing wrong, had a pragmatic yet alarming solution to the dilemma: "So it's going to turn into if you're going to fine me $40,000, I might as well put [the receiver] to sleep for real or I might as well blow his knee out."

Blowing out the knee of an otherwise defenseless player remains legal, but every receiver would prefer to take a high hit rather than a low hit upon catching a pass, even if it means being "put to sleep." Despite the potential long-term cognitive issues from blows to the head, concussions clear up relatively quickly. A blown-out knee wipes out a full season, and potentially the rest of a career.

And so for the first time in the history of the NFL, the league mandated playing rules that players and coaches deemed counterintuitive and potentially counterproductive. Tomlin became the most vocal of the coaches. He told the league office that the Pittsburgh defense was built to intimidate people, that the goal was to "beat you up" physically, and that the new rules would hurt the Steelers more than any other team. Eventually, Tomlin became persuaded that the rule changes advanced the best interests of the entire game.

Tomlin gradually became an advocate for complying with the rules. At one point, a defensive player who had been fined significantly for violating the rule regarding hits against defenseless receivers argued directly to members of the NFL Competition Committee that the provision was impractical. Tomlin answered bluntly, "Sometimes you're not going to be able to make that play."

Then and there, the league office knew that Tomlin had come around. It made it easier for the NFL to hold firm, forcing everyone involved to accept that certain hits would immediately draw a flag and expecting that players would adjust their behavior by lowering their target or suffering the consequences.

Quarterbacks, emboldened by the rule, now routinely serve up what once were dubbed "hospital balls," passes that put their teammates in danger of getting blasted in the helmet. On the rare occasions that the illegal hit happens, it comes with 15 yards of field position.

And so the adjustment to the rules has worked. The game has changed. It has changed for the better, protecting and preserving the health and safety of players who, frankly, are wired to sacrifice their health and safety in a wide variety of ways.

Even the most cursory inspection of NFL games from years before the sudden (and overdue) obsession with brain health immediately reveals a degree of brutality that simply no longer exists. Most have accepted, whether they like it or not, a kinder, gentler brand of pro football because what's the alternative? Still, others continue to (mostly) quietly long for the days when football was a game that entailed guys routinely getting *Jacked Up!*

THE CONCUSSION LAWSUITS

THE NFL BEGAN to take concussions seriously not only because of actual congressional pressure but also in recognition of potential legal jeopardy. Nothing levels the playing field between big business and the average person like the civil justice system, and the league and its owners justifiably feared massive liability to decades of players who would claim that the NFL had failed to properly warn them of the risks of repetitive blows to the head and to reasonably protect them from such injuries.

The lawsuits indeed came. Why wouldn't they? Lawyers balance three factors when assessing whether to take a case with the fee based on a percentage of the eventual settlement or verdict: (1) liability, (2) damages, and (3) collectability. In the concussion lawsuits, the second and third factors had potency; the challenge was to prove that the NFL had legal responsibility for any cognitive problems developed by a football player years after he had stopped playing football.

The actual litigation was settled long before the court system had occasion to resolve the various issues that the league could throw in the path of the lawyers representing former players. For many of them, it could have been argued that the applicable statute of limitations for filing suit had expired. For many of the former players, it could have been argued that they could not prove that their injuries had come from pro football versus the college, high school, or youth levels of the sport. For many of the former players, it could have been argued that an applicable CBA provides the exclusive remedy, barring any and all resort to the court system. For many, if not most (if not frankly all), of the former players, it could have been argued, and proven, that they would have continued to play football even if they had known everything there was to know about every potential risk they were assuming.

The NFLPA also loomed over the litigation. The plaintiffs had not sued the union for its role, if any, in failing to warn or protect them. Remember, the union had a seat at the table throughout the existence of the Mild Traumatic Brain Injury Committee. The union arguably, if not actually, knew or should have known everything that the league knew or should have known.

At some point, not targeting the union would have created a mess for the former players. With the union not a party to the litigation, and thus not represented at trial, the league could have repeatedly hammered on the union's responsibility for failing to protect the players, hopeful that the jury eventually would push all or most of the responsibility to the union, which necessarily was the players themselves.

Although the league had many persuasive and powerful arguments to advance, and given that the case would have taken years to slither and creak through the courts, the NFL was subject to a different kind of risk. If the litigation had proceeded, the NFL eventually would have produced documents and other evidence that would have shown what the league knew and when it knew it. This would have created a potential PR mess for the NFL as story after story emerged regarding memos and emails and testimony and other pieces of proof downplaying the risks of brain injuries or outright concealing them.

The various factors culminated in an effort to resolve the case, compromising in a way that balanced the plaintiffs' potential problems in proving the case against the league's potential problems in the case being proven. The league originally agreed to pay $765 million to settle it all, with $675 million going into a fund for former players and their families, who would be eligible to receive payment for certain specific diseases and conditions without having to prove that those maladies could be traced to playing pro football. As negotiated, the package worked out to roughly $24 million per team, an amount roughly equivalent at the time to one year of pay for a franchise quarterback.

Complaints quickly emerged regarding the sufficiency of the amount and, more importantly, the placement of a hard limit on the available funds. In order to secure court approval of the settlement, the league agreed to remove the cap and to assume the risk of, in theory, unlimited liability to all retired players who eventually could qualify for payment.

It still ended up being a good deal for the league, easily justifiable as supplemental compensation for men who had helped make the game the golden-egg-shitting goose that it had become. A settlement also greatly diminished the chances of any future concussion litigation given the alternative procedures contained in the CBA and the simple fact that moving forward, no one could contend that he hadn't known, understood, and assumed all short- and long-term risks of head trauma. Even with the league agreeing to reevaluate settled claims based on the impact of race-norming when determining the cognitive impairment suffered by Black players (when industry norms assumed a lower baseline cognitive capacity based on race, it became harder for Black players to show harm), the NFL will end up resolving these claims for far, far less than the cost of the worst-case outcome.

In the decade since the original concussion lawsuits were filed, no player has made similar claims against the NFL since the league's October 2009 concussion epiphany, for good reason. The risks are known, and the league has done much to make the game of football as safe as it can be while still preserving its essence.

Although the league faces other potential challenges arising from concussions (including but not limited to the fact that children are not playing football as much as they used to), liability has become a very small blip on the outer edge of the NFL's radar screen of concussion concerns.

THE MINIMIZATION OF THE KICKOFF

NO FOOTBALL PLAY entails more physical risk than the kickoff. Once the league began to publicly acknowledge that fact, dramatic changes became inevitable.

The kickoff, as the play was structured before 2018, endangered players because it entailed members of the kicking team and the receiving team running at full speed in opposite directions before suddenly colliding. At impact, football players instinctively dip their helmets. The physics of the crash of two large bodies moving at top speed in opposite directions coupled with the angle of the head can place significant pressure on the cervical spine, risking a broken neck, paralysis, or worse.

It happened to Bills tight end Kevin Everett in 2007. Fast action by doctors helped him avoid a permanent spinal-cord injury. It happened to Rutgers defensive tackle Eric LeGrand in 2010, confining him to a wheelchair for the rest of his life.

Starting in 2011, the NFL began to make the kickoff safer. Initial efforts focused not on changing the play but on having fewer kickoffs and kickoff returns. First, the kickoff point was moved from the 30 to the 35, setting the stage for more touchbacks. That year, the NFL also limited the running start for the kicking team to 5 yards, reducing the overall velocity and force with which players moving in opposite directions met.

Five years later, Giants co-owner John Mara set the stage for more changes by declaring that "the kickoff return remains the most dangerous play that we have in the game." Despite the reduced risk of liability given that all football players now know the risks associated with playing football, flagging one specific play as dangerous and doing nothing to make it safer is a potentially significant legal and ethical problem.

Later that year, the NFL decided to experiment with moving the touchback on kickoffs from the 20 to the 25 with the goal of persuading the receiving team to catch the kickoff in the end zone and not attempt to return it. The NFL continued this experiment in 2017 before making the rule permanent in 2018 despite the reality that some teams deliberately kicked the ball short of the goal line with the objective of tackling the returner before he could get to the 25. This ran counter to the idea that the kick return would be minimized by (1) more kickoffs going into the end zone and (2) more teams not trying to return a kick caught in the end zone.

In 2018, broader concerns lingered regarding the kickoff. The possibility of an alternative that would give the kicking team possession of the ball at its own 30-yard line, facing a fourth down and 15, had percolated ever since Commissioner Roger Goodell had floated it as a trial balloon in a 2012 *Time* profile. The kicking team could punt (simulating a kickoff) or go for it (simulating an onside kick). With a clear threat that this or some other replacement would be adopted for the kickoff, special-teams coordinators worked together to come up with an alternative that reduced the instances of players crashing into each other when running in opposite directions at high speed.

The league that year adopted an alignment that removed the running start for the kicking team, requiring all players except the kicker to start the play within a yard of the 35. Other specific requirements applied to the receiving team, mandating the placement and retention of eight players within 10 to 25 yards of the ball at kickoff, further reducing the chances for high-speed collisions.

The changes saved the kickoff, but they created a separate problem. Onside kicks became much harder for the kicking team to recover, making it much more difficult for a team trailing by more than one score to force overtime or win the game in regulation. It also rendered virtually obsolete the surprise onside kick, a quirk in the game made most famous by Saints coach Sean Payton at the start of the second half of Super Bowl XLIV against the Colts.

Coaches loved the onside kick as it was. Years ago, former Steelers coach Bill Cowher argued strongly against efforts to remove the mulligan that teams received if an onside kick attempt went out of bounds or was touched by the kicking team before it traveled at least 10 yards. Cowher called it a "courage drill" and lobbied aggressively against a rule that wiped out the second chance to recover an onside kick. Eventually (and reluctantly), Cowher gave in. If he were still coaching in 2018, he surely would have continued his efforts to preserve the onside kick as it used to be.

Thus, despite the reality that the most dangerous play in the game has become far less dangerous, the reduced likelihood of a late comeback has made the current onside kick configuration unacceptable. This, in turn, keeps a team trailing by more than one score late in the game from making things interesting. Asked in 2014 whether he roots for any given team, Commissioner Roger Goodell acknowledged that he always roots for the team that's trailing. The team that's trailing, given the current kickoff configuration, can't do as much about that as it could have done via the onside kick under the pre-2018 rules.

For that reason, the possibility of a fourth-and-15 play continues to hover over the game. But it's no longer regarded as a comprehensive replacement for the kickoff. Instead, it would replace the onside kick, enhancing the trailing team's chances of closing a late-game gap by keeping possession if 15 or more yards can be gained in one fell swoop.

Many believe it's just a matter of time before the fourth-and-15 play becomes the alternative to the onside kick. Some believe it unfairly rewards teams with great quarterbacks who run potent offenses. At some point, that argument (sound as it may be) won't be enough to save the onside kick in its current form because the onside kick no longer works as it once did.

LOWERING THE HELMET

EVERY MARCH, THE NFL releases to the media a list of proposed rule changes to be considered by owners at their annual meeting. The proposed rule changes are usually the product of careful discussion, debate, and vetting. Recently, one proposed rule change wasn't discussed, debated, or vetted at all.

In 2018, the league released to the media ten proposed rule changes before the annual meeting. Once in Florida for the event, a small group of league executives crafted an eleventh rule and presented it to ownership on the fly, with no advance consideration by the league's Competition Committee or notice to anyone outside the NFL. Specifically, the league's chief medical officer (Allen Sills) and its top health and safety executive (Jeff Miller) worked directly with Commissioner Roger Goodell and NFL general counsel Jeff Pash to push the rule through. The overriding goal became, as one person with knowledge of the internal dynamics has explained it, to "win the press conference in March" by unveiling a broad new rule that strongly promoted player safety.

News of the eleventh proposal emerged only after the owners had voted unanimously to pass it, and it broadly prohibited a tactic common to football at every level. In only a dozen words, the owners had created as dramatic an adjustment to the game as the game had ever seen: *Lowering the head to initiate contact with the helmet is a foul.*

Far broader than the long-standing prohibition on spearing or a 2013 rule that prevented the lowering of the helmet for use as a battering ram (which in many ways duplicated the long-standing prohibition on

200

spearing), this new rule as written would award 15 yards of field position whenever and however a player, on offense or defense, drops his helmet to any extent prior to hitting an opponent in any part of his body—the helmet, the shoulder pads, the arms, the torso, the thighs, the shins, the feet, anywhere.

The problems with the new rule were hidden in plain sight. With no language specifying that the rule applies to "forcible" or "punishing" hits, *any* contact initiated after the lowering of the helmet became a foul as the rule was written. For example, a defensive back pursuing the ball carrier at an angle will eventually make a last-ditch effort to knock him off his feet. When the defender makes his final move, will he lunge and roll with his shoulder? Or will he lower his helmet and dive, potentially initiating contact with his helmet in the ball carrier's lower body?

Because the NFL adopted the rule with no prior discussion, debate, or vetting, the league office and the owners never considered whether the on-field officials could officiate the new rule accurately and consistently. Early in the 2018 preseason, the officials tried to enforce the new helmet rule literally until the ensuing rash of fouls created an uproar regarding the fact that routine football plays had now become penalties. Amid much confusion and a cascade of complaints, the league's Competition Committee convened to address the rule before the 2018 regular season commenced.

"Inadvertent or incidental contact with the helmet and/or face mask is not a foul," NFL Executive VP of Football Operations Troy Vincent said in a statement after the emergency effort to address the rule had ended. In the same statement, however, Vincent insisted that the rule hadn't changed.

But the rule definitely had changed. The league had added language that hadn't previously existed in the rule as the original twelve-word standard had been crafted. The rule had now become very different. It was the closest the league would come to admitting that the rule as written was a bad rule.

The nonchange change to the rule significantly reduced the number of fouls. During the 2018 season, it largely became an afterthought. By 2019, however, the league had begun to insist on compliance not with the letter of the rule but with a more specific ban on dropping the helmet just before impact with the goal, intentional or not, of striking the opponent with any part of it.

The passage of time seemed to allow more players and coaches and officials to understand the true import and extent of the rule. The goal was, and is, to ensure that players never use their helmets as a weapon in any way. This protects both the player who is struck by the helmet and the player who does the striking, avoiding the application of force from the helmet to the neck and spine.

Over time, the rule has become less about the twelve broadly written words and more about a know-it-when-you-see-it standard. Would it be better if the rule had been written to specifically address the prohibited behavior? Absolutely. Even now, the league would be far better served by rewriting the standard in a way that makes the text of the rule match the manner in which it is applied.

That type of disconnect appears in several aspects of the NFL's broader collection of specific and at times convoluted rules. The language of the rule says one thing, and the application does another. The league should strive for something far more reliable, something far more clear than "Well, that's what the rule says, but that's not how the officials use it."

The current approach creates the potential for inconsistency and confusion. It gives those officials who have discretion when it comes to applying the rules a degree of flexibility that, in theory, can be wielded under certain circumstances to reach a desired result. Although, after more than twenty years of following the NFL extremely closely and writing and talking about it extensively, I firmly believe the officials and/or the league office don't try to get specific games to end a certain way, the league should strive to eliminate any situations in which those inclined to coat their craniums in Reynolds Wrap would have a semiplausible basis for arguing that the fix is in, even if it never actually is.

The lowering-the-helmet rule, with its baked-in ability to trigger a 15-yard foul without clear, bright, and narrow lines separating illegal techniques from legal ones, provides the kind of discretion that, when exercised to the literal extent of the language of the rule, could make the tinfoil-hat crowd suspect that something fishy is happening. That's not good for the game or for anyone connected to it.

THE PRO BOWL

THE NFL'S INCREASED sensitivity to player health and safety has had several casualties. The Pro Bowl definitely should be one of them. Amazingly, however, the Pro Bowl persists. It persists for one primary reason: it generates a profit.

The game has become an embarrassment. It's two-hand touch (at best) in full pads. No one tackles, no one hits. No one really tries to exert any real effort, determination, or will.

Not that they should. Long gone are the days of full-speed, high-impact collisions in an end-of-season exhibition game. And for good reason. Players who reach the end of a long preseason, regular season, and postseason healthy enough to suit up and play one more game should never, ever want to play one more football game.

Players on the precipice of free agency should always avoid the Pro Bowl at any cost. Any injury in late January quite possibly will implode the player's market value, causing him to lose millions and millions of dollars forever, or at least until the next time he becomes a free agent with the same value that he would have possessed without a Pro Bowl injury.

Even if a player remains under contract for one or more years, there's nothing to be gained by playing in the Pro Bowl. And there's plenty to be lost. With a limited slice of downtime in February and March before the voluntary (not really voluntary) offseason workouts commence, who wants to spend two months recovering from surgery and rehabbing an injury?

In early 2016, Bengals tight end Tyler Eifert suffered an ankle injury that wiped out his offseason. Eifert eventually underwent surgery. He vowed later that year to never play in another Pro Bowl. "It's just not worth it," he said at the time.

Indeed it isn't. But Eifert didn't need to play in a Pro Bowl and actually suffer an injury to realize that. He knew or should have known, even with a gentleman's agreement among the players to be gentle with each other, that injuries can happen. He assumed the risk, and he ended up regretting it.

That said, the risk remains small because football players simply don't treat the Pro Bowl like a football game. Although the commissioner several years ago spent some time whining about the quality of the Pro Bowl and threatening to pull the plug on the game if it didn't become more competitive, the absence of hard-nosed competition hasn't kept people from watching it. As long as people watch it—and they do—the NFL will tolerate the casual truce that the players have tacitly struck to enhance the likelihood that they'll emerge from the game with no more than a hangnail or, given the activities of Pro Bowl week, a hangover.

Would the NFL prefer something that looked more like real football? Sure. But the league has come to terms with the fact that players don't, won't, and shouldn't risk injury in a meaningless game. In an era that has featured the league ironing out of the game as many unnecessary hits as possible during football games with actual stakes and significance, the league seems to have realized that none of the contact in the Pro Bowl is necessary. So if the players are going to try to avoid any and all collisions, so be it.

Would the game be better if it looked like actual football? Of course it would, but since that won't appreciably increase its TV ratings, there's no reason to try to incentivize players to play hard.

Many football fans remember that the game at one point naturally and organically featured effort and contact and desire. It happened before free agency and the salary cap and the various business motivations that caused teams to always look for reasons to dump bloated salaries. The tipping point finally came after the NFL's concussion epiphany.

Fewer than three years before the NFL finally woke up to the challenges presented by head trauma, the Pro Bowl provided what ultimately became a final moment of sudden and jarring impact when Bills punter Brian Moorman ran with the ball instead of kicking it for the AFC and Washington safety Sean Taylor came out of nowhere and obliterated Moorman along the sideline.

"I told our Reebok rep that it was a perfect commercial for their shoes because they saw the bottom of mine immediately," Moorman told me a few years later, adding that the hit had actually ripped a hole in the jersey he had been wearing that day.

In today's Pro Bowl, there's no danger of anyone's jersey being ripped or of any other consequences from violent physical contact. Ultimately, that's a good thing. The Pro Bowl probably shouldn't be played at all. However, as long as what has become a watered-down version of a football game continues to draw a sufficiently large audience to justify its continuation, the Pro Bowl will survive.

THE IN-GAME
CONCUSSION CONUNDRUM

THE NFL HAS clear and specific rules that apply when a player has suffered a concussion. Things get murky when it comes to the question of whether a player has actually suffered a concussion during a game.

For most concussions, it's obvious. For others, it's not. For some of those concussions that aren't obvious, it's often not the best time to pull the player out of the game to be evaluated for a concussion that he may not have suffered. Sometimes the player who potentially has suffered a concussion plays quarterback. Sometimes the quarterback potentially has suffered a concussion during crunch time of a close game.

That's the lingering donut hole. That's the problem that eventually could blow up for the league. A player suffers a concussion, but the player isn't removed from the game by the officials or the doctors or the independent certified athletic trainers (known as "ATC spotters," a position adopted after Browns quarterback Colt McCoy wasn't removed from a game in 2011 despite suffering a concussion) or anyone else with the ability to bring the game to a halt for the purposes of giving the player who may or may not have suffered a concussion a more careful and exacting evaluation. None of the various people with the ability to remove the player from the game for a concussion evaluation exercise their prerogative to do so because plenty of other people have that power, too. For each of them, it makes more sense to wait for one of the others to do it than to be the one who calls for the player to be removed from the game during a key moment in the contest for a concussion evaluation that he potentially doesn't need.

The league has faced questions on multiple occasions regarding the failure to pull a player from the fray for a proper evaluation. The league always tries to do better when such circumstances arise, but those situations periodically persist.

In Super Bowl XLIX, played in early 2015, Patriots receiver Julian Edelman appeared disoriented after taking a helmet-to-helmet hit from Seahawks safety Kam Chancellor. Edelman never was pulled from the game, even though independent doctors tried to persuade the officials to remove Edelman for a proper evaluation. He'd later catch what became the game-winning touchdown pass before Seahawks quarterback Russell Wilson threw a game-sealing interception at the goal line.

In apparent response to the Edelman situation, the league thereafter gave the ATC spotter the ability to stop the game and to order a player removed for a concussion evaluation. During the first year of that rule, however, the system failed. In November, Rams quarterback Case Keenum's head slammed against the turf in Baltimore. No one took Keenum out of the game. The fact that so many different people had their fingerprints on the debacle made it hard to determine who, if anyone, should be punished for failing to immediately get Keenum off the field. So no one was punished at all.

"In the Case Keenum case, it was clear that there was somebody [from the Rams] giving him medical attention and that that was already done," Commissioner Roger Goodell said at the time in an interview with SiriusXM NFL Radio. "The problem we had is that the appropriate medical attention wasn't given. And there were several gates that frankly failed and didn't do the right things to our protocol, and so we're trying to make changes to that. We're going to continue to tweak that until we get that right and make sure the game is stopped so the player has the right medical attention, and that's always the issue."

That's fine, but the gates failed because the responsible people didn't activate them. The failure to punish any of the people who failed to do what needed to be done made the ultimate resolution confusing and unsatisfactory.

It happened again in the first game of the 2016 regular season. During a rematch of Super Bowl 50 (yes, the NFL temporarily ditched the Roman numerals for that one because it didn't like the look of "Super Bowl L") between the Panthers and Broncos, Carolina quarterback Cam Newton took a blow to the head that left him apparently in distress on the final drive of the night, a drive that ended in a field-goal attempt that decided the game. (Panthers kicker Graham Gano missed the kick.) Removing Newton would have thrust Derek Anderson onto the field with the game on the line. If Newton had been removed for a concussion evaluation and if it had been determined that he didn't have a concussion, the Panthers would have been forced to attempt to win the game with someone who was a second-stringer for a reason.

Other problems arose. In 2017, Seahawks quarterback Russell Wilson managed to essentially sneak back into the game after taking a brutal blow to the chin. Later that year, Texans quarterback Tom Savage briefly returned to the game after a blow to the head that caused him to assume what's known as the fencing posture, a concussion response that results in both arms shaking and pointing upward when the player is on the ground.

The NFL continues to circle the wagons regarding the curious inability or unwillingness to comply with the concussion protocol. Giants co-owner John Mara, regarded as one of the most powerful owners in the league, predictably defended the league in late 2017 after the Wilson and Savage misadventures.

"Whenever you're dealing with human beings, there's going to be mistakes made," Mara said. "And there were mistakes made there. . . . But in almost every case with the concussion protocol, we get it right. But those we get wrong end up being highly publicized, and that's what ended up here."

Of course they end up being highly publicized. They're highly publicized because someone somehow was allowed to keep playing when the league should have removed him from action—and because one of those incidents could bring to fruition the thing that Carson Palmer described in 2009: the death of a player during a game.

THE PANDEMIC

FOR THE ENTIRE nation, 2020 became the year of the COVID-19 pandemic. As with most American businesses, the situation affected the NFL. In contrast to most American businesses, it became business as usual, mostly, for pro football.

Yes, most stadiums welcomed few if any fans. Sure, the protocols changed the work experience for players and coaches. Indeed, the entire preseason was scrapped. Absolutely, the NFL lost billions in ticket sales. But the NFL found a way, with a few creative manipulations of the schedule, to play every regular-season game and every playoff game—and to collect its primary source of revenue: the cash from the television networks.

With uncertainties still lingering regarding a pandemic sparked by a virus that could become endemic to the population, the spirit of collaboration and cooperation between the NFL and NFLPA that allowed pro football to proceed in 2020 gave way to acrimony and rancor regarding the effort to get players vaccinated. The league opted first to create incentives for the vaccinated, allowing them to work under relaxed restrictions while the unvaccinated had to follow more restrictive procedures. Then, the NFL shifted from carrot to stick, squeezing the vaccine-reluctant to get the shot(s) in order to avoid creating a competitive disadvantage for their teams. The hammer came on July 22, 2021, when the NFL issued a memo explaining that any canceled games due to an outbreak among unvaccinated players and/or staff on a given team would result in a forfeit.

The union bristled at these tactics. The NFLPA feared that players not inclined to be vaccinated would lash out if they felt threatened by the league, posting antivaccination sentiments on social media and, in turn, influencing their followers to not be vaccinated, either.

Still, some players remained insistent on refusing the vaccine. Although the league's approach created a clear incentive to dump unvaccinated players (technically, players can't be cut due to their vaccination status), some players were simply too good to release based on their refusal to submit to the vaccine. As one GM told PFT in July 2021, his team had eight players who would never be vaccinated—and seven of them were too good to cut.

The league and the union could have simply agreed to make vaccination mandatory, but that would have exacerbated the complaints from players who wouldn't do it. Even if the players ultimately relented, the rants that would have emerged while they came to terms with the fundamental choice between being vaccinated and not playing football would have made their antivaccination noise even louder and potentially prompted more fans to avoid vaccination.

For many players, the question of whether to get vaccinated became pragmatic. With relaxed restrictions and no chance of forfeits for fully vaccinated teams, vaccination became just another box to check in the quest for a championship, along with lifting weights, eating right, studying film, and learning the playbook. The fact that plenty of players refused to see it that way illustrated the depth of the national division on the question of whether to get the vaccine.

The practice of identifying vaccinated and unvaccinated players at practice and during games also sparked controversy. The NFLPA deemed it unnecessary and believed it could become another way to drive players to sound off on social media. Some teams agreed, and some didn't. Through it all, the NFL focused on persuading more and more players to choose to be vaccinated.

Coaches found themselves caught up in the controversy, too. Patriots co-offensive line coach Cole Popovich left the team over the vaccination issue. Vikings offensive line coach Rick Dennison, after an erroneous ESPN report that he was out over a refusal to be vaccinated, eventually accepted a different position, given that he couldn't actually do any on-field coaching without first getting vaccinated.

The pandemic unfortunately became, and remained, a political issue for many months. Although everyone in the NFL seemed to be on the same page in 2020, the question of whether everyone connected to the game would choose to get vaccinated became an unexpected source of friction and dissent, proving that some issues are indeed strong enough for football players and coaches to deviate from the overriding obsession with doing whatever it takes to win.

PART VII

OFF-FIELD PLAYER MISCONDUCT

THE WHIZZINATOR

THE NFL, LIKE other professional sports leagues, decided long ago to police the private lives of its players when it comes to the use of street drugs. Unlike the prohibition against performance-enhancing drugs (PEDs), which necessarily give players who use them an unfair advantage, the rule against the use of marijuana, cocaine, etc. comes from broader PR concerns that first arose during the so-called war on drugs. In order to influence kids against using pot or cocaine or heroin or whatever, pro football cracked down on substances used by players when they aren't at work, often during the many months when it isn't even football season.

Compliance has never been very difficult for players who are smart and/or not chemically dependent on one or more of the banned substances. With only one test to pass each year and with full knowledge of the general time frame in which it will happen, a player needs only to take a well-timed break before providing a clean urine sample. After that, it's back to the mantra of "smoke 'em if you got 'em."

Problems arise once players test positive and land in the "program," which entails enhanced testing and increased penalties for additional positives. For some players who choose to keep using even when under extra scrutiny, the challenge is finding a way to continue to dabble in certain drugs while still passing drug tests.

For Vikings running back Onterrio Smith, who slid to the fourth round of the 2003 draft and who had been kicked out of the University of Tennessee for chronic marijuana use, the effort to stay on the right side of the league's substance-abuse policy entailed a specific device

215

aimed (pun absolutely intended) at helping the player provide clean urine. Smith, who had multiple strikes and faced a full-year suspension for another failed drug test, used a Whizzinator, a prosthetic penis through which clean urine was pumped during a drug test.

The NFL never actually caught Smith using the device while providing a sample; it was found in his luggage at an airport. The league insisted that its procedures, which require actual visual observation of the process, would never have allowed a Whizzinator to be successfully used. So why did Smith have one? The fact that he did suggests that it worked.

Without it, Smith eventually generated another positive result, suffered a one-year suspension, and never returned to the NFL. Eventually, the makers of the device faced prosecution because federal employees with safety-sensitive jobs had allegedly used the device to evade positive drug tests. Some believe the media coverage arising from Onterrio Smith's case, along with other incidents that put the device on the national radar screen, contributed to the decision to shut the company down.

Even without the Whizzinator, NFL players kept trying to find ways to beat drug tests. In 2013, Broncos linebacker Von Miller became embroiled in a controversy involving efforts to hide positive drug tests with the assistance of a sample collector based in Miami who, apparently for the simple reason of being starstruck, helped players pass urine tests.

Through it all remains the fundamental question of whether the league should care about players who smoke marijuana or use other non-PEDs. As more and more states have legalized marijuana for medicinal and/or recreational purposes, it has become harder for the NFL to justify its ongoing obsession with players who test positive.

Officially, the league continues to ban marijuana because it continues to be regarded as a controlled substance under federal law. Unofficially, the league won't unilaterally surrender the prohibition because it regards the issue as a matter of collective bargaining.

In other words, the league won't drop the ban for the benefit of the players without a concession from the players. But the players won't make a concession because the smart ones know how to beat the system. Nevertheless, the league in 2020 agreed to remove from the policy any possibility of suspensions for positive tests. Although players can still be fined for testing positive—and can still be suspended for blatant violations of their treatment plans—no player will ever again be suspended for testing positive.

It's a decent start, but it doesn't go nearly far enough. The NFL should mind its own business when it comes to players using non-PEDs in their own time, especially in the offseason. Given the increasing body of evidence regarding the benefits of marijuana for pain management and mental health, the league should encourage further research and acceptance of a compound that may work far more effectively than narcotics in helping players cope with the realities of pro football.

In short, the NFL has come a long way since the Whizzinator. However, the league still has a long way to go to get where it needs to be. It needs to no longer worry about what players smoke or otherwise use when not working. Whether they choose to use substances away from work that don't unfairly enhance their performance should be their own business, even if it can be argued that players who smoke pot become less able to do their jobs. In most respects, the NFL represents one of the world's most pure meritocracies. The best players usually play and get paid based on their performance. If a player's use of marijuana or other drugs impairs his ability to perform, then he'll pay the price for his behavior by losing playing time and/or his roster spot.

THE LOVE BOAT

ON THE EVENING of October 6, 2005, a Minnesota woman called police to complain that a group of men had urinated in her yard. Thus began the incident that would come to be known as the Love Boat scandal.

During a bye-week excursion featuring players from the Vikings and certain guests, one thing led to another, and—as it soon became clear—to another and another and another. The guests turned out to be prostitutes flown in specifically for the party. Graphic accounts and allegations quickly emerged, and four Vikings players eventually faced criminal charges.

It could have been much worse, and it's still not clear why it wasn't. Federal law provides clear and specific penalties on the subject of prostitutes crossing state lines. Perhaps that explains former Vikings cornerback Fred Smoot's ongoing insistence that the fifty-five women who came to Minnesota from all over the country were strippers, not prostitutes.

That line can easily become blurred, especially in light of the allegations arising from the Love Boat incident. Stephen Doyle, the attorney representing the company that chartered the boat, provided graphic details from the get-go.

Doyle said witnesses shared with police the things they had seen during the party. Doyle rattled off the various types of behavior witnessed by workers on the boat: "Masturbation, oral sex, woman on man, woman on woman, toys, middle of the floor, middle of the couches, middle of the room," Doyle said at the time, claiming that "enormously detailed" photos of the events had been taken by participants and that the crew members were in a state of shock.

"They got frightened," Doyle said. "They got petrified. They couldn't believe people did this."

The allegations, involving Smoot, tackle Bryant McKinnie, and others, were shocking. For the tawdry details, I'll defer to your Google-equipped digital device. Suffice it to say that it will be hard to forget the specifics, especially regarding Smoot, no matter how badly you may want to.

The incident infuriated Vikings owner Zygi Wilf, who had purchased the team earlier that year and commenced a delicate effort to finagle considerable amounts of taxpayer funding for the construction of a new stadium. Wilf tore into the players for the embarrassment that churned through days of news cycles.

"I expressed my anger, and I expressed my embarrassment, my embarrassment on behalf of my family and for the people who work hard here," Wilf said, vowing at the time to institute a team code of conduct that demands "high standards, high morals, and success."

No more was ever heard about the code of conduct, presumably because the rules of collective bargaining prohibit teams from unilaterally imposing such provisions. Likewise, the league took no action against any of the players.

In 2005, Paul Tagliabue was the commissioner, and the Personal Conduct Policy wasn't wielded as aggressively as it eventually would be by Tagliabue's successor, Roger Goodell. As a result, punishment from the league office—which has become virtually automatic in recent years—was never even seriously mentioned.

The only consequences for the off-duty misbehavior of the players who faced charges happened within the confines of the criminal justice system. Smoot and McKinnie pleaded guilty to charges of disorderly conduct and "being a public nuisance on a watercraft." They each agreed to pay a $1,000 fine and to perform forty-eight hours of community service.

Running back Moe Williams fought the case all the way through trial. A jury convicted him on one count of disorderly conduct. The jury acquitted him on charges of indecent conduct and lewd or lascivious behavior. Williams received a $300 fine and a mandate to perform thirty hours of community service.

For star quarterback Daunte Culpepper, charges based on the allegation that he had groped the buttocks of a naked dancer were dropped. All of the men will forever be associated with the Love Boat scandal, and they definitely faced other issues in their personal lives at the time.

"Some guys almost lost their families," Smoot said in a 2018 *Barstool Sports* documentary on the incident. "Some guys even lost their jobs. Like, guys got cut."

Guys on NFL teams get cut all the time for all sorts of reasons. Given the interchangeable nature of most roster spots in any NFL franchise, however, it's easy to see why a player who was tied to the scandal would have been let go by the team if, all else being equal, someone who hadn't found himself in a boat full of strippers/prostitutes on Lake Minnetonka was available to be employed.

REGGIE BUSH

IN 2005, USC tailback Reggie Bush was regarded as a can't-miss NFL prospect. Many viewed him as the next Gale Sayers, an all-time great whose name was routinely mentioned with hushed reverence and to whom comparisons never were lightly made.

Bush won the Heisman Trophy that year, but the Trojans lost an epic Rose Bowl to Texas. The fact that Bush didn't dominate as he had throughout the season (he had "only" 177 yards from scrimmage along with a boneheaded downfield fumble) didn't change the presumption that he'd enter the NFL as the first overall pick in the 2006 draft.

Indeed, ESPN reported without equivocation that the Houston Texans, who had bottomed out in their fourth year of existence and thus had earned the No. 1 selection, would draft Bush. Everything pointed in precisely that direction in the days, weeks, and months preceding the draft.

Then came a report that Bush's family had allegedly received $54,000 in free rent from a group of agents who had hoped to represent Reggie at the NFL level. The situation came to light because Bush didn't hire the agents to represent him once he entered the NFL.

The timing complicated matters for Bush. The news emerged only days before the 2006 draft. The Texans drafted pass rusher Mario Williams instead of Bush. Although GM Charley Casserly insisted that the disclosure hadn't influenced the process, many connected to the NFL believed it had. Likewise, and as PFT reported at the time, Casserly had no remaining juice; after the draft, he'd resign to pursue a job in the league office (he didn't get it), which looked better for him and for the team

221

than the team firing the first coach (Dom Capers) and GM in franchise history in bang-bang fashion after the end of the 2005 season.

By falling to No. 2 in the draft, Bush made less money than if the Texans had made him the first pick. But Bush made it all back and then some via endorsement deals with the likes of Adidas, Pepsi, Subway, and more.

The situation created other problems for Bush. The NCAA investigated and found widespread violations; as a result, it vacated USC's victories from December 2004 through 2005, took away the team's BCS win from January 2005, and triggered the forfeiture of Bush's Heisman Trophy. The NCAA initially required USC to permanently disassociate itself from Bush.

The NCAA later reduced the ban to ten years, and it expired in 2020. By the time that happened, however, college athletics had changed dramatically. As major college football programs have earned more and more and more money, the hypocrisy has become more and more and more obvious. Players responsible for the generation of billions of dollars essentially have received peanuts in comparison. Most recently, and in the immediate aftermath of the June 2021 US Supreme Court characterizing the entire NCAA business model as a nationwide antitrust violation, the NCAA abandoned all prohibitions on players making money from their names, images, and likenesses.

Those intent on the preservation of the college sports model and/or oblivious to the unfair compensation provided to athletes continue to argue loudly that the athletes receive a free education. But what does that free education really cost the schools? More accurately, what is the actual out-of-pocket cost of allowing a football player to be a college student? Setting aside the jewelry-store markup that every university applies before handing out scholarships based on accomplishments such as breathing on one's own and/or accurately spelling one's own name, how much money does a university spend on letting an athlete attend class (or, in many cases, not attend class)? In turn, how much money flows from the sport the athlete plays?

Another problem with big-time college football comes from the fact that many who sign up to play at a big-time college have clear designs on doing so professionally. Because the NFL and the NFLPA have agreed to create an artificial three-year waiting period between high school gradu-ation and draft eligibility, aspiring pro football players have no choice but to play at the college level. Although some periodically raise the ridicu-lous notion that eighteen-year-old football players need to be protected from getting hit by men in their twenties and thirties, any team that would draft an eighteen-year-old would have every reason to ensure that he is safe when competing against older and more developed teammates and opponents. In reality, the three-year rule comes from one motivation and one motivation only: protection of the NFL's free farm system.

It's just another roadblock to the reckoning that may never come, but should. Year after year after year, football players go to college and, as a practical matter, major in football. Despite the reality that only a small percentage of college football players ever make it to the NFL, high school players who find themselves recruited by Alabama, Clem-son, Florida State, Texas, or other major institutions believe that they're destined for the next level. Even if they fully understood the long odds they face, they shrug and say they've already beaten the odds—why not keep beating them?

Against this inherently corrupt backdrop that consistently entails players being exploited because they can be, individual players should get whatever they can, whenever they can, however they can. Whether it comes through rules allowing them to profit from their fame or whether it comes in the form of a cash handshake from a booster, it's not wrong. The system is what's wrong, and in hindsight, it was very wrong for the NCAA to demonize Bush for daring to get for himself and his fam-ily a sliver of what he was giving to USC specifically and to college football generally.

PACMAN JONES

AS THE 2005 draft approached and NFL scouts began to gather information on highly regarded West Virginia prospects Adam "Pacman" Jones and Chris Henry, one scout who later would become a GM told me, "It's amazing no one was killed when they were in Morgantown."

Jones, extremely talented but prone to finding trouble (and/or to having trouble find him), became the sixth overall pick thanks to an aggressive effort by his agent, the late Gary Wichard, to sell Jones over the other top defensive backs, Antrel Rolle and Carlos Rogers. The Titans wanted to include safeguards in Jones's contract to protect against off-field misconduct, and he balked. Eventually, the two sides reached a compromise that would invalidate certain future payments if Jones were convicted of a crime.

To his credit, he wasn't convicted of a crime. To his detriment, he was involved in a string of incidents that didn't result in any convictions but that still got him into trouble with the league. Pacman's incidents included a July 2005 arrest for assault and felony vandalism; a February 2006 arrest for possession of marijuana, misdemeanor obstructing of police, and felony obstruction; an April 2006 incident at a gas station where a fight broke out and shots were fired (Jones wasn't arrested or charged); an August 2006 arrest for disorderly conduct and public intoxication; an October 2006 assault allegation for spitting in the face of a college student; and a February 2007 incident in Las Vegas that happened after Jones "made it rain" at a strip club, sparking a brawl that culminated in a shooting. (Eventually, a jury ordered Jones to pay $12.4 million to victims of the shooting.)

In March 2007, NFLPA Executive Director Gene Upshaw (who runs the organization that defends players accused of wrongdoing) made an unavoidable public concession. "How is it possible to be in the wrong place at the wrong time so many times?" Upshaw said.

In April 2007, barely seven months into his tenure, Commissioner Roger Goodell lowered the boom on Jones, suspending him for a year. At the same time, Goodell suspended Chris Henry for eight games after his own string of incidents, including the alleged brandishing of a firearm *while wearing his Cincinnati Bengals jersey*. Goodell used the occasion to beef up the league's Personal Conduct Policy, with a focus on enhanced penalties for repeat offenders.

Upshaw acknowledged the importance of making the changes, as did players such as Henry's teammate, Bengals receiver T. J. Houshmandzadeh. "You would think it's necessary just because of the negative publicity the NFL is beginning to receive because of what's happening," Houshmandzadeh told ESPN.com at the time. "It was going on for an extended period of time. Each day, each week, something was happening."

Jones complied with the league's expectations during his suspension, with the only real drama coming from an effort to dabble in pro wrestling and ensuing litigation from the Titans to keep him from putting himself in harm's way given that the team still held his contractual rights. In April 2008, the Titans traded those rights to the Cowboys, who hired (essentially) a full-time babysitter to keep Jones out of trouble.

It didn't work. In October 2008, Jones became involved in an altercation with his full-time babysitter, triggering a six-game suspension from the league and sparking the Cowboys to cut him after the season ended.

Jones didn't play football in 2009. He planned to join the Winnipeg Blue Bombers for a portion of the season, but the Blue Bombers backed off when Jones referred to the Canadian Football League as the "United Football League." (The then fledgling UFL promptly offered Jones a contract, but he passed.)

Things soon changed. In 2010, Jones ran a 4.42-second 40-yard dash in a workout for scouts from six teams, and the Bengals decided to give him his latest second chance. He remained in Cincinnati from 2010 through 2017, an eight-year stay that would have seemed inconceivable during his ultrarocky early NFL seasons. While he didn't stay entirely out of trouble (the league suspended him for the first game of the 2017 season for a fresh violation of the Personal Conduct Policy), Jones stayed in the league and on the team well beyond his expected shelf life.

Yes, Jones could have had an even better career if he'd been smarter and more mature in his early years. He entered the NFL at the age of twenty-one, and he suddenly had millions of dollars at his instant disposal. As he tore through the money, agent Gary Wichard explained the mindset to me in blunt, candid terms. "Jones made it through his whole life with nothing," Wichard said. "He has no concerns about having nothing again."

To his credit, Jones ended up with a lot more than nothing, playing in the NFL through 2018 and retiring the following May at the age of thirty-five.

MIKE VICK

IN APRIL 2007, police began investigating a man named Davon Boddie for possession of marijuana with intent to sell. They found something else entirely.

Boddie lived at the Surry County, Virginia, home owned by his cousin. His cousin played football for the NFL's Atlanta Falcons. His cousin is Mike Vick.

The property contained extensive evidence of a dogfighting operation, from kennels to a fighting pit to treadmills to pry bars used to break up dogfights to malnourished fighting dogs to a "rape stand" for breeding more dogs to fight. Vick instantly claimed that he never went to the property and didn't know what went on there.

At the 2007 draft, only days after authorities discovered the dogfighting operation, Vick lied to Commissioner Roger Goodell's face about the situation. "He was very direct and impassioned," Goodell said of Vick's response in an ESPN documentary regarding Vick's career.

Given the extent of the dogfighting operation, a flat, broad denial was Vick's only option. It also made it much easier to prove that he knew about the dogfighting and was directly involved in it.

Immediately after Vick said he had no role in or knowledge of the criminal activities, contradictory evidence emerged. He had been there. He was involved. He and a group of other men actively maintained a dogfighting operation.

The local prosecutor, sixty-six-year-old Gerald Poindexter, didn't seem to be interested in pursuing the matter. Poindexter downplayed the evidence, calling it all hearsay. Whether he wanted to protect Vick or had no interest in taking on the legal dream team that Vick had the money to amass, Poindexter created a clear impression that he ultimately wouldn't pursue charges.

That was when the feds got involved. Some still believe the NFL, which had quickly learned plenty about Vick's previously secret activities, instigated the federal investigation given the apparent likelihood that local officials would do nothing. From a June 7 raid to July 17 indictments to guilty pleas from his three partners in the dogfighting operation—Quanis Phillips, Tony Taylor, and Purnell Peace—the walls soon collapsed on Vick. On August 24, Vick struck a deal to plead guilty to federal dogfighting and gambling charges.

The paperwork confirming the guilty plea acknowledged that Vick and his cohorts in the enterprise known as "Bad Newz Kennels" (a reference to the nickname of Vick's hometown of Newport News, Virginia) had "killed by various methods, including hanging and drowning" dogs that did not perform well in "testing" sessions conducted at Vick's property. After pleading guilty, Vick told federal investigators that dogs had indeed been hanged, shot, and electrocuted.

On December 10, less than eight months after police first discovered the dogfighting operation, Vick received a sentence of twenty-three months.

Many called Vick's misadventures a "mistake." That's by far the wrong term to use. It was a lifestyle. In Falcons owner Arthur Blank's 2020 autobiography, *Good Company*, Blank wrote that Vick admitted, "I never thought I'd get caught." In the ESPN documentary regarding Vick's rise and fall, Vick said, "Man, if I [had] just walked away, maybe a year ago, this wouldn't be happening."

Maybe he wouldn't have been prosecuted and imprisoned if he'd walked away a year earlier, but he still would have engaged in multiple years of fighting dogs and killing dogs deemed unworthy of fighting. Who's to say it wouldn't have come to light at some point? Who's to say someone else from the world of dogfighting wasn't already using knowledge of Vick's activities against him as a rough-and-tumble form of football kompromat?

What comes next is speculation, and it's speculation I've previously articulated on radio programs and in podcasts. Look up Vick's game-by-game performances from the 2006 season, his last in the NFL before the discovery of the dogfighting operation. Statistically, Vick showed wild swings from great games to horrible games. In this world of dogfighting, which fundamentally was a platform for gambling, is it ridiculous to think that another dogfighter might have threatened to blow the whistle on Vick's secret lifestyle if he didn't agree to have a well-timed poor game that contributed to his team's failure to win or inability to cover whatever point spread applied?

That question, by all appearances, was never even pondered by the NFL. When Vick's sentence expired in July 2009, Goodell promptly reinstated Vick on a conditional basis. The Eagles quickly signed him, potential boycotts and demonstrations from animal-rights groups be damned. (The protests never materialized in any significant fashion.) After one season spent backing up Donovan McNabb, Vick eventually became the starter. In 2010, Vick won the annual Comeback Player of the Year award. Next came a five-year, $80 million contract with the Eagles.

Vick had secured his redemption, and Vick had changed his life. Whenever criticism emerges regarding Vick's past misconduct, defenders will insist that he paid his debt to society. As far as the federal government is concerned, he did. As far as the Commonwealth of Virginia is concerned, it's fair to ask whether he actually did.

Often overlooked in the broader Vick saga is the failure of Gerald Poindexter to indict Vick on eight counts of killing or causing a companion animal to be killed. The charges, based on Vick's own admissions to the federal government, would have exposed him to up to forty more years in prison.

So, yes, Vick served time for fighting dogs and betting on dogfights. He avoided significant criminal scrutiny for admitting involvement in the electrocution, drowning, and hanging of dogs deemed too docile to fight other dogs. The best the naysayers can say in response is "It's just dogs." Anyone who has ever had a dog knows that's a woefully inadequate excuse for a multiyear pattern of gruesome misconduct premised on killing innocent animals that are beloved and important members of families throughout the world.

PLAXICO BURRESS

HE CAUGHT THE championship-clinching pass in Super Bowl XLII despite a shower mishap that sprained his knee and nearly knocked him out of the game. Later that same year, Giants receiver Plaxico Burress would suffer a far more serious off-field leg injury.

The season after the Giants became an unlikely Super Bowl winner, making it to the title game and beating the previously unbeatable Patriots, the Giants started 10–1 and appeared to be on track for another potential Super Bowl run. Then, on the Friday after Thanksgiving, Burress went to a nightclub in Manhattan. He went to the nightclub with a gun tucked into the waistband of his jeans.

The weapon fired, blowing a hole through Plaxico's leg. Here's how Burress later explained the moment in an item for *The Player's Tribune*. "The stairway was narrow and dark and everything was black," he wrote. "I had a drink in my left hand and I was walking right behind the security guard. The music was loud and I could feel the bass thumping the stairs under my feet. But I could barely see and I guess I missed a step and my foot slipped. My gun came unhooked from my belt and went sliding down my right pant leg. My instant reaction was to catch it before it hit the floor, and I reached down with my right hand to grab it. And I guess my finger hit right on the trigger, because it went off."

Indeed it did, even though no one heard the crack over the sonic booming of the club. Burress saw the flash, but he didn't realize he'd shot himself until he felt something wet on his leg. It could have been worse; prosecutors claimed that the bullet nearly struck a security guard standing inches from Burress.

The projectile entering and exiting Plaxico's thigh became just the beginning of the player's problems. Although he may not have known the full extent of the legal jeopardy he'd face, Burress instinctively knew that it would be better to keep it all quiet. He went to New York Presbyterian Hospital for treatment under the pseudonym "Harris Smith," a name with far less cachet than "Ron Mexico" (a lawsuit once alleged that Mike Vick used that name to obtain herpes treatment). The hospital failed to report the gunshot to authorities, resulting in the firing of at least one employee and public calls for prosecution of the institution. The Giants also participated in the attempted cover-up, failing to inform New York City officials of the shooting that had occurred in their city.

Manhattan authorities eventually learned of the incident, which was bad news for Burress. The city had passed strict laws regarding the illegal possession of firearms. Mayor Michael Bloomberg made it clear that in order to protect innocent citizens from accidentally getting shot, individuals guilty of illegally carrying a gun in New York would face serious consequences.

"If you are convicted, you will serve a minimum of three and a half years behind bars," Bloomberg said in 2007, "no exceptions."

Bloomberg wanted no exception to be made for Burress; rather, he wanted an example to be made of him. The mayor, reportedly "fuming" over the incident, wanted Burress prosecuted "to the fullest extent of the law" and to end up "in the slammer."

"It's pretty hard to argue the guy didn't have a gun and that it was loaded," Bloomberg said at the time. "You've got bullet holes in and out to show that it was there."

Many think that the rich and famous get special treatment from the criminal justice system. Just as often, if not more frequently, those with significant notoriety find themselves under hyperaggressive scrutiny given that the ensuing media coverage goes a long way toward deterring the average person from committing similar violations.

Burress ultimately caught a break, relatively speaking. Instead of facing the mandatory forty-two-month prison term, he pleaded guilty to reduced charges and received a two-year sentence, which with good behavior was reduced to twenty months.

The league, applying a Personal Conduct Policy that at the time focused more on punishing repeat offenders, gave Burress no penalty beyond a suspension coinciding with his time behind bars. In 2011, Burress signed with the Jets, catching forty-five catches for 612 yards and eight touchdowns primarily as a red-zone target. The following season, his career ended where it had begun twelve years earlier, joining the Steelers for four late-season games.

Burress ended up losing more than two seasons of his NFL career. The incident arguably derailed the Giants' 2008 playoff run. They lost three of their last four regular-season games, and they fell at home in the divisional round to the Eagles.

Would they have fared better with Burress that year? Possibly, if not probably. It ultimately worked out for the Giants, however. In 2011, the same season that saw Burress return and sign with the same-stadium Jets, the Giants won another Super Bowl.

BRETT FAVRE

HALL OF FAME quarterback Brett Favre had a magical season with the Vikings in 2009. The effort to win a second Super Bowl fell one level short of the biggest game in the sport, with Minnesota losing to New Orleans in the NFC Championship. For multiple reasons, Favre in hindsight should have called it quits then and there.

Favre retired for the third time and eventually unretired for a third time, committing to another season with the Vikings. Beyond the fact that Favre, now closing in on forty-one, was becoming what the kids would called "washed," his decision to continue to play made an unexpected off-field issue a much bigger deal than it otherwise would have been.

On August 4, 2010, Deadspin.com ran a story accusing Favre of sending lewd photos to Jenn Sterger, a former Jets sideline reporter who had crossed paths with him in 2008 during the one season he had played in New York. Setting aside the question of whether the story was ripe for publication (or whether Sterger had actually authorized the attachment of her name to it), it grew legs. Quickly.

Favre had allegedly pursued Sterger, who had spurned the much older and extremely married athlete's advances. Eventually, Favre allegedly sent Sterger a photo of his penis. The original article, written by A. J. Daulerio, noted, "Sterger claims that, in one of the photos Favre allegedly sent to her, he's masturbating—while wearing a pair of Crocs."

Favre actually hadn't decided to keep playing when the story first broke. Absent photos of Favre or voice messages he had left Sterger, the story fizzled out.

Then came an October date with the Jets, and Deadspin.com coincidentally (or not) published audio of two snippets of Favre's voice from messages he had sent to Sterger. When reporters asked him about the developments, Favre said, "I've got my hands full with the Jets."

The audio evidence forced the league to deal with the situation. "One can assume that we look into everything that is relevant, whether we say so or not," NFL spokesman Greg Aiello said at the time before admitting shortly thereafter that the league was indeed reviewing the matter. The league had no choice but to do so, especially since the Jets had created a stir with their construction-worker treatment of TV Azteca reporter Inez Sainz in September 2010.

The story accelerated. Favre addressed his Vikings teammates. Minnesota kicker Ryan Longwell said Favre "broke down in tears" while apologizing for being a distraction. Favre didn't appreciate Longwell's comments, saying that the conversation was "between me and my teammates, apparently not all of them."

Questions lingered regarding when the league would interview Favre and whether Sterger would meet with the league. Without her cooperation, the investigation of Favre would ultimately go nowhere.

Favre and his agent, Bus Cook, eventually met with the NFL on October 19. Sterger, at that point, had not cooperated. The league made it clear that it still hoped to talk to her. The *St. Paul Pioneer Press* reported that Sterger would decline to meet with the league if Favre agreed to a financial settlement, a legitimate method for buying her silence.

When Favre didn't respond to multiple apparent efforts to get him to settle any claims in exchange for Sterger not talking to the league, she did. The first meeting happened on November 11. The following month, she met with Commissioner Roger Goodell in a session that reportedly became "heated."

Favre's camp became exasperated with Sterger's tactics, eventually challenging her representatives, repeatedly, to "give us a lawsuit." But Sterger never did, letting the two-year statute of limitations pass with no civil complaint against Favre or the Jets for sexual harassment or any other alleged wrongdoing.

Ultimately, the league took no action against Favre for violating the Personal Conduct Policy in connection with his interactions with

Sterger. The NFL instead fined him $50,000 for refusing to cooperate with the investigation into whether sexual harassment had happened.

The punishment made no sense then, and it makes no sense now. The league explained that Favre faced monetary punishment for not being candid during the interview and that if it had determined that Favre had violated workplace conduct policies, a higher level of punishment would have been imposed. However, Favre's lying (the league didn't call it what it was, but it was lying) could have been coupled with Sterger's version of the events to lead to a conclusion that she was telling the truth.

Favre should have been punished for his behavior toward Sterger, not simply for lying about it. He arguably should have been suspended. Lesser players with shorter NFL tenures and far fewer accomplishments likely would have been. Favre, apparently benefiting from his homespun charisma, three league MVP awards, a Super Bowl win, and (at the time) every major career passing record, amazingly got a pass.

AARON HERNANDEZ

THE PATRIOTS CREATED the platinum standard when it comes to building and maintaining a high-quality team. But even the best organization the NFL has seen in decades, if not ever, has had its share of awkward moments. None were more awkward than the decision to draft, employ, and give a big-money contract extension to a man who killed at least one and maybe three people.

By the summer of 2012, tight end Aaron Hernandez had become a key member of the New England offense. A skilled route runner, pass catcher, and blocker, Hernandez had enhanced value because of his ability to play multiple positions. His Swiss Army knife–style skills allowed the Patriots to slide into a no-huddle offense without warning, moving players around and creating mismatches against a defense that couldn't react by shuttling in replacements.

In 2011, the NFL changed the rules regarding second contracts for new players, forcing teams to wait three years before rewarding draft picks. The Patriots would have benefited from that policy in relation to Hernandez. In August 2012, they gave the 2010 fourth-round pick a five-year, $40 million extension after only two NFL seasons—and possibly at a time when he'd already murdered two people.

Few knew about Hernandez's double life until June 2013, when authorities discovered a corpse not far from his home. A vibe instantly emerged that Hernandez may have had something to do with it. Within days, the tall, chiseled football star made an awkward perp walk from his home, white T-shirt pulled over his torso with hands cuffed behind his back, as he faced murder charges.

The Patriots immediately severed ties with Hernandez. The team took the PR effort to the next level, offering to buy back any and all Aaron Hernandez jerseys. As the investigation into the death of Odin Lloyd continued, investigators became intrigued by Hernandez's potential role in an unsolved drive-by double murder from July 2012. One thing led to another, and formal charges landed against Hernandez for the two additional deaths.

Hernandez's lawyers said all the things that defense lawyers always say. *Hernandez didn't do it. Hernandez looks forward to returning to the NFL.* Yada, yada, yada. Although investigators never found the handgun used to shoot and kill Lloyd, the circumstantial evidence became overwhelming, including the fact that Hernandez had left a shell casing matching the bullets that had struck Lloyd in a rental car used to pick up Lloyd and to take him to the place where he had been executed.

Prosecutors believed that Hernandez feared Lloyd knew too much about the double murder from the prior July, the culmination of an incident that allegedly began after one of the two victims bumped into Hernandez at a club in Boston, spilling his drink. As more information emerged regarding Hernandez's alleged exploits while at the University of Florida and the secret life he had led throughout his career—including news of a flophouse where drugs and guns and anything other than the Patriot Way prevailed—it seemed plausible, if not likely, that the photogenic football player was a cold-blooded triple murderer.

In 2015, a jury convicted Hernandez of killing Lloyd, and Hernandez received a life sentence for the crime. Nearly two years to the day later, a jury acquitted Hernandez of killing Safiro Furtado and Daniel de Abreu. Two days after that, Hernandez committed suicide in prison.

It was a sad and sordid story, and an eventual Netflix documentary meandered through various potential excuses for the fact that Hernandez had killed at least one and possibly as many as three people. The best explanation may be the simplest. Like any other murderer, Hernandez was a high-level asshole/narcissist/sociopath who believed he'd get away with it and who had no apparent feelings of genuine guilt for the things he had done.

Through it all, the NFL and the Patriots somehow managed to avoid having any of the ugliness stick to the league or the team. The Patriots employed the guy, and yet they surely knew nothing about his hidden world of drugs and guns and crime or they wouldn't have given him a gigantic contract the month after he had allegedly killed two people.

Even at a time when the Patriots had become sufficiently polarizing within a clear segment of the media and the broader NFL fan base was looking for any reason to criticize the team, few wagged a finger at the Patriots for not knowing that they had given such a prominent role and lucrative contract to such a troubled and malignant person. Maybe it was because the Patriots moved so quickly to sever ties. Maybe it was the hand-washing gesture of refunding fans for Hernandez jerseys. Whatever the reason and whether or not even the Patriots believed it would work, swift and decisive action mixed with a clear gesture of contrition allowed them to avoid having the franchise dragged down by its close association with Hernandez.

It also helped that from the time of Hernandez's arrest to the time of his suicide, the Patriots won two more Super Bowls. Nothing deflects scrutiny for off-field entanglements better than on-field success.

RAY RICE

FEW NFL CONTROVERSIES have threatened the employment of the commissioner. In 2014, an NFL controversy threatened the employment of the commissioner.

It started on February 15 in Atlantic City. Ravens running back Ray Rice and his fiancée, Janay Palmer, allegedly fought in a hotel elevator. Authorities charged both with simple assault. The truth was far more complicated.

Four days later, TMZ released a video of Rice dragging Palmer's unconscious body out of the elevator. The case percolated for three months before Rice entered into a diversion program to resolve what had grown into aggravated assault charges. During that period, no one wondered whether the video from outside the elevator after the incident could be supplemented by video from inside the elevator before and during the incident.

Then, on the Friday of Memorial Day weekend, the Ravens conducted a press conference during which Rice apologized for "the situation" and Palmer expressed "regret" for her role in it. The team received widespread criticism for sanctioning the awkward event.

Rice and Palmer met the following month with Commissioner Goodell. In late July, Goodell imposed a two-game suspension on Rice.

The public and media reaction stunned the league. Given the images of Rice standing next to his knocked-out fiancée, a belief persisted that Rice deserved a harsher punishment. Besieged by reporters while attending Hall of Fame festivities in Canton, Ohio, Goodell justified the suspension by pointing out that the criminal justice system allowed Rice to enter into a diversion program that would ultimately result in no incarceration or even house arrest.

Not long after that, I got into a fairly heated argument with a league executive regarding the potential existence of video evidence of the knockout blow. The executive insisted that the league didn't have the video and had no way to compel law enforcement to release it. My response was fairly straightforward. If a video existed, it would have become part of the file in the criminal case, Rice's lawyer would have possession of it, and Rice would have an absolute right to direct his lawyer to turn the video over to the league. The NFL's leverage was clear. If it told Rice that he couldn't play until he directed his lawyer to produce the video, Rice would direct his lawyer to produce the video immediately.

My explanation was met with condescension, frankly, along with the stubborn reiteration of the contention that the league had no way to get the video. The conversation ended with this prediction: *You should go get the video now because TMZ eventually will.*

TMZ eventually did. The Monday after the start of the 2014 regular season, TMZ released the footage. Graphic, brutal, and shocking, the video triggered an immediate seismic reaction.

The Ravens cut Rice, and the NFL suspended him indefinitely. The league also engaged in damage control, claiming that it had tried to get the video from law enforcement and that law enforcement had not produced it. The league continued to ignore the obvious reality that it could have ordered Rice to instruct his lawyer to produce the video.

Two days later, scrutiny of the league reached a fever pitch. The Associated Press (AP) reported that a law enforcement officer had sent the video to the NFL in April. The league reacted by hiring former FBI director Robert Mueller to investigate the situation. (The league insisted that the investigation was independent; however, Mueller worked for a law firm that had a business relationship with the league and that presumably intended to preserve if not expand it. That fact alone undermined the independence of the investigator, no matter who the investigator was.) Although Mueller would eventually conclude that the AP report was not accurate, Goodell spent a couple of weeks in the aftermath of the

AP report worrying about the possibility that the league's owners would decide to replace him.

During that stretch, a number of people argued that many could do Goodell's job for far less than the $40 million or so paid annually to him. The fumes of that take undoubtedly contributed to the eventual showdown between Goodell and Cowboys owner Jerry Jones, who would take a stand three years later based on the belief that the league was overpaying its commissioner.

The situation eventually died down, but not until after the league had revamped the Personal Conduct Policy to impose a baseline suspension of six games for first-offense domestic violence and created (thanks to off-field issues involving Panthers defensive end Greg Hardy and Vikings running back Adrian Peterson) a system of paid leave aimed, quite candidly, at helping the NFL manage the PR problems associated with allowing players with unresolved charges to play football, despite the presumption of innocence.

Amazingly, the league argued at the time and still believes that paid leave does not harm a football player. This argument ignores the fact that football players want to play football and to generate statistics and other achievements that enhance their standing and future earnings.

None of that mattered to the league. Goodell became determined to never again be accused of being too lenient with players who committed domestic violence. Although the league would be tested (and would fail that test) in connection with the decision to impose only a one-game suspension on Giants kicker Josh Brown in 2016 (the team released him under the weight of public pressure and after the release of new evidence of misconduct), the NFL has otherwise adhered to the precedent created by Rice and cemented by Hardy and Peterson.

The best news for the league is that the new approach generally has worked. Players have finally gotten the message that off-field misbehavior will prevent them from playing football. As a result, far fewer players have been suspended in recent years for violating the Personal Conduct Policy.

EZEKIEL ELLIOTT

THE RAY RICE situation caused the NFL to push the pendulum too far in the other direction. The commissioner's determination to never again be accused of being too lenient caused him, in the case of Cowboys running back Ezekiel Elliott, to be too aggressive, imposing punishment even though Elliott was never arrested or even sued for his alleged misbehavior.

Elliott's former girlfriend Tiffany Thompson accused him of five separate incidents of domestic violence between July 17 and July 22, 2016, fewer than three months after the Cowboys had drafted Elliott. Thompson pressed charges against Elliott, but prosecutors decided in September 2016 not to pursue the matter.

Pre-Rice, the decision not to prosecute Elliott would have ended the case from the league's perspective. Post-Rice, the NFL activated the in-house justice system created to supplement if not supersede decisions made by the authorities.

The league investigated the situation, meeting with Elliott and interviewing Thompson six times. Along the way, NFL director of investigations Kia Roberts developed an opinion about the matter: she believed Elliott should not be suspended.

Elliott eventually alleged in court proceedings challenging his suspension that someone in the league office had kept Kia Roberts's opinion from the commissioner. The league vehemently denied this, creating the impression that the commissioner eventually punished Elliott with a six-game suspension *despite* being aware of the misgivings of a person who had spoken directly to Tiffany Thompson on multiple occasions.

The flaws in the investigation were compounded by the results-driven kangaroo court convened by the league. The commissioner, who at the time had the power to make both the initial disciplinary decision and either handle the appeal personally or delegate the process to a person of his choosing, appointed Harold Henderson—a league-friendly arbitrator—to preside over the appeal. Henderson surprisingly didn't direct the league to make Thompson available to testify at the appeal hearing. Even though she agreed to submit to at least six interviews with league personnel, the league never even asked whether she would appear at the appeal hearing.

In a controversy that fundamentally hinged on assessing and reconciling the credibility of Elliott and Thompson, especially since there were no third-party witnesses to the alleged misconduct, Elliott's inability to confront and cross-examine Thompson and Henderson's inability to scrutinize her words and demeanor while testifying undermined the validity of the entire exercise. How can anyone make a reliable decision as to whether Elliott committed domestic violence without hearing both parties testify and having the testimony of each witness challenged via skilled and probing questions?

The flaw allowed Elliott to secure some preliminary success in court, as a federal judge in Texas found that the inability to cross-examine Thompson prevented the process from being fundamentally fair to Elliott. The judge also concluded that the confusion regarding the Kia Roberts situation made Commissioner Roger Goodell's testimony critical to a fair hearing. Also, the judge determined that Henderson should have required the league to produce all notes of the various interviews of Tiffany Thompson and that Henderson should have compelled the league to produce Kia Roberts for testimony at the hearing.

Unfortunately for Elliott, the federal judge's decision didn't last. Knowing that the NFL would immediately file a lawsuit to affirm the suspension in New York (a favorable forum for the league), Elliott's lawyers got a head start, suing before the suspension became official. The federal appeals court with jurisdiction over Texas eventually found that Elliott had sued too early.

Given that the law has developed in the federal appeals court with jurisdiction over New York in a way that makes it much, much easier for the NFL to win there, and given that the league always knows when it will be issuing a suspension, it can simultaneously drop the gavel and file the paperwork aimed at getting the courts to rubber-stamp the suspension. Additionally, it can rely on its own in-house investigation to reach whatever decision it wants to reach, with whatever inherently unfair process it wants to use, without fear of having the decision overturned.

In 2020, the league agreed to revise the Personal Conduct Policy procedure to involve a neutral decision-maker. However, the neutrality comes not at the appellate stage but at the initial level. The commissioner still has final say over the process, which means that the league can still do whatever it wants to do and that, as long as the league files the lawsuit in New York federal court to uphold the outcome immediately upon issuing the decision, it will always win.

ANTONIO BROWN

THE STEELERS HAVE had three coaches since 1969. Their most recent hire, Mike Tomlin, has plenty of detractors despite many years of success. Whenever the Steelers stumble, a chunk of the fan base—and some of the team's limited partners—begin jostling for change.

If change ever happens, Tomlin would instantly find a head-coaching job with another team. He continues to be one of the most respected figures in the NFL for, among other things, his ability to reach players who, absent Tomlin's influence, could become problematic. He has done so with players such as linebacker Lawrence Timmons and most notably with receiver Antonio Brown.

For a decade, Tomlin kept Brown from imploding by finding a way to indulge his ego and diva disposition. A separate set of rules applied, and no one resented it because Brown delivered. From missing meetings to having his own off-site rental house during training camp while team-mates were crammed into dorm rooms to showing up ridiculously late for games, it was fine as long as Brown delivered. And deliver he did.

Some coaches get rid of players a year too early, and some coaches get rid of players a year too late. As for Tomlin and Brown, it happened at absolutely the right time.

Two days after Brown had torched the Saints for 185 yards and two touchdowns on fourteen catches in a critical game that the Steelers lost when second-year receiver JuJu Smith-Schuster fumbled the ball, the team announced that Smith-Schuster had won the team MVP award for 2018. Brown blew a gasket, storming out of practice, going AWOL, and then making a belated, and unsuccessful, effort to play in the regular-season finale.

Brown spent the next two months agitating for a trade, behaving increasingly erratically in what some regarded as a crazy-like-a-fox effort to obtain more guaranteed money. The Steelers played it cool in an effort to finagle the best possible trade before getting third- and fifth-round draft picks from the Raiders. Brown got his new team, along with $30 million in guaranteed payments.

The move had promise, pizzazz, potential. And then training camp rolled around. First, Brown couldn't practice due to a mishap in a cryogenic chamber that had frozen the flesh on his feet. Next, a controversy over his desire to wear a helmet the league had deemed to be insufficient resulted in a failed legal fight and, eventually, capitulation by the player.

Then things got really goofy.

Brown had missed practices during the helmet kerfuffle. The Raiders fined him for his failure to follow the rules. Brown became incensed by the imposition of discipline, accosting GM Mike Mayock and calling him a "cracker." The Raiders moved to suspend Brown for the regular-season opener. Brown then launched an effort to be released. He got his wish, with the sudden and abrupt decision coming one day before the first Sunday of the season.

Then things got even goofier.

The Patriots immediately swooped in to sign Brown, giving him a $9 million signing bonus on a one-year deal that paid up to $15 million. Three days later, Brown's former trainer sued him for sexual assault and rape.

Although the Patriots had moved quickly to cut tight end Aaron Hernandez after his murder arrest six years earlier, they declined to summarily release Brown based only on allegations made in a civil lawsuit. As the Patriots saw it, anyone could be sued at any time for anything. Making employment decisions based solely on the content of a civil complaint, especially when the player had never faced criminal charges, would establish a tricky precedent.

And so Brown played for the Patriots in their Week Two game against the Dolphins. He established an immediate bond with quarterback Tom

Brady, and they connected on a touchdown pass in their first game as teammates. It would be their only game together in 2019.

Days later, SI.com reported on another allegation against Brown, and Brown allegedly retaliated against the woman who had made the accusation via hostile and intimidating text messages. That prompted the Patriots to sever ties with Brown.

Enter the NFL. As it commenced an investigation regarding the various allegations that had been made against Brown, the league used the vague threat of a paid suspension to keep other teams, as a practical matter, from signing him. With the league declining to tell teams whether Brown would be placed on paid leave if signed, no one wanted to sign him (and incur the associated PR hit) if that team would ultimately be paying Brown to not play while the league investigated the claims against him.

The league successfully dragged its feet on the various Antonio Brown investigations for the balance of the 2019 season, essentially imposing a fourteen-game unpaid suspension by failing to reach a decision or to tell teams whether he'd be placed on paid leave. While Brown was shunned by the league, his behavior became more erratic, culminating in a January 2020 incident with the driver of a truck moving Brown's belongings from his temporary home in the Oakland area back to his permanent home in Miami. Brown didn't want to pay the bill, one thing led to another, and Brown ended up facing criminal charges.

Along the way, agent Drew Rosenhaus fired Brown unless and until he got the help that so many believed he needed.

Brown eventually pleaded no contest to a felony charge arising from the incident with the moving-truck driver, and the league imposed an eight-game suspension for everything but the September 2019 allegation of sexual assault and rape. On that matter, the league curiously punted, opting to wait for the court system to resolve the case before making any decisions—even though the league routinely makes such decisions in the absence of judgment rendered by a court of law, civil or criminal.

Operating under the reduced standard of proof that had allowed the league to find that Cowboys running back Ezekiel Elliott had committed domestic violence two years earlier, the league could have, and should have, made a decision based on the available evidence. Either Brown hadn't committed sexual assault and/or rape, or he had. If the league believed he did, how could he ever play in the NFL again?

The most likely explanation is that the league believed, based on its investigation, that he hadn't done it, but the league didn't want to risk another Ray Rice situation by exonerating Brown and then having the civil justice system reach a different outcome. So the league decided to put a pin in things while the courts did their work, even though in the aftermath of the Ray Rice case, the league had resolved to never again defer to the conclusions reached, or not reached, by the justice system.

This allowed Brown to return to the NFL in 2020 after serving his eight-game suspension. He played for the Buccaneers and won a Super Bowl ring after the trial date for the pending civil case was moved from December 2020 to December 2021. Then, he settled the lawsuit, ending the matter for good.

DESHAUN WATSON

AT A TIME when the Houston Texans seemed to be creeping toward accepting the fact that the team had no choice but to trade disgruntled quarterback Deshaun Watson, Watson disclosed on social media an unexpected twist. After making what Watson called a "baseless six-figure settlement demand," a lawyer had filed a lawsuit against Watson.

The lawyer was Tony Buzbee, a prominent plaintiff's attorney in Houston who had tried to resolve a claim of alleged misconduct during a massage-therapy session by making an opening demand of $100,000. Watson's lawyers opted not to respond with an offer (which based on the opening position could have resulted in a settlement in the range of $50,000 to $75,000), asking instead that Buzbee make a new, lower demand.

This unconventional approach served only to piss Buzbee off. And it resulted in Buzbee finding more and more (and more) women who claimed that Watson had engaged in misconduct during massages. Buzbee filed the lawsuits on a near daily basis until twenty-two in all landed on the docket. A full-blown, gloves-off battle ensued in the court of public opinion. Buzbee attacked relentlessly. Watson, represented by famous Houston lawyer Rusty Hardin, initially didn't engage. In time, Hardin did.

It got loud. It got nasty. The NFL launched an investigation. With twenty-two women claiming misconduct during massages, how could an investigation not have happened? Even though only a few of the women alleged any type of forcible action, the sheer volume of complaints and

249

the similarities of the allegations made it extremely difficult to accept that each and every one of them was lying. Hardin has nevertheless persisted in that position, eventually proclaiming publicly that Watson, and in turn Hardin, does not believe that the women are telling the truth.

The situation prevented a Watson trade from happening in March 2021 given the strong possibility that the league would eventually use its broad discretion to place Watson on paid leave pending the resolution of the legal situation. Multiple women made complaints with the Houston Police Department, raising the possibility of a prosecution—which would virtually guarantee paid leave.

But then, after several weeks of press conferences and Instagram posts and public comments, things fell eerily quiet. The two sides took a step back because they were trying to resolve the cases out of court. The thinking was that a settlement would facilitate a trade. Even with the league likely to suspend Watson without pay for several games due to the sheer volume of allegations, it was believed that a new team would be far more likely to give real value for Watson's contract if the prospect of an extended stay on paid leave could be extinguished.

With the settlement talks came an unexpected glitch. Usually in cases of this nature, the party paying for legal peace wants everything to be kept confidential. Here, Buzbee wanted confidentiality; Watson and Hardin insisted on full transparency.

The fact that talks broke down on the issue of confidentiality implied two significant facts: (1) the two sides had already reached a tentative deal on the far more important question of the amount to be paid to settle the twenty-two civil claims, and (2) the amount was sufficiently small to give Watson and Hardin no concerns about having it freely and publicly known. This also suggested that once the actual litigation began to unfold, a settlement could be reached based on the tentative deal that had been struck.

It seems likely that at some point, the cases will indeed settle. (By the time you read this, there's a chance a settlement will have already occurred.) Assuming that settlement happens, the challenge for the league will be to determine the proper penalty to be applied to Watson if (as it appears given the high bar that applies in criminal cases) none of the allegations ever results in a conviction or guilty plea for something more than a simple misdemeanor, such as "lewd conduct."

Between the sheer volume of women accusing Watson, the even greater number of massage therapists he used (more than forty), and Hardin's admission that some of these encounters had resulted in consensual sexual activities, the league will have little choice but to take action. In 2010, the NFL suspended Steelers quarterback Ben Roethlisberger for six games (reduced to four) based on two allegations of sexual misconduct, neither of which resulted in criminal charges. In the letter informing Roethlisberger of the suspension, Commissioner Roger Goodell explained that Roethlisberger's "conduct raises sufficient concerns that I believe effective intervention now is the best step for your personal and professional welfare" and that the league had the power under its Personal Conduct Policy to impose discipline "'even where the conduct does not result in conviction of a crime' as, for example, where the conduct 'imposes inherent danger to the safety and well being of another person.' More broadly, the policy authorizes punishment for behavior that 'undermines or puts at risk the integrity or reputation of the NFL, NFL clubs, or NFL players.'" As Goodell told Roethlisberger, "By any measure, your conduct satisfies that standard."

Based on the standard that the league applied to Roethlisberger, Watson's conduct does as well—even without a verdict against him in a civil case or any type of criminal prosecution. So whether it already has happened or will happen in 2022, it would be a surprise if Watson isn't ultimately required to sit out multiple games without pay.

It also would not be a surprise if Watson, like Roethlisberger, eventually returns to the game and continues a career that could result in Super Bowl berths and potentially a bronze bust in Canton. Unless Watson ends up being convicted of one or more felonies and incarcerated for a decade or longer, he'll continue to play football. And, as happened with Roethlisberger, the memory of Watson's misbehavior will fade for everyone except those who believe he acted improperly.

PART VIII
MAJOR SCANDALS

THE JANET JACKSON INCIDENT

IF YOU USE YouTube, you can partially thank Janet Jackson for a moment that helped inspire the creation of the online video behemoth. More on that in a bit. For now, let's focus on the intermission of Super Bowl XXXVIII.

Most of the first two quarters of the championship game between the Patriots and the Panthers had been uneventful. Neither team had scored for nearly twenty-seven minutes of clock time until a 24-point outburst in the final three minutes and five seconds of the half. Then came the real eruption.

Michael Jackson's youngest sibling had become a superstar through her own talent. The NFL invited her to perform at halftime of the game, a continuation of a pattern that had started eleven years earlier when the NFL had hired Michael in order to prevent other networks from siphoning a portion of a massive audience during the break in the football action.

For Super Bowl XXXVIII, the halftime show featured multiple musical acts, from Jackson to P. Diddy to Nelly to Kid Rock to Justin Timberlake. The NFL had growing concerns, however, about the MTV-produced show. The league thought the budget for the halftime performances had become bloated and had specific worries about the performers and the show's messaging. Commissioner Paul Tagliabue eventually received a personal assurance from CBS president Les Moonves that he would work directly with MTV, a CBS affiliate, to minimize the possibility of any problems.

Moonves didn't sufficiently minimize the possibility of any problems. The show ended with Jackson and Timberlake performing Timberlake's "Rock Your Body," a tune that culminated with Christmas-album lyrics: "I'll have you naked by the end of this song." As Timberlake uttered the words, he grabbed Jackson's costume, pulling off a piece of material and exposing her breast.

The timing and the lyrics and the fact that Jackson happened to be wearing a piece of jewelry that (mostly) concealed her nipple made it all seem planned. The storm that immediately emerged resulted in the official version eventually becoming that Jackson had experienced a "wardrobe malfunction," perhaps the first time in the history of the English language that those two words were deliberately used in direct juxtaposition.

After it happened, reports of the incident made their way to people who were at the game but hadn't seen the TV feed. A small group of league executives (led by Tagliabue) went directly to the booth used by replay officials to watch the end of the show. "They quickly saw all they needed to see," one source who was present for the screening said.

Gloom descended over Tagliabue and his top lieutenants. The initial statement came not from Tagliabue but from communications executive Joe Browne, who said that the league was "extremely disappointed by elements of the MTV-produced show," that those elements were "totally inconsistent" with "assurances" the league had received, and that it was "unlikely that MTV will produce another Super Bowl halftime."

Jackson repeatedly apologized, insisting that the end result had been accidental. She described the outcry as hypocritical in light of the proliferation of sexualized beer and erectile dysfunction commercials, she repeatedly said that having her breast exposed to the worldwide audience of millions had caused her significant embarrassment, and she explained that the argument that she had done it to boost sales of her new album made no sense because the album (unlike her breast) wouldn't come out for two months.

Timberlake initially embraced the situation, flashing more than a hint (but less than a breast) of impishness in his initial comments on the situation. ("Hey, man, we love giving you all something to talk about," he told *Access Hollywood*.) Timberlake eventually pivoted to an apologetic tone, and he eventually expressed frustration that his character (as reflected by, say, the lyrics to "Rock Your Body") had been called into question.

Complaints were made (the league received between twenty thousand and twenty-five thousand emails and letters), fines were imposed, and lawsuits were filed. Changes were made. The NFL took the Super Bowl halftime show in a far different direction, at least for a while, opting for acts that were much less likely to have wardrobe malfunctions or sexual connotations and implementing a several-second delay. (By the halftime show of Super Bowl LIV, featuring Shakira and Jennifer Lopez, everything but the wardrobe malfunctions had returned.)

Accountability for the Janet Jackson debacle was also meted out internally. Tagliabue's initial public comment on the matter, made the day after the game, hinted at the consequences: "We will change our policies, our people, and our processes before the next Super Bowl to ensure that this entertainment is far more effectively dealt with." As one person with knowledge of the dynamics explained it, the use of "our people" was "jarring" to NFL executives whose fingerprints were on the show.

The NFL usually doesn't fire league-office executives; it sends them to work for one of the teams. Senior VP of Marketing John Collins, who had initially arranged for Janet Jackson to perform at Super Bowl XXXVI (she withdrew after the 9/11 attacks), had ultimate internal responsibility for the situation. By the end of April, he faced a fate worse than termination: he took a job as president of the Browns. (Relax, Clevelanders, it's a joke.)

This part is definitely no joke. The Janet Jackson incident (which happened in February 2004) coupled with the horrific Asian tsunami (which happened in December 2004) helped inspire the website that in 2005 would revolutionize the Internet. Jawed Karim, one of the founders of YouTube, explained to USA Today in 2006 that difficulty finding online clips of the Janet Jackson incident and the earthquake-triggered tidal wave contributed to the creation of a destination where users could upload their own videos.

So if you like YouTube, you can thank Janet Jackson. If you hate YouTube, you can blame Janet Jackson. Either way, if Jackson's wardrobe malfunction moment had happened after YouTube had been created, it might have contributed to a full-blown meltdown of YouTube's server farms. And the NFL might have had a much different reaction to it if those billions of views could have been traced to league-owned accounts from which the NFL would have profited mightily.

As the Internet has matured, the NFL has found more and more ways to monetize its content, both by slapping preroll advertising onto (and within) official video properties and by aggressively slapping around anyone who would dare to use that footage without authorization. The Janet Jackson incident surely would have prompted a robust debate at league headquarters regarding the balance between honoring appropriate standards and raking in the cash that would have flowed from You-Tube in the minutes, hours, and days after the word "song" emerged from Timberlake's mouth—and Jackson's breast malfunctioned its way out of her wardrobe.

SPYGATE I

STARTING IN 2001, the Patriots began to set the standard for NFL achievement. By winning three Super Bowls in four years, the franchise led by coach Bill Belichick and quarterback Tom Brady became the envy of the rest of the league. Envy eventually became something more tangible.

It's a simple process. When opposing owners interrogated their coaches and GMs regarding their team's inability to compete with the Patriots, the coaches and GMs couldn't and wouldn't say to the people who sign their checks, "They work harder than us. They're smarter than us. They're better than us." It's far easier (and safer) to shrug and say, "They cheat."

And so that became the suspicion and, eventually, the narrative. *The Patriots succeed because they cheat. Now all we need to do is catch them cheating.*

This strategy for minimizing New England's achievements overlooked the fact that the NFL has long adhered to the old NASCAR adage "If you ain't cheatin', you ain't tryin'." Cheating in creative and effective ways had become for NFL teams not a scarlet letter but a badge of honor, from stealing playbooks to spying on practices to anything and everything that can be done to gain an edge over the other team because the other team is doing unto others with the knowledge that they may as well do it while they can because it eventually will be (if it isn't already being) done unto them.

That dynamic provided the foundation for the scandal that would engulf the Patriots and the rest of the NFL after the first week of the 2007 regular season. Enhancing the circumstance was the relationship between New England coach Bill Belichick and New York Jets coach Eric Mangini, a former Belichick lieutenant who had taken a job with the franchise that Belichick despised above all others. Mangini knew Belichick's tricks and simply didn't want Belichick to use them against Mangini. Specifically, he didn't want Belichick to videotape the hand signals that the Jets' coaches used to communicate play calls to their defense.

At the time, offensive coaches could speak directly to quarterbacks via a speaker in their helmets. Defensive coaches had to rely on gestures from the sideline. Opposing teams could watch and take notes on the signals used and the defenses that resulted from them. The rules, clarified in September 2006, prohibited videotaping the signals and then matching them to the ensuing defensive formation and approach, which would allow an offense to crack the code the next time it faced that defense, often later in that same regular season or postseason.

Mangini had told Belichick not to do it. Beyond that, Mangini had told others in the organization (specifically GM Mike Tannenbaum) that Belichick liked to illegally videotape defensive coaching signals. Mangini has since said that he didn't want it to become a big deal, but a big deal it became. The Jets, after alerting the league to Belichick's habits, caught the Patriots camera-handed during the first game of the 2007 regular season.

The league hammered the Patriots, fining the team $250,000, imposing a separate $500,000 sanction on Belichick, and taking away the team's 2008 first-round draft pick. Belichick eventually admitted that he had interpreted the rules aggressively—and incorrectly—and that he was indeed in the wrong.

After catching the Patriots, the NFL decided to explore the depths of the New England rabbit hole. That's where the controversy gets vague and confusing. For years, rumors and reports have persisted that the league destroyed the evidence provided by the Patriots. At least one source with knowledge of the manner in which the events unfolded contends that Belichick provided the league with a treasure trove of proof of cheating of all shapes, sorts, and sizes committed by the Patriots and by many other teams. Belichick, per the source, also suggested to the NFL (in his own understated way) that if it came after him in the future for cheating, he'd take everything he knew public.

As another source put it, Belichick's overriding message to the league was simple: "When in Rome."

Belichick's disclosure of evidence and explanation, along with the punishments imposed by the commissioner, may have settled the matter with the league. It definitely didn't end the issue regarding other alleged victims of the videotaping scheme. Players from teams such as the Steelers wondered whether cheating had influenced AFC Championship losses in 2001 and particularly in 2004, when a regular-season meeting won by Pittsburgh preceded the postseason victory by New England. Multiple Steelers have asked aloud whether the Patriots won a game that determined a berth in Super Bowl XXXIX by using videotaped defensive coaching signals from the prior meeting or through other forms of cheating.

It also didn't end the issue for Belichick's boss. Patriots owner Robert Kraft grilled Belichick regarding the extent to which the rules violation had aided the team.

"How much did this help us on a scale of one to 100?" Kraft asked Belichick, as explained by Kraft to Gary Myers in the book *Coaching Confidential: Inside the Fraternity of NFL Coaches.*

"One," Belichick said.

"Then you're a real schmuck," Kraft replied.

Plenty of people in NFL circles think Belichick is a real schmuck for a variety of reasons. Most think it because for nearly two full decades, they couldn't compete with him, regardless of whether either or both teams were cheating.

SPYGATE II

THE PATRIOTS RESPONDED to the original Spygate scandal in the best way possible: by winning. And win they did. They won every game, making them the first team in NFL history to finish the regular season with a record of 16–0. Next, they won a pair of playoff games, giving New England its fourth Super Bowl berth in seven seasons.

Only one thing stood in the way of the Patriots and 19–0 perfection: the New York Giants, the NFC's fifth seed and a whopping 14-point underdog. Heavy betting on the Giants caused the line to fall to 12, but even the wisest of wiseguys couldn't have foreseen the eleventh-hour wrench that would be suddenly chucked into the effort to supplant the 1972 Dolphins as the primary example of pro football perfection.

On the day before Super Bowl XLII, the *Boston Herald* reported that on the day before Super Bowl XXXVI, New England had secretly re-corded a St. Louis Rams walk-through practice at the Louisiana Super-dome. The report, which reduced to writing a rumor/urban legend that had ricocheted around the league for six years, sent shock waves through the sport.

The Patriots first learned of the looming *Herald* report on Friday night. The team's top outside litigator, Dan Goldberg, made it clear to the *Herald* that the team would seek to hold the newspaper accountable if it published the report. The *Herald* published it anyway.

The NFL decided to launch an immediate investigation. On the day before Super Bowl XLII.

Some in the league office believed the investigation should wait until after the Super Bowl. "Someone was pushing it," a source with knowledge of the situation said, suggesting that the effort came from Commissioner Roger Goodell, NFL general counsel Jeff Pash, or both.

Although the Patriots never would and never will attempt to excuse the stunning 17–14 loss to the Giants by pointing to the league office's decision to disrupt final preparations by conducting a probe that distracted the organization, that's exactly what happened. With Super Bowl XLII set for the following day, the NFL—instead of waiting until after the game to explore the allegations—opted to delve into the issue at a time when the Patriots should have been focused solely on the upcoming game.

The investigation found nothing. Former Patriots video employee Matt Walsh, believed to be the source of the *Herald* report, eventually met with Commissioner Roger Goodell after delicate negotiations that included the Patriots paying for Walsh's legal fees and his travel expenses from his home in Hawaii to NFL headquarters in New York. Walsh gave Goodell and the league eight videotapes. None of the items contained images from the Rams' walk-through practice prior to Super Bowl XXXVI, and Walsh insisted that he was not the source of the *Herald* report.

Belichick reacted sharply to Walsh's claims, telling the *CBS Evening News* that Walsh had embellished his role with the team and had been fired for "poor job performance."

The *Herald* and reporter John Tomase later retracted the story. For the first time ever, a major US daily newspaper issued a full front-page apology. In the accompanying article, Tomase explained that he had "failed to keep challenging" the information he had been given and that he had accepted the allegation of the taped walk-through practice as "fact and stopped questioning the assertion." He admitted to making a "devastating leap of logic" that a camera set up by the Patriots at the walk-through practice was actually capturing video.

The Patriots attempted to put the matter to rest once and for all, issuing a one-paragraph statement that decried the team having to defend itself against "assumptions based on an unsubstantiated report rather than on facts or evidence" and expressed hope that, given Walsh's comments, everyone would finally believe that the suggestion that the Rams' walk-through practice had been videotaped by the Patriots was "absolutely false."

Good luck getting the Rams to accept that. Former Rams running back Marshall Faulk continued to complain about the situation years after the fact.

"Am I over the loss?" Faulk asked NBC Sports Boston in 2013. "Yeah, I'm over the loss. But I'll never be over being cheated out of the Super Bowl. That's a different story."

Faulk said that the Rams had new plays for the Super Bowl—plays they hadn't used during the 2001 season. Plays that the Patriots seemed ready to defend against.

"It's either the best coaching in the world when you come up with situations you had never seen before," Faulk said, "or you'd seen it and knew what to do."

More recently, Faulk insisted in a session with reporters that the taping of the walk-through practice was "a fact."

Former Rams quarterback Kurt Warner was more tactful and vague, calling the situation a "huge unknown" that "leaves this cloud over the top of everything."

The cloud still lingers, at least for those who would rather not attribute New England's success to "the best coaching in the world" and who prefer to make themselves feel better about their own failure to compete with the Patriots by shrugging and saying authoritatively despite dispositive evidence, "They cheat."

BOUNTYGATE

BY EARLY 2012, the NFL faced thousands of claims from former players that the league had failed to properly warn them about the risks of head injuries and also had failed to protect them from such harm. The league needed to show that it took player health and safety seriously. An opportunity to do so fell into its lap late on a Friday afternoon in March.

The NFL announced that twenty-two to twenty-seven defensive players on the Saints had maintained, in 2009, 2010, and 2011, a "bounty" program that provided payment for hits that knocked opponents out of games. Saints linebacker Jonathan Vilma had allegedly offered $10,000 as a bounty on Vikings quarterback Brett Favre before the 2009 NFC Championship, and Saints defensive coordinator Gregg Williams had administered the program.

The word "bounty" was always misleading. Players weren't being commissioned to kneecap opponents, Nancy Kerrigan style. The cash payments came from the application of clean, legal hits that kept opponents from continuing to play. Players already had the incentive to do just that, especially to the opposing quarterback—and especially with a berth in the Super Bowl on the line.

In the immediate aftermath of the disclosure by the league, reporters began to chase the question of whether and to what extent Williams, a veteran coach, had utilized similar programs in the past. For example, former Washington safety Matt Bowen said that Williams had a similar program when he worked there. Former Bills safety Coy Wire said that

Williams promoted "financial compensation" for hits that injured opponents in Buffalo.

But the league had no desire to look backward—other than to look
backward at the Saints. As one source familiar with the events explained
it, the league feared what it would find if it explored evidence of other
bounty programs.

Undoubtedly, the NFL knew that widespread evidence of similar
programs would undermine the perception that the Saints had a rogue
operation and that, instead, the issue of extra payment for big hits that
knocked an opponent out of the game had become a cultural reality in the
NFL. Admitting that most if not all teams had a similar system, given
the still new sensitivity to player health and safety, would have created
a major PR and/or legal problem for the NFL—far bigger than the one
flowing from the notion that the basket contained only one bad apple.

By the end of the month, Commissioner Roger Goodell had suspended Williams indefinitely, Saints coach Sean Payton for a year,
Saints GM Mickey Loomis for eight games, and Saints linebacker coach
Joe Vitt for six games. The team was fined $500,000 and lost a pair of
second-round draft picks. Goodell also meted out suspensions to four
players: Vilma (a full season), defensive end Anthony Hargrove (eight
games), defensive end Will Smith (four games), and linebacker Scott
Fujita (three games).

The fact that the coaches and executives had no union gave them virtually no right to meaningfully challenge the penalties imposed upon
them. The players, in contrast, had rights under their CBA and aggressively pursued those rights in various forms and forums. Beyond fighting
the suspension, Vilma sued Goodell for defamation. Goodell became
the central figure in the legal fight given his effort to serve as both the
person issuing the punishment and the person responsible for the internal appeal of the punishment he issued, sparking sharp criticism of his
persistent desire to at all times serve as judge, jury, and executioner in
matters of player discipline.

After months of briefs, testimony, and argument, Goodell agreed to
delegate his power to resolve appeals of player discipline to someone else.
He selected his predecessor, Paul Tagliabue, to handle the case. And
Tagliabue surprised everyone, including Goodell.

In a carefully crafted decision that allowed Tagliabue to tactfully stick a knife into Goodell's rib cage, the former commissioner explained that the NFL had a cultural issue and that cultural issues are best changed not by hammering one team but by making it known, going forward, that all are expected to change their ways. Tagliabue compared the situation to the manner in which his own predecessor, Pete Rozelle, had handled the steroids problem in the 1980s. Instead of putting the head of one franchise on a pike in the hope of scaring all other teams straight, Rozelle made sure that all teams knew that the past was in the past and that in the future, a new approach would be expected. As a result, Tagliabue overturned all discipline imposed on the Saints players who had been involved in the bounty program.

The outcome undoubtedly angered and frustrated Goodell, whose league office had diligently and zealously tried to secure suspensions not only of coaches and executives but also of players. The effort included hiring Mary Jo White, a respected former prosecutor who was retained ostensibly to provide an independent analysis but who quickly became an advocate of the league's position. Most importantly, she misrepresented to reporters a key piece of audio that was used to incriminate Anthony Hargrove.

For me, the moment of realization that White was flat-out wrong in her contention that it was Hargrove who yelled, "Give me my money," when it was actually a different player, was an important epiphany in regard to covering NFL-imposed discipline on teams and/or players. From that moment forward, I resolved to always assume that bullshit was lurking somewhere in the allegations or the characterizations of the evidence being pushed by a league that all too often selects a preferred outcome and works backward. More than once, that instinct has proven to be incredibly valuable.

BULLYGATE

PRO FOOTBALL'S CULTURAL problems went far beyond the so-called bounty issue. The game in many ways had remained stuck in the 1950s, with behavior that would never be tolerated in normal civilized society remaining commonplace in football locker rooms.

In 2013, multiple lingering caveman tendencies came to light in Miami thanks to offensive lineman Richie Incognito. Straight out of central casting for the role of stereotypical nerd-hating (and everyone-else-hating) jock, Incognito was big, fat, large, loud, rough, tough, and mean and (unfortunately) suffered from an obvious mental health issue that required intervention by appropriate medical personnel.

From college into the NFL, Incognito had had multiple behavioral issues that had caused multiple teams to decide that his skills didn't justify dealing with the headaches he brought with him. In 2010, he landed with the Dolphins and became both a very good player and, initially, not enough of a problem to outweigh his abilities.

He remained in Miami for 2010, 2011, and 2012. In 2012, the Dolphins used a second-round pick on Jonathan Martin, a tackle from Stanford who lacked the mean streak that so many coaches and executives believe is critical to success in the NFL. The Dolphins knew that Martin needed to be "toughened up"; indeed, the team conveyed that sentiment to his agents, and efforts were made to find ways to instill more of a badass mindset into Martin.

Within the confines of the Miami Dolphins facility, Incognito became one of the men on whom the Dolphins relied, expressly or implicitly, to help Martin enhance his size and strength and agility and brainpower into the total package by making him more of an on-demand asshole. So that was what Incognito did, allegedly (or actually) bullying Martin consistently, zealously, and relentlessly.

Incognito's behavior went beyond hazing, although there was plenty of that. Among other things, the Incognito-Martin situation brought to light the fact that veteran players routinely make rookies buy lavish dinners with exorbitant charges that the rookies must pay without complaint if they know what's good for them. Whether the incident in Miami caused the practice to end or simply compelled everyone involved to be more discreet about it remains largely unknown, mainly because the players have stopped talking about it or the media has stopped paying attention to it.

The Dolphins and the NFL moved quickly to address the problem, with the team suspending Incognito and the league hiring attorney Ted Wells to investigate. Wells, who would become much better known for his next NFL-related project, found that Incognito and other Dolphins players (offensive linemen Mike Pouncey and John Jerry) had engaged in harassment that in any normal workplace would be regarded as beyond over the top. For the NFL, however, a certain amount of that kind of behavior and language was accepted. In plenty of locker rooms, it undoubtedly still is.

Here's a key passage from the Ted Wells report: "Incognito told us that Martin (and other offensive linemen) all recognized, accepted and, indeed, actively participated in 'go-for-the-jugular' teasing, and that vulgarity and graphic sexual comments were not only a staple of their locker-room culture but also helped them bond." The language directed at Martin included some of the most offensive four-, five-, and six-letter words in the vernacular. Again, no normal American workplace would tolerate that type of conduct. NFL teams have, and many surely still do.

The problem was exacerbated by the fact that Incognito and others didn't confine their taunts and insults to other players. An Asian American member of the training staff found himself repeatedly harassed by the trio based on his race.

"On December 7, 2012 (the anniversary of the attack on Pearl Harbor), Incognito, Jerry and Pouncey donned traditional Japanese headbands that featured a rising sun emblem and jokingly threatened to harm the Assistant Trainer physically in retaliation for the Pearl Harbor attack," Wells wrote in his report. "Martin reported that the Assistant Trainer confided to him that he was upset about the Pearl Harbor prank, finding it derogatory and demeaning. Jerry and Pouncey each admitted that they repeatedly used racial language toward the Assistant Trainer—including calling him a 'Jap' and a 'Chinaman'—and acknowledged their Pearl Harbor Day stunt."

For Incognito, the issues went well beyond the locker room. The Martin controversy brought to light sexual harassment in which Incognito had engaged at the team's annual golf tournament in 2012. Incognito had reportedly rubbed a golf club against the crotch of a female hole monitor, rubbed his private parts against her buttocks, and poured water in her face. He reportedly wrote a check in the range of $30,000 to settle any civil claims the woman could have made in court.

Still, talent ultimately wins when it comes to the NFL. Incognito had plenty of it, and after spending all of 2014 out of football, he continued to play in Buffalo for three seasons. Then, after another year out of football fueled by a contract standoff with the Bills and a pair of off-field incidents following the passing of his father (one at a funeral home and one at the house of his ninety-year-old grandmother), Incognito got yet another chance. He signed with the Raiders, where he reestablished himself in 2019 before injuries limited him to two games in 2020. Martin, on the other hand, was traded to the 49ers in 2014. He'd spend one more year in the NFL before ending up out of the league.

The other two players found responsible for misconduct in Miami also continued to play because they were good enough to keep playing. And that continues to be the moral of a story that will play out in different forms and fashions well into the NFL's future. The desire for raw football talent will overcome plenty of potential problems, especially when those problems fall into the broad and deep bucket of "boys will be boys" excuses into which coaches and GMs will routinely dip when it comes to the one thing that will keep them gainfully employed: winning games.

MICHAEL SAM

THE NFL'S TEAMS surely have employed hundreds of gay players over the years. Prior to 2021, the NFL's teams collectively have employed only one openly gay player in the league's 102 seasons of existence. That player never actually played in a game that counted.

In early 2014, Missouri defensive end Michael Sam made his sexuality known after concluding his college career. Given that no prior NFL player had ever made such a disclosure, the issue drew intense media interest. And it created what many football coaches routinely refer to as a distraction—especially when the coach prefers not to deal with the issue.

NFL players and coaches usually thrive in a storm of distractions. Every snap of every game involves a series of endless distractions, with the offensive player attempting to execute an assignment and a defensive player trying to keep that from happening. Nothing ever unfolds perfectly, and the more players learn how to function amid constant adversities, both expected and unforeseen, the better equipped they will be to thrive when it counts.

Or so it would seem. But plenty of coaches prefer to avoid certain types of distractions under certain specific circumstances. It's a balancing act driven by the skill of the player; the better he is, the more any distractions he brings to the table will be tolerated. Hall of Fame linebacker Lawrence Taylor, for example, created constant havoc for Giants coaches through drug use and hard living. But Taylor, despite his problems, continued to be a force of nature on the football field. His distractions were regarded as a small price to pay for his greatness.

Sam wasn't nearly good enough to get a pass for the perceived distractions that he brought to an NFL locker room. Right or wrong (wrong), coaches didn't want players to constantly deal with questions about Sam's sexuality—as if the questions would have been that big a deal.

Of course, the media tried to make it a big deal. Josina Anderson, who at the time worked for ESPN, quoted on the air an unnamed Rams teammate who said that Sam had been "waiting to kind of take a shower, as not to make his teammates feel uncomfortable." (ESPN later apologized for the report.) Regardless of whatever nonsensical angles reporters may have pushed, Sam would have earned a spot on the Rams' roster if he had been a sufficiently good player.

The fact that the Rams used a draft pick on Sam created the impression among the most casual of fans that Sam was sufficiently good to play in the NFL. But Sam arrived via round seven, and seventh-round picks routinely don't make it past the final roster cuts of their rookie season.

Actually, Sam came within seven picks of not being drafted at all. And a belief still lingers in league circles that Commissioner Roger Goodell urged Rams coach Jeff Fisher to draft Sam and to keep him through the offseason program, training camp, and preseason. One source with knowledge of the dynamics estimated a 98 percent certainty that Goodell had asked Fisher to help the league prevent the bad look that would have come from Sam going undrafted. Although Goodell would say that he has zero influence over decisions of that nature, common sense would suggest that the commissioner has plenty of ways to get what he wants and that unofficial deals are made all the time.

Any lingering suspicions were likely validated after the Rams released Sam in the days prior to the start of the 2014 regular season. Peter King of NBC Sports reported that the league office called around to the various teams in an effort to persuade one of them to give Sam a spot on the practice squad, a group of players who aren't on the official roster but are part of the team. The Cowboys bit, and Sam remained with the Cowboys until October 21 of that same year. After that, Sam never returned to the NFL.

It's unclear whether he ever would have been good enough to play. He considered following the lead of defensive end Cameron Wake, who had been undrafted nine years earlier, hadn't made the Giants' roster, had gone to the Canadian Football League and become a star there, generated plenty of NFL interest, joined the Dolphins, and become a star in the NFL. Sam had a very short stint with the CFL's Montreal Alouettes, and he eventually admitted in an appearance on Dan Patrick's radio show that he "never really wanted to go to the CFL."

So that was that for Sam's football career. Would he have gotten more chances to develop in the NFL, via practice squads and offseason workouts and training camps and preseason games, if he weren't openly gay? Most likely yes. With the exception of the quarterback position (although that's changing), the supply of competent football players far outweighs the demand. For every Michael Sam, there are dozens of defensive ends who aren't openly gay and thus won't bring a host of extraneous issues into the locker room.

Again, coaches shouldn't care about that. But they do. While some teams that otherwise would have given Sam a chance undoubtedly were influenced by feelings of homophobia, the bigger issue from Sam's perspective is that in a sport that thrives on players who behave like interchangeable robots, Sam stood out. He simply wasn't talented enough to stand out.

Seven years after Michael Sam declared his sexuality, a player who had spent five years in the NFL did the same. Raiders defensive end Carl Nassib made his statement, it was covered for a day or two as a news event, and everyone quickly moved on. Hopefully, this means that the issue has become a nonissue for the NFL.

DEFLATEGATE

ON JANUARY 18, 2015, the Patriots easily manhandled the Colts for the AFC Championship, outclassing the Indianapolis upstarts en route to a 45–7 win and a berth in Super Bowl XLIX. After midnight, Indianapolis sportswriter Bob Kravitz posted a tweet that would become the first hint of a scandal that would linger for nearly two years.

"Breaking," Kravitz said. "A league source tells me that the NFL is investigating the possibility the Patriots deflated footballs Sunday night. More to come."

More came. Quickly. In order to best understand what came next, it's important to understand what had already happened. The prior weekend, the Patriots had defeated the Ravens in a divisional-round playoff game, wiping out a pair of 14-point deficits along the way. In so doing, they used a creative offensive formation that stretched the limits of the rules, mixing players who were and weren't eligible to catch a pass. After the game, Ravens coach John Harbaugh complained loudly about the Patriots using "a substitution type of a trick type of thing." Patriots quarterback Tom Brady trolled the Ravens, saying that "maybe those guys got to study the rule book and figure it out."

The Ravens had the last laugh regarding both the Patriots and Brady. In the days before the next round of the playoffs, Baltimore's equipment manager told the Colts that the Patriots had used footballs inflated below the minimum air pressure of 12.5 pounds per square inch (psi). Colts GM Ryan Grigson then raised the issue before the game with the league office via email. No one from the league office, however, raised the issue with the Patriots. Whatever the reason for not alerting them to the concern and advising them that the air-pressure rule would be strictly enforced, the failure to flag the issue directly with the Patriots created the impression that someone was hoping to catch them in the act.

According to a source with knowledge of the situation, the league's head of officiating at the time, Dean Blandino, anticipated no issues because the league had assigned referee Walt Anderson to handle the Colts-Patriots game. Anderson had a reputation for being extremely conscientious, and when it came to checking the air pressure in the twelve footballs used by each team's offense before the game, Anderson handled the assignment personally. Walt was "very strict with the process," the source said.

Anderson wasn't strict enough. The New England footballs temporarily went missing, leaving Anderson "beside himself." Still, nothing was regarded as amiss until Colts linebacker D'Qwell Jackson intercepted a Brady pass, and the Colts (in violation of the rules) checked the air pressure in the ball and found it to be under the minimum allowed air pressure of 12.5 (psi).

If Kravitz's initial tweet sparked widespread curiosity, a subsequent tweet from ESPN's Chris Mortensen prompted rampant condemnation. "NFL has found that 11 of the [twelve] Patriots footballs used in Sunday's AFC title game were under-inflated by 2 lbs each, per league sources," Mortensen said in the message that would in many ways come to define the scandal. The claim, repeated in a separate column posted on the ESPN website, created a clear impression that the league had caught the Patriots cheating—again.

Mortensen's report, however, was incorrect. Someone at the league office had given bad information to him and to other reporters, including Peter King, who wrote at the time for *Sports Illustrated.* Per a source with knowledge of the situation, that bad information came directly from NFL Executive VP of Football Operations Troy Vincent.

The footballs technically were underinflated, but not to the level that the league office had characterized the numbers. Through a Mutt-and-Jeff-ish effort to gather the footballs and check the pressure with a pair of mismatched needles (one short and straight, one long and crooked), league officials found at halftime that the air pressure in the New England footballs fell below the 12.5 psi minimum limit.

The reduced numbers nevertheless fell within the range of where they should have been given the weather conditions that night in Foxborough, Massachusetts. Over the ensuing months, football fans learned more than they had ever wanted to know about the ideal gas law, a mathematical equation that stands for the simple proposition that as the air temperature drops, so does the air pressure within a football.

The outcome of the investigation run by Ted Wells (yes, the Ted Wells of the Richie Incognito–Jonathan Martin imbroglio) should have been that the evidence of cheating was inconclusive at best. But the NFL—which put the cart of cheating before the horse of truth—wanted the investigation to conclude that the measurements hastily made in a clunky fashion at halftime of the AFC Championship game revealed foul play, not atmospheric reality. Put simply, as the mob of league officials who wanted to gin up evidence of New England cheating inserted a pressure gauge into the footballs at halftime of the Colts-Patriots game and saw that they were under the minimum limit of 12.5 psi, they assumed the worst and then spent the next several months scrambling to prove it. (Among other things, the effort to work backward and prove cheating included rejecting referee Walt Anderson's best recollection regarding which of two different gauges had been used to check the air pressure in the New England footballs before the game.)

Unfortunately for the Patriots, the league found circumstantial evidence of wrongdoing. Text messages exchanged by team employees John Jastremski and Jim McNally created the impression that the two men had developed and maintained a system for removing air from footballs at the behest of quarterback Tom Brady. McNally, who worked as the locker-room attendant for the game officials and thus had access to the footballs, apparently was the one who normally removed the air from ("took the top off," in NFL parlance) the balls. In one text message to Jastremski, McNally referred to himself as the "deflator." (The men implausibly claimed during the league's investigation that the term "deflator" related to losing weight from their bodies, not air from the Patriots' footballs.) Other text messages suggested that McNally had received shoes and autographed memorabilia from Brady for his efforts.

Further complicating matters for the Patriots was the fact that surveillance video showed McNally taking the bag of Patriots footballs into a bathroom for roughly ninety seconds while on his way to the field. As the hypothesis goes, McNally usually doctored the footballs in the officials' locker room. Because, however, a crowd had gathered there to watch the overtime period of the Seahawks-Packers NFC Championship, McNally took the bag of balls to the separate bathroom. Once inside (again, as the hypothesis goes), he actually decided not to put the bag on the floor, open it up, remove each of the twelve balls, take air out of them, put them back in the bag, and zip it up. That would have taken more than ninety seconds.

Indeed, one NFL head coach who was fascinated by the story actually conducted his own experiment. Twelve footballs in a bag. (Not necessarily in a bathroom.) Open the bag, remove each ball, insert a needle into each ball, replace each ball in the bag, and close the bag in ninety seconds. The coach determined that it couldn't be done.

So perhaps McNally planned to try to deflate the balls in the bathroom but realized that he couldn't pull it off quickly enough to avoid raising red flags. Or maybe he just peed. Regardless, if McNally had taken air out of the balls, the combined effect of deliberate deflation and atmospheric reduction would have resulted in the numbers being where they definitely weren't—two or more pounds below the 12.5 psi minimum.

None of this stopped the league from declaring the Patriots guilty, fining the team $1 million, stripping first- and fourth-round draft picks, and suspending Brady for four games. Brady, whose case was complicated by the perception/reality that he had failed to properly cooperate with the investigation and deliberately destroyed his cell phone, managed to delay the suspension by a full year via litigation. Eventually, a US appeals court sided with the league and upheld the four-game suspension as a product of the league's internal arbitration procedures.

What actually happened? My best informed guess is that Brady, Jastremski, and McNally had a scheme in place to reduce the air pressure in footballs, the NFL failed to catch the Patriots in the act, the NFL commissioned an investigation that incorrectly concluded that the Patriots had been caught in the act, the NFL hammered the Patriots based in part on a lingering belief in league circles that they hadn't been sufficiently punished for Spygate I, and the NFL regarded Brady's behavior as an effort to conceal guilt—even if the league couldn't actually establish that he was guilty.

Here's the postscript. Starting in 2015, the NFL began to randomly gather footballs at halftime of games, measuring the air pressure inside each ball and recording the numbers. Per a source with knowledge of the situation, the full collection of numbers generated in 2015 showed, as expected, air pressures below 12.5 psi at halftime of games played in cold conditions. "Numerous" games, per the source, resulted in halftime measurements outside the permitted range of 12.5 to 13.5 psi, with the measurements showing a direct correlation between temperature and air pressure.

So what happened with those numbers? As a source with knowledge of the situation has explained it, NFL general counsel Jeff Pash directed that the information be gathered and deleted. The reason for erasing the numbers is obvious: they looked a lot like the numbers generated when the NFL inartfully measured New England's footballs on January 18, 2015, and erroneously assumed the worst in order to justify whacking Brady and the Patriots, again.

COLIN KAEPERNICK

COLIN KAEPERNICK JOINED the NFL as a second-round pick of the 49ers in 2011. In 2012, starting quarterback Alex Smith suffered a concussion, which opened the door for Kaepernick. He seized the opportunity, led the 49ers to the Super Bowl, and nearly won it.

The next year, ESPN's Ron Jaworski created several days of content for his employer by proclaiming that Kaepernick could become the greatest quarterback of all time. After a solid 2013 season, Kaepernick received a long-term, big-money (but not as big as his agents characterized it) contract.

As the team regressed in his fourth season, so did Kaepernick. In 2015, the 49ers replaced coach Jim Harbaugh with an overmatched Jim Tomsula. Kaepernick's fifth season ended with three different injuries that required offseason surgery.

As Kaepernick entered his sixth season, things changed. Dramatically.

August 26, 2016. Kaepernick was spotted sitting on a bench during the national anthem prior to the team's third preseason game. (He had also sat for the first two, but it hadn't been noticed because he hadn't been in uniform.) The issue quickly became a major story, with Kaepernick explaining, "I am not going to stand up to show pride in a flag for a country that oppresses Black people and people of color. To me, this is bigger than football and it would be selfish on my part to look the other way. There are bodies in the street and people getting paid leave and getting away with murder." He would later point out (accurately) that it's easier to achieve a license to use lethal force as a police officer in California than to wield a curling iron as a cosmetologist.

The 49ers supported Kaepernick, who would shift from sitting to kneeling in an effort to make the gesture more respectful to the military, throughout the 2016 season. He initially served as the backup to Blaine Gabbert while continuing to recover from the trio of offseason surgeries. Eventually, Kaepernick played, throwing sixteen touchdown passes and only four interceptions for a team that simply wasn't good enough to compete.

After the season, the 49ers cleaned house, firing one-and-done coach Chip Kelly, hiring Kyle Shanahan to replace Kelly, and bringing in John Lynch to serve as GM. Kaepernick's contract gave him the right to opt out of the final year and become a free agent. He did; however, Lynch told me at the time that if Kaepernick hadn't opted out, the 49ers would have released him.

Kaepernick then became a free agent in March 2017. And nothing happened. Not a thing. Not a sniff. Not an offer. Not a contract. Not a team.

In lieu of expressing interest in Kaepernick, teams whispered to willing media members a slew of false narratives that were blindly passed along as fact. Those who had decided not to employ him came up with phony reason after phony reason to not pursue him: Kaepernick had rejected an offer from the Broncos in 2017 (false—he had declined a trade opportunity in 2016 before he ever protested during the anthem); Kaepernick had demanded a starting job (false—discussions never got to that point); Kaepernick had demanded starting-quarterback money (false—discussions never got to that point, either); there were concerns about his vegan diet (Tom Brady is a vegan, too); and he preferred social-justice efforts to playing football (also false). Multiple media members reported those reasons without questions, scrutiny, or skepticism.

Kaepernick, unsurprisingly, drew little interest. The Seahawks brought him in for a visit but didn't offer him a contract. The Ravens planned to bring him to town for a possible contract offer, but after his girlfriend posted a meme on social media comparing team owner Steve Bisciotti to a slave owner and legendary Ravens linebacker Ray Lewis to a slave, nothing happened.

Kaepernick eventually filed a collusion grievance against the NFL, arguing that the league office had dissuaded teams from signing him by tying him to the controversy arising from players not standing for the anthem. As the litigation unfolded, Kaepernick's lawyers grilled owners and coaches and GMs and Commissioner Roger Goodell on various specific topics regarding the alleged shunning of Kaepernick. Evidence obtained by Kaepernick's lawyers showed that the anthem issue had equally strong and sizable constituencies on each end of the spectrum of football fans but that the league (for whatever reason) had opted to kowtow only to those fans who insisted on standing.

The league, for its part, couldn't insist on standing because of a defect in an internal policy that requires players to be on the sideline for the playing of the anthem but does not compel them to stand. Unwilling to take the issue to the bargaining table with the players' union (where concessions would have been required to change the rules), the league tried to come up with ideas that would persuade players to choose to stand. Discussions resulted in meetings between owners and players that at times became more awkward than an average episode of *The Office* and that ultimately did not conclusively resolve the question of whether players would or wouldn't protest during the anthem.

Although protests continued, and still do, Kaepernick's role as the robot who made the other robots self-aware turned him into a pariah. Even after his collusion grievance was resolved for roughly $10 million with the ability to seek further NFL employment, no one bit.

The last-ditch attempt to get Kaepernick considered for a job came in a November 2019 guilt-assuaging effort by Commissioner Roger Goodell to set up a workout for Kaepernick that all teams could attend. Although teams routinely bring players to town for workouts, no one had ever done so for Kaepernick in more than two and a half years. The league nevertheless persisted with an out-of-the-blue gesture that quickly bogged down in a cloud of bilateral mistrust. The suspicions came directly from clunky negotiations over an injury waiver that possibly would have released any legal claims Kaepernick may have had based on his ongoing shunning by the league after the settlement of his collusion case. Kaepernick refused to sign it, and the league refused to proceed.

In the end, the Kaepernick situation proved that if the NFL and its teams don't want someone in their league, he won't be. While it could get delicate and/or ugly and/or expensive, the billionaires who run the NFL are used to getting their way. With Colin Kaepernick, they definitely did.

JERRY RICHARDSON

BUSINESSES AND BUSINESSPEOPLE who have resolved actual and threatened legal claims have written often sizable checks in exchange for not only a waiver of those claims but also an agreement to keep the payment and all other facts relating to the resolution confidential. It's a fair and proper term, usually the topic of arm's-length bargaining between the lawyers representing the parties.

For Panthers founder Jerry Richardson, multiple recipients of confidential settlements opted to break their promises in 2017 by sharing with *Sports Illustrated* details covered by their contracts. The amounts paid were reportedly "significant," and the recipients had been the subject of sexually suggestive language and behavior (in one case) and of a racial slur (in another case).

When the settlements came to light in December 2017, no one said, "Why are these people breaking their promises to remain silent?" Instead, momentum quickly gathered for Richardson to sell the team, whether he wanted to or not.

The allegations underlying the settlements reflected inappropriate behavior. But if the individuals who made those allegations wanted to have their contentions heard and evaluated in open court, they should have refused to enter into a confidential settlement and pressed forward with litigation. They each chose to take the money and, in return, to commit to silence.

They didn't have to take the money; likewise, they didn't have to commit to silence. But they did, and they ultimately had it both ways—getting the money and eventually breaching the confidentiality provision.

The court system loves settlements, even if they come with confidentiality. Every case resolved privately becomes one fewer case that the justice system must resolve. Starting in the 1980s with *The People's Court* host Doug Llewelyn's familiar admonition, "Don't take the law into your own hands; take 'em to court," America became more litigious than ever. Judges who are paid not by the hour or by the case but by the year want to see as many cases settle as possible. If it takes a confidentiality agreement to make it happen, so be it. And if confidentiality agreements can't be trusted, that will make business and individuals less inclined to settle claims.

None of that mattered to Richardson. He promptly sold the Panthers for $2.2 billion, and the league eventually fined him $2.75 million. So he still basically got $2.2 billion.

Despite the significant financial package received upon selling the team, Richardson suffered the slap in the face of having to surrender the franchise he had founded in 1995. For billionaires, who almost always get their way, forcing them out of the club is the only way to impose meaningful punishment.

In the aftermath of the Richardson situation, many league observers wondered whether and to what extent other owners had entered into similar confidential settlements that had not come to light because the promise of confidentiality had been observed. In late 2020, for example, reports indicated that Washington owner Daniel Snyder had paid $1.6 million in 2009 to confidentially settle a claim of sexual assault. The league already knew about the settlement, however. This meant that the league hadn't investigated the situation or punished Snyder for it; rather, the league had decided at or about the time the settlement was reached that Snyder had done nothing wrong. (The allegations resulting in that settlement and any other specific details learned by the lawyer who eventually investigated claims of misconduct within Snyder's organization never saw the light of day because the lawyer never prepared a written report. In turn, that kept the league from even considering the possibility of forcing Snyder to sell his team.)

The aftermath of the Richardson situation resulted in a suggestion by investigator Mary Jo White (you may remember her from the clunky effort to spin the Bountygate evidence in the light most favorable to the NFL) that the league should limit the ability of teams and owners to enter into confidential settlements. It's unclear whether the NFL ever adopted that suggestion, and the NFL has consistently declined to address the subject. Owners may not want to forfeit the ability to write a big check that buys silence because the alternative means having dirty laundry aired in a court of law—and potentially inaccurate conclusions being made in the court of public opinion.

That's precisely what Snyder did in early 2021, paying an undisclosed amount of money (likely not insubstantial) to end, before it could get started, a lawsuit filed by multiple former cheerleaders who had unwittingly starred in a video compilation of outtakes from calendar shoots that showed them in various states of undress. Snyder asked for and received a broad confidentiality provision, and the NFL allowed him to do it. Coupled with a formal investigation that swept far more broadly but resulted in no written report, the league avoided the precedent created by Jerry Richardson's decision to sell the Carolina Panthers.

SPYGATE III

GIVEN THEIR MISADVENTURES with the original Spygate, the Patriots became the team least likely to find itself embroiled in another scandal involving the recording of an opponent's sideline with video. Therefore, naturally, the Patriots once again found themselves embroiled in another scandal involving the recording of an opponent's sideline with video.

It happened on December 8, 2019, at a game that didn't even involve the Patriots. That day, the Browns hosted the Bengals in Cleveland. The Patriots sent an outside video crew to the game to record footage for an online documentary series dubbed *Do Your Job*, a title taken directly from the mantra the Patriots and other teams have used for years to ensure that people focus on their own responsibilities and never think about anyone else's. The video crew followed an advance scout, a person who attends the game of an upcoming opponent to study it for relevant information. The advance scout attended that Cincinnati-Cleveland game because the Patriots would play the Bengals one week later.

The video crew, ostensibly trying to show what the advance scout does, aimed the camera in the direction of the thing the advance scout was studying—the Cincinnati sideline. They did it openly and obviously, without trying to conceal their activities or affiliations in any way. The Bengals became aware of it and allowed it to keep going, giving the Patriots representative more than enough rope.

Jay Glazer of Fox Sports, who had made his bones in the insider business in large part by finagling the original Spygate video, tracked down

286

the Spygate III footage. The Patriots representative, after being caught video-handed, offered to "delete this right here for you." Said the Bengals representative, "The damage is done."

The damage may have been done, but it took a while to figure out the proper punishment. Patriots coach Bill Belichick insisted that no connection existed between the football operation and the video operation. Thus, even if the Patriots had broken the rules (and indeed they had), they hadn't done so with a broader plan to turn ill-gotten video footage into game-day advantage.

The league investigated aggressively. Multiple Patriots employees interrogated by NFL officials perceived that the investigators became upset by the inability to prove a link between the football department and the video department. Ultimately, the league neither disclosed publicly nor leaked through preferred members of the media (i.e., those with a large platform who accept what they're told and pass it along without asking questions) any proof connecting anyone on the video crew to anyone in the football operation.

Absent such proof, many believed the punishment would amount to a slap on the wrist. But then something happened. More specifically, nothing happened. The situation sat for months with no action taken.

Some reasonably believed that if the Patriots lost a draft pick over it, the league would have stripped the draft pick before, you know, the draft. The 2020 draft came and went, however, with no decision announced and no penalties revealed.

The situation lingered until a Sunday night in late June 2020, when the Patriots floated word that they'd reached an agreement with quarterback Cam Newton on a one-year deal moments before the league's decision on Spygate III emerged.

The NFL imposed a whopping $1.1 million fine and removed from the Patriots a third-round draft pick. The magnitude of the punishment implies that the league found a link between the video operations and football operation. The league, however, never addressed that point.

Did the league find a connection? We don't know. What justified a seven-figure fine and a third-round pick? We don't know. Was there any proof that a system existed to transform the video footage collected one Sunday into a tangible strategic edge the next Sunday? We don't know.

If nothing else, those details regarding the basis for the sanction are relevant to deterring the Patriots and other teams from engaging in similar behavior in the future. Absent such details, what impact does the punishment have? Other teams don't know where the line is because the league didn't bother to tell anyone where the line is and/or what the Patriots did to cross it.

The inescapable conclusion is simple and clear: the punishment represented another effort to reach back to 2007 and whack the Patriots again for a violation that, in the opinion of some of the owners who pull the strings and push the buttons of the commissioner, didn't generate sufficient consequences at the time. If/when the Patriots ever find themselves in another cheating scandal, they can assume that they'll get hit harder than any other team would be because there will still be some people in positions of power who believe that the Patriots should have gotten it worse way back when the Spygate saga began.

JON GRUDEN AND THE WFT EMAILS

IN JUNE 2021, the commissioner and a small group of owners gathered with Washington owner Daniel Snyder at league headquarters in Manhattan for a hearing regarding the punishment that would be imposed on Snyder as a result of an extensive investigation into chronic misconduct in the workplace over which he presided. On July 1—the Thursday before a four-day Fourth of July weekend—the NFL announced the sanctions, while also making it clear that no specifics would be released regarding the probe.

Some of the specifics would unexpectedly emerge three months later.

In one of the most bizarre and troubling off-field developments in the 102-season history of the NFL, the league initially buried the results of the Washington Football Team (WFT) investigation, with no documents released and no written report generated by the lawyer who conducted the probe, which lasted nearly a full year. The league claimed that it needed secrecy to protect the confidentiality of the current and former employees who came forward. (The NFL apparently isn't aware of the concept of redaction.) The goal, as many in league circles believed, was to protect Snyder and, in turn, to protect other owners who could find themselves in the throes of an investigation triggered by allegations with which they fundamentally disagree. Not everyone, however, would enjoy such protections.

At some point during the investigation, the NFL became aware of emails that raised issues falling beyond the question of whether WFT employees endured mistreatment. Only a few very powerful people had access to the emails (i.e., the commissioner, the owners involved in determining the punishment of Snyder, and their lawyers). From July into early October 2021, senior NFL executives reviewed more than 650,000 emails for items that created specific concerns. Early in the week of October 4, 2021, those executives presented a summary of the review to Commissioner Roger Goodell. The summary flagged Raiders coach Jon Gruden as sending multiple inappropriate emails to former Washington coach Bruce Allen in the years before Gruden's second stint as Raiders coach began in early 2018. While writing any of the emails that came to light in early October 2021, Gruden worked for no NFL team. (At the time the emails were sent, Gruden served as the lead analyst for ESPN's Monday Night Football, after the Buccaneers fired him in early 2009.)

The league gathered the emails written by Gruden and delivered them to the Raiders. (It's debatable whether that was the right move to make, and whether it was the right time to do it.) On one hand, one of the emails contained a racist trope regarding NFLPA Executive Director DeMaurice Smith and antigay slurs, and others contained content that was homophobic, transphobic, and misogynistic. Among other things, Gruden questioned the league's alleged decision to broker a deal with the Rams to draft Michael Sam, the first openly gay prospect in NFL history. (At the time the emails surfaced, Gruden's Raiders employed Carl Nassib, who came out as gay in June 2021.) On the other hand, none of the emails were written by Gruden at a time when he was employed by the NFL or any of its teams.

Someone leaked the disparaging email regarding DeMaurice Smith to the *Wall Street Journal* on Friday, October 8, after the league initiated the process of sending the emails to the Raiders. Some in league circles believe the initial leak flowed from a desire by the NFL to save Smith's job by garnering sympathy and support from his constituents. Coincidentally (or not), hours after the *Wall Street Journal* report emerged, Smith barely secured approval from the NFLPA's board of player representatives for an extension of his contract, which otherwise would have expired in March 2022.

It appeared at first that Gruden would survive the firestorm. He expressed near-defiance regarding his purported absence of racist thought, despite writing to Allen during the 2011 lockout that "Dumborris" Smith has "lips the size of michellin [*sic*] tires." Then, on the evening of Sunday, October 10, after Gruden coached the Raiders in an upset loss to the Bears, the league sent more Gruden emails to the Raiders. Far more importantly, someone leaked additional emails to the media on Monday, October 11. Within an hour after the next wave of leaked emails landed in an article posted on the *New York Times* website, Gruden resigned.

The fact that someone not employed by the Washington Football Team lost his job as a result of an investigation regarding the Washington Football Team created plenty of confusion and frustration. Although Gruden got what he deserved, the league had hidden 650,000 emails, but then someone selectively had used a small sliver of them to take out Gruden. Basically, the emails had become weaponized. Others' emails could be used to target anyone who landed on the enemies list of anyone who had access to them.

That potential became even more apparent after someone (possibly the same person who leaked the Gruden emails, possibly not) released to the media on Thursday, October 14, various emails that NFL general counsel Jeff Pash had sent to Allen. Although containing none of the overt hate found in the Gruden emails, Pash's correspondence to Allen illustrated an overly chummy relationship that undermined competitive integrity and nonchalantly expressed derision in various directions, from players resisting efforts to reduce their pay, to Mexican fans who could be alienated by the building of a border wall, to players who don't exercise their right to vote.

Through it all, the league refused to release the full trove of emails so that all cards could be put on the table and all bad actors could simultaneously be exposed. The league eventually claimed that the 650,000 emails came exclusively from messages sent to or by Bruce Allen during a tenure with the team that lasted almost exactly one decade. That works out to 178 emails sent or received per day every day for ten full years. Many find the league's suggested intake and output from Allen to not be credible.

Even though the NFL refused to release information regarding the investigation in order to protect those current or former employees who came forward to cooperate, the NFL also admitted that the 650,000 emails fell beyond the scope of the investigation. Thus, why not release them?

The NFL's stubborn refusal to embrace transparency allowed the small handful of people who had access to the documents to hold power over anyone who sent or received email messages to Allen. At any given time, more documents could be leaked—regardless of whether those materials contain content that would be clearly offensive or inappropriate.

Although the league's effort to hide the results of the WFT investigation in July largely had succeeded, a surprising number of fans and media reacted negatively to the use of some of the 650,000 emails to take out someone who never worked for the organization. Again, Gruden got what he deserved. Others, however, may have deserved a similar fate; they received ongoing protection at a time when Gruden endured exposure, embarrassment, and ultimately unemployment.

The league office has persistently denied leaking the Gruden emails. Still, only a small number of people within the broader NFL structure had access to them. The league declined in October 2021 to say whether it's investigating the source of the leaks. Frankly, any such investigation would entail only a few suspects.

And the damage done was obvious. If no one had leaked any of the emails to the media, Gruden likely would have continued coaching the team. The leaks made his situation untenable; he definitely had to go. Without the leaks, he could have stayed.

That's why some in league circles believe that someone deliberately leaked the Gruden emails in an effort to get him to quit or be fired. The initial leak, while believed to have been intended to help Smith save his job, didn't do the trick. The second leak, which included multiple offensive terms used in connection with Commissioner Roger Goodell, did. If Gruden hadn't resigned at that point, would more emails have been leaked? It's safe to believe that, yes, it would have happened.

Of course, the league had no incentive to leak the Pash emails. It's entirely possible that the Gruden and Pash emails were disclosed by two different parties with access to the documents. The possibility of multiple leakers reinforces the very real concern that others, in time, would find themselves similarly targeted by one of the people with the keys to the full set of emails.

In other words, the league tried to treat 650,000 emails like nuclear waste, burying the materials under 300 feet of reinforced concrete. Then, someone slipped into the sarcophagus for a handful of documents, engineering the resignation of Jon Gruden five games into the season and necessarily creating significant competitive issues for the Raiders. Additional competitive issues could still arise if/when others in positions of power with other teams find themselves targeted by someone with access to the stack of emails that remains secret only until it isn't.

By the time you read this, there's a chance that the 650,000 emails will have been released. It's a slim one, at best. Even though the league's original reason for keeping the results of the WFT investigation secret has no relevance to the 650,000 emails that by the league's own admission fall beyond the scope of the investigation, the league had, as of late October 2021, no inclination to change its mind. Likewise, no one with the power to get the league to change its mind seemed to be interested in trying to force it to do the right thing.

PART IX
OFFICIATING

REPLAY REVIEW

SOME WOULD ARGUE, accurately, that the "L" in "NFL" stands for Luddite. The league has for decades resisted the development of applications based on technology that would improve the accuracy of officiating football games. Instead, for most of the NFL's existence, all decisions have come from officials equipped with naked eyes and thirty feet of chain link between a pair of metal poles.

That changed in 1985 when the NFL first adopted a system of video replay for reviewing certain rulings on the field, focusing on possessing or touching the ball, the boundaries of the field, and the goal line. Initially an experiment for the preseason, it went so well that some wanted to implement the system in the 1985 postseason. Instead, the owners voted in early 1986 to make replay review part of the preseason, regular season, and postseason.

It didn't last. In 1991, the sixth season of the replay system, the replay official stationed in a booth at each stadium erred in nine of the ninety calls that were overturned. Thus, starting in 1992, officiating returned exclusively to judging games based on things seen and not seen by middle-aged men focused primarily on not being trampled by gladiators in various shapes and sizes of armor.

That didn't last, either. A horrible call at the end of the 1998 season—a mistaken assessment that Jets quarterback Vinny Testaverde had scored a touchdown against the Seahawks when he hadn't—created an immediate groundswell to reinstitute replay review. By 1999, the replay system had returned.

The new system worked much differently than the first one. Instead of a nameless, faceless replay official making the decision from on high, the referee walked to the sideline to watch the play on a monitor under a hood and decided whether indisputable visual evidence existed to change the ruling on the field. Put very loosely, indisputable evidence exists when fifty drunks in a bar watching the play would agree unanimously that a mistake has been made.

Activation of the new replay procedure hinges in many instances on a coach throwing a red flag onto the field. Each coach could initially make two challenges per game, with certain circumstances (the final two minutes of each half and all of overtime) subject to automatic review by the referee if activated by an in-stadium replay official. If a coach's challenge failed, his team lost a timeout; thus, the coach's team needed to have at least one timeout remaining in a given half before the coach could challenge a play.

The list of reviewable plays in Replay 2.0 started fairly small. The list has grown over time, typically after a bad call is made that can't be reviewed because the rules don't allow it. In the next cycle of rule-making, the league often expands the replay system to include that wrinkle.

The circumstances for automatic review have also expanded. Scoring plays and turnovers now trigger automatic review, allowing the process to activate without a red flag thrown or a timeout risked. (However, plays that would have been touchdowns or turnovers if ruled correctly can still be changed only through a challenge unless the play happens in the final two minutes of a half or overtime.)

At its core, the challenge system conflicts with the fundamental desire to get calls right. Although coaches who successfully use their first two challenges now get a third, they shouldn't need any; the desire to fix mistakes should make all replay reviews automatic, as in the procedure the league used from 1986 through 1991.

The range of circumstances for replay review can be limited in order to limit delays. Plays subject to automatic replay should be scoring plays or plays that would have resulted in a score if ruled correctly, turnovers or plays that would have resulted in a turnover if ruled correctly, and first downs or plays that would have resulted in a first down if ruled correctly.

That's all that needs to be subject to the automatic, full-blown replay-review system.

The second iteration of replay review has also evolved to remove the replay decision from the referee and delegate it to the league office. Aimed at ensuring that the same standard applies in all circumstances, the shifting of final say over the review from the stadiums to a centralized location has reinstated the concern that decisions are being made not by the referee assigned to the game but by someone disconnected from it.

Coaches and executives have wondered privately about the people present in the room at the league office when big decisions are made in important games. Is the person charged with making the decision being influenced by his or her supervisor or possibly by the commissioner?

Then there's the question of the competence of the person making the replay decisions. Although the language of the standard has changed to "clear and obvious," the practical rule of thumb (fifty drunks in a bar) still controls. Is the senior VP of officiating properly skilled to reliably apply that standard over and over again?

That's not an insignificant question. Dean Blandino, the person for whom the current system was designed but who left the league office to become a rules analyst at Fox, told me during an interview following his departure that the league doesn't properly "value" the position. In other words, the league is being cheap about it—and as with anything else, you get what you pay for.

Blandino left the NFL for more money and reduced responsibilities. Unless the NFL streamlines the job of resolving replay review for all 272 regular-season games and another 13 postseason games and pays that person a lot more money, the league will continue to get what it pays for. And that's something far less accurate than the modern game of pro football needs and deserves.

THE TUCK RULE

RAIDERS FANS LIKELY utter a one-syllable word that rhymes with "tuck" when pondering the now-defunct portion of the rule book providing that when a quarterback loses possession of the ball while attempting to throw a pass, it's not a fumble if possession is lost at any time from the moment the arm begins moving forward until the ball is tucked back into his body. In something a little closer to English, the rule used to provide that the quarterback can't fumble once his arm starts moving forward—even if he's just tucking the ball back under his arm.

The NFL adopted the rule because it provided a clear, bright-line standard for officials to apply. Instead of having to figure out whether the ball had been dislodged before the movement of the arm stopped, the officials knew that the process of attempting to throw the ball didn't end (and thus a fumble couldn't happen) until the ball had been retucked.

The divisional round of the 2001 playoffs included the last game ever played at Foxboro Stadium in Massachusetts, a Saturday-night snow globe between the Raiders and the Patriots. With 1:50 to play and New England trailing by 3 points, the Patriots had the ball on the Oakland 42. Quarterback Tom Brady lined up in shotgun formation. Barking signals, he didn't notice Raiders cornerback Charles Woodson creeping toward the line of scrimmage in the slot to Brady's right.

At the snap, Brady looked to his left and Woodson sprang into the backfield untouched. Brady pumped the ball, and Woodson struck Brady after he finished his throwing motion—but before Brady had tucked the ball back into his body.

Brady lost his handle on the ball. It landed on the snow covering the ground. The Raiders recovered. With fewer than two minutes to play and the Patriots out of timeouts, the Raiders simply needed to take three knees to end the game.

Fans streamed for the exits, leaving Foxboro Stadium for the final time as the latest shoulder shrugging sparked by a long-disappointing franchise took root. After many of them had cleared the perimeter of the building, they heard a fairly important announcement echoing through the public address system.

The replay assistant monitoring the game from a booth above the field had activated the review process, and referee Walt Coleman had gone to the sideline to watch the play. (At the time, the referee personally inspected the available angles and determined whether indisputable visual evidence existed to overturn the ruling on the field.) Coleman had determined that the decision to call the play a fumble amounted to a reversible error.

"After reviewing the play, the quarterback's arm was going forward," Coleman announced. "It is an incomplete pass."

Fans on the way to their cars did an about-face and tried to return to the venue. Stadium employees, despite the well-established "no re-entry" rule that applies at all NFL events, relented.

The Raiders, led by longtime owner Al Davis, were confused, and for good reason. Coleman's explanation didn't mention the tuck rule. Instead, Coleman said that Brady's arm was going forward. It wasn't. The arm had gone forward, the process had ended, and Brady had not yet tucked the ball back into his body.

The visual evidence (just pull up YouTube and search for "tuck rule") seems to support the conclusion that Brady hadn't finished the throwing motion and pulled the ball back to his body. The lingering controversy regarding the decision to overturn the play and, eventually, change the outcome of the game comes from the fact that the play looks like a fumble and feels like a fumble, but thanks to a rule that hadn't been reduced to writing until just one year earlier, it technically wasn't a fumble.

The specific circumstances of the play made the outcome even more excruciating for the Raiders.

"Football is a game of seconds and a game of inches, and in this instance, that was certainly borne out," former Raiders CEO Amy Trask told me. "The play in question happened with less than two minutes left in the game, so it was subject to league review. Had the play occurred twenty or so seconds earlier, there would have been no review, as New England was out of timeouts. A game of seconds, indeed."

Specifically, if the play had started only eleven seconds earlier, no replay review could have happened. (At the time, turnovers were not subject to automatic replay review.) In order to challenge a play, the team making the challenge needs to have a timeout since an unsuccessful challenge results in the team that initiated the process losing a timeout.

The passage of time hasn't made the Raiders any less convinced that they were screwed, giving the franchise a twenty-eight-year bookend to the Immaculate Reception from the 1972 playoff loss to Pittsburgh. After the tuck game, some Raiders employees in some departments added a photo of Woodson forcing the Brady fumble to the team's official fax cover sheets, the predigital means for quickly communicating letters and other documents.

Was Trask, the team president, sufficiently disturbed by the tuck rule to include the image on her fax cover sheets?

"Not all the time and not often," she said, "but there were times I did—maybe, just maybe, when sending something to the league office."

The league office eventually got the message, but not before the passing of longtime Raiders owner Al Davis in 2011. Two years later, and more than twelve years after its most controversial application, the owners voted to abolish the tuck rule. The change didn't happen sooner because, as one source with knowledge of the internal processes explained, to do so would have amounted to admitting that the tuck rule was indeed a bad one.

Said Patriots owner Robert Kraft at the time, "I love the tuck rule, and forever will, and I know Al Davis, may he rest in peace, is probably smiling."

SUPER BOWL XL

IT YOU'RE INCLINED to cover your scalp with tinfoil and fantasize about conspiracy theories, this book isn't for you. The NFL, contrary to the beliefs of plenty of fans, doesn't fix games. It just doesn't.

First, there's no real reason to do so. The TV ratings are what they are, and the money from networks is what it is. Second, and far more importantly, the NFL isn't nearly competent enough to rig games without anyone finding out about it.

Consider for a moment the number of people who would have to be involved in a full-blown plot to rig games and who would have to take their secrets to the great beyond. Consider the potential impact on the sport if the league decided, WWE style, to predetermine winners—and if the fans and/or the media became aware of it. The NFL enjoys tremendous popularity without having to risk the downside that would come from having a scheme in place to push the outcome of a game in a given direction.

This reality doesn't keep people from thinking it happens. When officials make mistakes, and they routinely do, fans become more inclined to suspect foul play rather than poor performance. They believe that someone is always up to something, even when, from the NFL's perspective, there's no reason to be up to anything (and many reasons not to be).

The notion of a big game being rigged reached its peak in February 2006 when the Seahawks and Steelers met for the second-ever Michigan Super Bowl. A series of officiating mistakes helped Pittsburgh and hurt

Seattle, creating the widespread belief among Seahawks fans (and Steelers haters) that the league "wanted" Pittsburgh to win.

It didn't help that Steelers fans traveled in droves to Detroit and that not many Seahawks fans made the trek from Seattle. It didn't help that retiring Pittsburgh running back Jerome Bettis had grown up in Detroit, making him a sentimental favorite to win the Super Bowl in his final career game.

It definitely didn't help that once the game began, a Seahawks touchdown pass came off the board due to a questionable offensive pass interference foul. It didn't help that a late second-quarter run from Steelers quarterback Ben Roethlisberger at the goal line became a touchdown even though it appeared that the football hadn't broken the front plane of the end zone.

It didn't help that a Steelers defensive player jumped early, that a Seahawks offensive lineman grabbed the Steelers defensive player to protect quarterback Matt Hasselbeck, and that the officials called a holding penalty on Seattle but not an offside foul on Pittsburgh. It didn't help that officials flagged Hasselbeck for a low block on an interception return by Steelers defensive back Ike Taylor, giving Pittsburgh 15 yards of field position beyond the spot to which Taylor took the ball. Hasselbeck's hit didn't come against some random Steeler; he struck Taylor—who had the ball—low, and legally, in an effort to tackle him.

It didn't help that Seahawks coach Mike Holmgren opted to accuse the officials of bias. "We knew it was going to be tough going against the Pittsburgh Steelers," Holmgren declared after the game. "I didn't know we were going to have to play the guys in the striped shirts as well."

And it definitely didn't help that referee Bill Leavy later admitted that mistakes had been made.

"It was a tough thing for me," Leavy said while visiting Seattle training camp in 2010. "I kicked two calls in the fourth quarter, and I impacted the game, and as an official, you never want to do that. . . . It left me with a lot of sleepless nights, and I think about it constantly. I'll go to my grave wishing that I'd been better."

That didn't, and shouldn't, make fans of the 2005 Seahawks feel any better. However, it helps show that the outcome didn't happen because Leavy or anyone else wanted the Steelers to win or the Seahawks to lose.

It happened because NFL game officials are human. Like other humans, they make mistakes. That's it. It's that simple. Mistakes, not malevolence. Incompetence, not conspiracy.

That still hasn't extinguished the urban legend. In 2019, for example, a football handicapper named Dennis Ranahan claimed that Leavy was one of Ranahan's clients and that Leavy bet on games. This contention, which surfaced (coincidentally) in the days preceding Super Bowl LIII, was never substantiated. And even if a referee were betting on games (we'll address that later), it's still too difficult to fix an NFL game. It would be even more difficult to fix an NFL game and ensure that no one ever found out about it.

SCOTT GREEN'S IRRELEVANT
(NOT REALLY) MISTAKE

OFFICIATING ERRORS DON'T always affect the outcome of a game. They can affect, however, the outcome of a wager on the game. Or, as the case may be, plenty of them.

One such blunder happened on November 16, 2008, in Pittsburgh. Chargers at Steelers. The Steelers took the lead, 11–10, on a field goal with eleven seconds left in the game.

With time left for a desperation play, the Chargers launched a predictable last-ditch series of laterals aimed at somehow busting through the Steelers defense for a touchdown. After a couple of exchanges, Steelers safety Troy Polamalu got his hands on the ball at the San Diego 12 and took it to the end zone.

The score meant nothing to the game. It meant everything to anyone who had bet on the Steelers giving the Chargers 4.5 points.

That was when things went sideways. Referee Scott Green, at the behest of the replay assistant, looked at the play. Green initially decided that the ruling on the field should be upheld and that the touchdown—and the cover—would count.

But then Green and the other officials huddled to discuss the situation. Eventually, Green explained that one of the laterals executed by the Chargers had actually amounted to a forward pass, ending the play on the spot and nullifying the touchdown.

Green erred, badly; the illegal forward pass hadn't ended the play. If the Chargers had scored, the foul would have wiped it out. Because the Steelers scored, the penalty could have been declined, with the touchdown standing and the cover surviving.

The game ended in an 11–10 win for the Steelers. Pittsburgh won but didn't cover the spread. Estimates at the time suggested that the decision swung $64 million in wagers.

To make matters worse, Green admitted after the game that he and his crew had blown it and that he should have upheld the ruling of a Pittsburgh touchdown because the illegal forward pass hadn't hit the ground.

"We should have let the play go through in the end, yes," Green said. "It was misinterpreted that instead of killing the play, we should have let the play go through."

The situation created an uproar, but since most of the bets had been placed illegally, aggrieved gamblers had limited options for being heard. Now, with the US Supreme Court opening the door in 2018 for states to adopt sports wagering, more and more of the money that was bet illegally on a game such as Chargers-Steelers in 2008 will be bet legally.

Next time, then, the outcome very likely will create a much greater furor, with legislators and/or prosecutors demanding recompense for the bettors who sacrificed hard-earned money on a wager tainted by a horrible mistake at the end of the game. At a minimum, pressure to change the outcome will emerge. At worst, politicians may try to exercise external oversight of the NFL with the goal of ensuring integrity, security, and reliability for the placement of wagers.

Governmental regulation happens. It happened with the stock market after the crash in 1929. It could happen for the NFL and other pro sports at any time.

In many respects, the prospect of a federal agency that oversees the NFL constitutes the league's biggest concern. The NFL cherishes the ability to make its own decisions, to determine its own path. That will go out the window if/when Congress decides that the NFL can't do a sufficient job on its own to ensure that bets will be determined by the skills and abilities of players and coaches rather than by any whims and inaccuracies of the people who officiate games.

Fortunately for the league, Green's blunder happened more than a decade too early. If/when something like that happens again, it could spark a major change in the way the NFL does business.

THE SANTONIO HOLMES
MISSED CALL

IN 2017, THE NFL tried to shed its "No Fun League" label by dramatically relaxing the rules regarding celebrations. Group displays returned. Going to the ground resumed. The ban against using props relaxed.

The last of those provisions—the rule that previously prevented players from using the football as a prop in celebrations—had existed for years. The NFL had a reason for it, even if some wondered whether the reason made sense.

"This is a rule that was put in place to prevent things from escalating," former NFL Senior VP of Officiating Dean Blandino said in 2015. "We had situations where players were using the ball as a prop. It was getting elaborate; it was getting extensive. And we were creating this animosity with the team that scored and then the team that got scored upon, and we were ending up with altercations, and this got out of control."

As a result, the pre-2017 rule resulted in scrutiny after touchdowns when a player, for example, put the ball under his jersey as a tribute to his pregnant wife, used the ball as a pillow when pretending to take an on-field nap, used the ball as a horse he pretended to ride, used the ball as a golf ball and a pylon as a putter, and squatted and dropped the ball from behind his buttocks as if it were, well, you get the point.

Seahawks receiver Doug Baldwin performed the pigskin-as-poop maneuver in Super Bowl XLIX. (Presumably, the gesture would violate even the less constipated celebration rules.) Six years earlier, when the rules plainly prohibited the use of the football as a prop, another receiver committed a similar violation that went unnoticed. And if the violation had been noticed, it could have resulted in the league crowning a different champion.

The fact that you're likely confused by this revelation shows that the NFL did a great job of turning the page on the infraction and that the reporters who cover the NFL did a poor job of focusing sufficient attention on it. Regardless, it happened.

The Cardinals qualified for the 2008 postseason by winning the NFC West with a 9–7 record. Some described Arizona as the worst team ever to earn a berth in the playoffs. Then the playoffs began, and the Cardinals started winning.

First, the Cardinals beat a Falcons team that had won 11 of 16 games, 30–24. Next, Arizona crossed the country to Carolina, stunning the 12–4 Panthers on a night that saw quarterback Jake Delhomme's career disintegrate amid a sextet of turnovers. Then came an even bigger stunner, with the Cardinals reversing a 48–20 Thanksgiving-night loss to the Eagles by beating Philadelphia for the unlikeliest of berths in the Super Bowl.

The upstart Cardinals had set the stage for a showdown with the Pittsburgh Steelers. Arizona had never before played for a Lombardi Trophy, whereas the Steelers had done so six times before, winning five.

Pittsburgh, favored to win by nearly a touchdown, found itself in an unlikely fight with the Cardinals. Down 20–7 in the fourth quarter, the Cardinals rallied. Larry Fitzgerald caught a short touchdown pass from Kurt Warner. The extra point made it 20–14. Pittsburgh offensive lineman Justin Hartwig committed holding in his own end zone: 20–16. Then, with fewer than three minutes to play, Warner found Fitzgerald for an iconic shot-from-a-cannon catch and run that gave the Cardinals a 23–20 lead.

From the Tampa Bay press box, I muttered at that moment, "Holy shit, the Cardinals are going to win."

But the Steelers, despite squandering a 13-point lead, weren't ready to surrender. They moved the ball in position to at least force what would have been the first overtime in Super Bowl history. From the Arizona 6 with 48 seconds to play, quarterback Ben Roethlisberger threaded a needle in the back of the end zone. Receiver Santonio Holmes did, or didn't, get both feet on the grass before going out of bounds.

The officials on the field called it a touchdown. The replay official called for a review. The officials didn't notice in the aftermath of the Super Bowl–winning play that Holmes had paid homage to the talcum-powder toss made famous by NBA great LeBron James. Holmes used the football as a prop in place of the powder.

Yes, by rule, the No Fun League's bat signal should have activated. The Steelers should have kicked off from their own 15, not from their own 30. And the Cardinals, with forty-two seconds to play and a pair of timeouts left, may have had a better chance to pull off one of the most amazing finishes in Super Bowl history.

Mike Pereira, who served at the time as the league's VP of officiating, later acknowledged that the officials should have penalized Holmes. The league office, confirming that Holmes had violated the no-prop rule, fined him $10,000.

Asked at the Pro Bowl (at the time, it was played after the Super Bowl) about the failure to call a penalty on Holmes, Commissioner Roger Goodell tried to downplay the situation by explaining that the violation "happened about fifteen seconds after the play" and that this was "something the Competition Committee is going to have to look at—is there a period of time where it really doesn't have the same impact that it would if it was done immediately?"

By all appearances, the Competition Committee never applied an egg timer to the rule against props. More importantly, no such exception existed at the time. Goodell, frankly, was trying to avoid the obvious implication: that the officials had screwed up, that the Steelers should have kicked off only 45 feet from the end zone they'd be defending, and that the Cardinals should have had an enhanced opportunity to score a potential championship-clinching touchdown.

In the end, the league's handling of the situation worked. The NFL, as one source with knowledge of the situation explained it, was surprised at how quickly the issue went away. The source also acknowledged that if social media had been in early 2009 what it is today, the issue surely wouldn't have disappeared quite so quickly.

THE FAIL MARY

BUOYED BY THE NFL's ultimate victory in the 2011 lockout of the players, which accomplished the owners' goal of replacing the 2006 CBA with terms far more favorable to management, the league set its sights on vanquishing the game's officials. The sequel didn't go quite as smoothly.

In 2012, as the contract with the NFL Referees Association (NFLRA) approached expiration, Commissioner Roger Goodell shrugged at the prospect of locking out game officials and replacing them with others of a necessarily lower level of quality. Pointing out that the league had turned to replacement officials a decade earlier, Goodell acknowledged that some calls would be missed but that the officials hired to replace the regular officials would do an acceptable job.

"Safety is such a focus for us," Goodell said in early August 2012. "They've been training on that basis."

Others disagreed. Referee Walt Anderson, who had a vested interest in the labor dispute being resolved, questioned whether the replacements would experience the same degree of vetting that the regular officials had experienced. "Back whenever I first applied to the NFL, it was five years that they spent, not only scouting me but going through the vetting process of looking into my background, talking to people who knew me," Anderson told Houston's Fox affiliate at the time. "They wanted to know a lot more about my character, my work ethic, the things that you were going to do off the field from that standpoint. . . . The whole integrity of the game is put in our hands, and the last thing [Goodell] wants to have out there on the field are people that are of potential questionable character."

It ultimately wasn't questionable character but questionable skill that doomed the 2012 lockout. With the best of the best officials locked out, the NFL turned to officials who hadn't been good enough to graduate to the place all football officials aspire to be. At the same time, the NCAA—whose officials are accustomed to the pressure and other challenges of large crowds and high stakes—became reluctant to guarantee that any of its officials who accepted replacement assignments with the NFL would have employment waiting for them after the lockout ended. This prompted most to decline the opportunity to replace the best officials in the sport, forcing the NFL to dig even deeper. The league had separate concerns about using high-level college officials who would otherwise graduate to the NFL and who would still be regarded as scabs by their pro-level colleagues. (That was precisely what happened when replacements from a 2001 lockout later became NFL officials.)

As replacement officials worked preseason games, others with a clear interest in causing the NFLRA to cry uncle, such as Texans founder Bob McNair, claimed that there was no difference between the regular officials and those the NFL had hired to take their place. "We have complaints; it doesn't matter who's officiating," McNair said at the time. "And we look back at it as to those calls that we think were bad calls, and we don't have any more now than we had before."

McNair nevertheless acknowledged the obvious, that the replacements "are not as good professionally as the ones we've had; otherwise, we would have had the others all along." Still, McNair insisted that he saw no difference in the quality of the calls or the number of calls with which teams disagreed. "We have the same situation—we have some calls we don't like, we have some that should have been made that weren't made, but we don't have any more, and the players are just as well protected," McNair said. "So I don't think that safety is an issue at all."

While safety may not have been compromised, quality clearly was. And multiple league-office employees knew it would happen. As the lockout endured through the preseason and into the regular season, the differences between the regular officials and the folks the NFL were able to find to replace them became increasingly obvious, notwithstanding Goodell's claim that the replacements would "do a very credible job."

Goodell echoed that belief when the regular season commenced with a game between the Cowboys and the Giants. "Our officials did a more than adequate job," Goodell insisted. "I think we've proven we can train officials, get them up to NFL standards, and we've done that in a three-month period. These officials will get even better as time goes by. The game is not going to stop."

The game didn't stop, but the problems quickly became apparent. Replacements from the collegiate level were treating defensive pass interference as a 15-yard penalty (which it is in college) and not as a spot foul. An early-season Monday-night game between the Broncos and Falcons featured Denver center J. D. Walton grabbing an official without the automatic ejection that usually accompanies such an indignity. Falcons coach Mike Smith yelled and screamed at officials, resulting in a flag for unsportsmanlike conduct that mysteriously was picked up. The replacement officials, put simply, were over their skis.

As one source with knowledge of the concerns created by the lockout explained it, some in the league office expected that the situation would eventually get messy. "It's not a matter of if but when," the source said regarding the prevailing mood during the lockout. "The shit's gonna hit the fan. This is not sustainable."

The shit hit the fan on Monday, September 24. At the conclusion of a Monday-night game between the Packers and Seahawks, Seattle receiver Golden Tate committed a blatant shove of a Green Bay defensive back on a last-second Hail Mary play, allowing Tate to catch the ball and win the game. The obvious incident of offensive pass interference went uncalled.

The play, and the outcome of the game, quickly became known as the Fail Mary. Packers fans held a protest at Lambeau Field. And the league finally blinked, promptly working out a new eight-year deal and returning the regular officials to the field before the very next game, three nights after the Fail Mary.

The lockout ended with stunning speed. The league had anticipated that upon resolving the lockout, roughly a week would be needed to get the regular officials properly prepared to return to action. The Fail Mary accelerated the process by creating a clear sense that the replacements had to go.

"We're sorry to have to put our fans through that," Goodell admitted after the league buckled. "I believe in accountability, not excuses. And I regret we were not able to secure an agreement sooner in the process and avoid the unfortunate distractions to the game. You deserve better."

They got better once the regular officials returned. The first game, pitting the Browns against the Ravens, featured images of a cocksure Gene Steratore, back in his role as referee. "Well, you had your Maximus moment," Steratore was told at the time.

Although the Fail Mary solved the problem, the damage was done. The unwarranted Green Bay loss kept the Packers from earning a bye in the postseason, forcing them to play in the wild-card round and to face the 49ers on the road in the divisional round. The Packers should have had a week off and a home game in the round of eight.

Of course, it's impossible to know how things would have turned out if the Packers had hosted a game in the divisional round, whether against the 49ers or someone else. Still, the league's aggressive effort to get the officials to capitulate marred the 2012 season, and it may have cost the Packers a chance to face—and to beat—the Ravens in Super Bowl XLVII.

THE INDEX CARD INCIDENT

THE NFL'S FUNDAMENTAL officiating function has not changed in decades. A group of individuals in black-and-white stripes armed with whistles, yellow flags, blue bean bags, and two poles connected by 10 yards of chain preside over each game. From the days of radio to the dawn of television to the proliferation of cable to the advent of the Internet to the full-blown digital age, nothing has changed when it comes to administering the rules of a football game.

The low-tech nature of the officiating of the game goes on display every time the call comes for those two poles connected by 10 yards of chain to be brought onto the field to determine whether the offense has earned a new set of four downs. The process generates drama, with the ball sitting on the field as one of the officials pulls on the slackened links until the pole stops, lowering the point of it to the ground and allowing the referee to then decide whether enough territory has been secured to earn a first down.

If the ball meets or passes the pole, the referee signals that a first down has been secured. If the ball falls short of the pole, the referee provides the crowd with a loose approximation of the gap, either by holding up both hands or, when it's really close, using a thumb and an index finger. Once, the outcome of this low-tech measuring process was sufficiently unclear to require the use of an external prop.

It happened in December 2017, roughly a week before Christmas. *Sunday Night Football*. Dallas Cowboys at Oakland Raiders.

With Dallas clinging to a 20–17 lead, the Cowboys faced fourth down and one from their own 39, with five minutes and six seconds to play. Quarterback Dak Prescott ran the ball up the middle.

The spot put the ball extremely close to the line to gain. Referee Gene Steratore called for a measurement. Out came the sticks. With the back pole stationary, umpire Roy Ellison pulled the front one taut while field judge Mike Weatherford held the ball in place.

Once the front pole landed, the gap looked more narrow than any gap ever had.

"Look at this," NBC's Al Michaels said. "Look at this."

Steratore leaned over, placing his own hand on the ball and straightening it slightly.

"Back it away," Steratore said to onlookers as he stood upright before hunkering down again to inspect whether the ball had made it far enough.

Ellison inched the pole as close as he could to the ball, and Steratore then stood again. He retrieved a folded piece of paper from his pocket and attempted to drop it between the ball and the pole. When the folded paper (which became widely known as an index card, even though it wasn't) didn't fit, a smirking Steratore stood to signal that the Cowboys had secured a first down. As the referee moved, Cowboys tight end Jason Witten walked by and gave Steratore an approving pat on the ass.

"Here we are across the [San Francisco] Bay from Silicon Valley, the high-tech capital of the world, and you got an index card that determines whether it's a first down," Michaels declared over images of an apoplectic Raiders coach Jack Del Rio. Cowboys coach Jason Garrett also seemed to disagree with the approach (but not the outcome), believing that the pole wasn't quite positioned at 90 degrees.

The NFL dubbed the exercise "very unusual," but the league said that it violated no rules.

Still, the incident illustrates the stubborn refusal of the NFL to find a better way. Years ago, a company developed a laser-based system for determining whether a first down had been earned, creating a four-inch green line that could be seen by coaches, players, and fans in the stadium. The NFL never embraced it.

Coaches have argued for the placement of digital technology inside the football, which would allow for a quick and easy determination regarding whether the ball had moved 10 yards from the starting point. The NFL continues to drag its feet on such possibilities.

Whatever the ultimate form of the device, it would be very easy to remove the poles-and-chain approach. And so the question becomes whether the league *wants* it this way.

If the league were to replace the century-old system with something that would generate a quick, clear, and reliable answer, the pulled-pole drama would disappear from the game. Those two or three seconds of wondering where the front pole will land in relation to the ball would be stripped from the game. Indeed, some within the league office prefer the extra suspense that comes from the old-school measuring process. Making the measurement system digital would entail a quid pro quo of certainty that would make the effort far more reliable but also far less compelling.

Thus, the league persists with a substandard method that can lead to unfair results, simply to preserve a moment of intrigue that easily could be engineered out of the game. Put in those terms, it's ridiculous. As legalized gambling spreads, it becomes increasingly unacceptable.

At some point, the league will have no choice but to shift to a new approach. Some within the league office accept that it's inevitable. The only question is whether the league will make the move on its own or whether it will happen at the behest of those who will exercise the power to regulate the sport.

THE CATCH RULE

IN JANUARY 2000, as the Buccaneers tried to upend the high-powered Rams for a berth in the Super Bowl, Tampa Bay receiver Bert Emanuel caught a pass. As he landed, the ball hit the ground while in Emanuel's possession. The catch was ruled incomplete based on a bright-line rule that made any catch incomplete if the ball struck the ground.

The league decided to alter the rules, allowing a catch to be a catch if the ball touches the ground but doesn't move. That good deed definitely didn't go unpunished; instead, it unlocked nearly two decades of confusion regarding what is and isn't a catch.

The examples of questionable calls quickly piled up, and the confusion regarding what is and isn't a catch increased. The first major controversy happened in Week One of the 2010 season when Lions receiver Calvin Johnson caught what appeared to be a game-winning touchdown pass. Falling to the ground in the end zone, he smacked the ball against the ground, left it behind as he got up, and commenced the celebration. It was ruled not a touchdown, however, and referee Gene Steratore upheld the decision via replay review, creating plenty of confusion as to whether Johnson had actually caught it.

The catch rule periodically reared its ugly head over the next few years, culminating in a moment from the 2014 playoffs known simply as "Dez caught it." Down 5 points with fewer than five minutes to play and facing fourth and 2 from the Green Bay 32, Cowboys quarterback Tony Romo opted not for a short pass that would have secured a first down but to throw it deep down the left sideline to star receiver Dez Bryant.

Bryant leaped high over Packers defensive back Sam Shields, snatched the ball out of the air, took two steps, and lunged for the goal line. When Bryant struck the ground, the ball popped up.

Field judge Terry Brown immediately ruled the play a valid catch, giving Dallas a first down inside the Green Bay 1. Packers coach (who later would become Cowboys coach) Mike McCarthy threw a red challenge flag.

Referee Gene Steratore (he shows up a lot in these situations, doesn't he?) announced that the ruling on the field would be overturned. Steratore, who by rule at the time made the decision with input from the league office, explained to a pool reporter after the game that in his view, Bryant hadn't performed an act "common to the game" while falling, that the ball had struck the ground, and that Bryant's ability to repossess the ball became irrelevant because the ball had struck the ground.

The available replay angles suggested otherwise. Arguably, Bryant had performed an act common to the game (lunging for the goal line), and the ball hadn't actually hit the ground. That was where the replay standard became particularly relevant. The ruling on the field? A catch. To overturn it, Steratore needed clear and obvious evidence that Bryant wasn't performing an act common to the game along with clear and obvious evidence that the ball hit the ground. There seemed to be clear and obvious evidence of neither.

The outcome defied the commonsensical know-it-when-you-see-it examination of the play, and the ruling on the field definitely didn't satisfy the loose notion that it should be overturned only if fifty drunks in a bar all believed an error had occurred. It looked like a catch, and to this day a large number of football fans believe it was.

"It was a great catch I can say now," McCarthy said in the press conference that introduced him as the Dallas coach in early 2020. "It wasn't technically then."

The outcome forced the league to keep striving for a solution to the catch rule, hoping to find an amalgamation of words that captured the know-it-when-you-see-it reality of a great catch like the one Bryant had made.

After two more years of groping, the league finally solved the problem. At the 2017 annual meeting of all NFL teams, the Competition

Committee recommended—and the owners adopted—a new formula-
tion of the definition of a catch. The player must secure the ball in his
hands or arms before the ball strikes the ground, must touch the ground
with both feet or any part of the body other than his hands, and (most
importantly) must perform an act common to the game, which includes
tucking the ball, extending it forward, taking a third step, turning up-
field, or avoiding or warding off an opponent.

As a practical matter, the notion that a third step completes the catch
has become the most easily applied objective measurement. For that reason (and others), the new rule has worked. The NFL finally has crafted a
definition of a catch that meshes with the expectations of fans and media
when seeing what they believe to be an actual catch.

Under the current rule, Dez Bryant undoubtedly caught it. Under
the current rule, Calvin Johnson undoubtedly caught it. Under the current rule, Bert Emanuel undoubtedly caught it. While nothing can be
done to change those outcomes, they've paved the way for what hopefully
will be a future of football filled with reliable rulings regarding what is,
and isn't, a catch.

THE RAMS-SAINTS DEBACLE

WITH THE QUESTION of defining a catch finally resolved, the NFL involuntarily shifted to a thornier, albeit unexpected, problem. It confronted the intersection of officiating and instances of interference with the opportunity to make a catch.

Long a point of periodic consternation, pass interference—offensive or defensive and called or uncalled—never became part of the replay-review process. The justification for omitting it arose from the notion that pass interference entails the application of judgment and that judgment of the officials should not be second-guessed through the frame-by-frame micromanagement of the decision after the fact.

But the judgment of the officials can sometimes be botched in a clear and obvious way. Sometimes in a way that would prompt fifty drunks in a bar to instantly see the error and agree that the ruling should be changed.

On January 20, 2019, the Saints hosted the Rams with a berth in Super Bowl LIII up for grabs. With the game on the line, fifty drunks in a bar (and everyone else) saw the error and agreed that the ruling should be changed. In a 20–20 game, with 1:49 to play, the Saints faced third and 10 from the LA 13. Quarterback Drew Brees received the snap in shotgun formation. Receiver Tommylee Lewis, who had lined up to the right of Brees in the backfield, sprinted to the flat.

Rams cornerback Nickell Robey-Coleman had the assignment to cover Lewis, and the defender realized too late that his man was on the other side of the formation. Robey-Coleman sprinted across the field toward Lewis, ignoring the ball and deciding to disrupt what could have been a walk-in touchdown by blasting Lewis.

Brees floated the ball a bit, giving Robey-Coleman a chance to intercept it—if he hadn't already committed to wiping out Lewis. Robey-Coleman clearly arrived before the ball, hitting Lewis high as he was preparing to catch the pass.

Despite multiple officials seeing what the rest of the world saw, no flags were thrown. The Saints settled for a field goal, creating a 3-point lead. The Rams tied the game before the end of regulation, and then they won on a field goal in overtime.

The Saints and their fans were justifiably livid. Coach Sean Payton, despite the ever-present possibility of a fine or other punishment from the league for criticizing officiating, pulled no punches at his postgame press conference.

"They blew the call," Payton said. "That call makes it first and ten, and we'd only need three plays. It was a game-changing call."

Indeed it was. It also became a rule-changing call.

Faced with an outcry that included a New Orleans boycott of the ensuing Super Bowl (the local TV ratings plunged from 53.0 in the prior year to 26.1 for Patriots-Rams), the NFL worked hard to figure out a way to prevent that kind of outcome from happening again. The easiest fix, of course, would have occurred if NFL Senior VP of Officiating Al Riveron had instructed referee Bill Vinovich to drop a flag through the real-time communication system used for conducting replay review. (While such a directive would have violated the rules, it would have avoided the ensuing shitstorm and thus would have been worth the trouble.)

Some in league circles argued that the incident should be treated as a once-per-century aberration and thus ignored. The Competition Committee, led by Falcons president Rich McKay, ultimately proposed a half measure that would have allowed pass interference calls to be reviewed via the replay process. However, it would not have allowed replay review of situations where, as in the Rams-Saints game, no foul was called.

Hiding behind vague notions of "unintended consequences," the Competition Committee simply opted to assume that what had happened in New Orleans wouldn't happen again, at least not during their own membership in the group responsible for recommending rule changes. The owners, influenced by input from coaches and executives who found that proposal unacceptable, crafted a standard that made all calls and noncalls of pass interference, offensive and defensive, subject to replay review.

That ended up being the easy part. As the season approached, it became clear that Riveron intended, when the replay system was properly activated, to perform a slow-motion analysis of each reviewable instance of uncalled interference, searching for proof that one player had impeded another. Riveron raised eyebrows in a session with employees of NFL Media by pointing out several past noncalls of interference that had created no controversy but would have resulted in a flag being thrown via the new replay process.

Once the games started, the bar shifted multiple times, with the standard for determining interference (or noninterference) changing throughout the season. Some began to regard Riveron's replay process as something as random as the rattling of a Magic 8-Ball. By the end of the year, Riveron seemed to have settled on a test that changed only egregious errors of judgment.

It wasn't enough to save the system. After the 2019 season, the owners decided to ditch replay review for calls and noncalls of offensive and defensive pass interference. The league thus reverted to the same standard that had applied during the Rams-Saints NFC Championship, setting the stage for another unfixable blunder that will consume the league with controversy, alienate a fan base, and potentially trigger Congress to provide external oversight and regulation of pro football.

The last part alone is more than enough reason for the NFL to take care of the problem on its own. If it doesn't, someone else definitely will.

THE WORST RULE IN FOOTBALL

THE WORST RULE in football continues to hide in plain sight, with no effort to revise a nonsensical provision that arbitrarily penalizes effort. And the worst rule in football will continue to be the worst rule in football until it sparks the worst-case scenario for the NFL.

The worst rule in football applies when an offensive player, while approaching the goal line, fumbles the ball and it enters and exits the end zone unrecovered. If the offensive player fumbles the ball and it exits the field short of the end zone, the offense keeps the ball at the spot of the fumble. If, however, the ball makes it into the end zone and then bounces out of any portion of it, the defense—not the offense—gets the ball. And the defense doesn't get the ball at the spot of the fumble. The defense gets the ball at its own 20.

No one from the NFL has ever managed to articulate a sensible explanation for the worst rule in football. The best explanation for the worst rule in football essentially comes from the last of the three sentences that Homer Simpson shared with his son, Bart, when Homer believed he was dying after eating poison blowfish (that's a hell of a windup, I know): "Cover for me," "Good idea, boss," and "It was like that when I got here."

It was like that when I got here. That's it. That's the reasoning. What else can there be? At the absolute best, it can be argued that the end zone is some sort of sacred territory around which the offense should take care not to fumble the ball. (In the very early days of the NFL, an incomplete pass by the offense that landed in the end zone resulted in a touchback for the defense.)

That's still a weak justification for unfairly penalizing the offense and giving the defense an unwarranted advantage. When a player closes in on the end zone, he wants to score. Sometimes he reaches the ball forward by extending his arms. Sometimes he dives with his body. And if, in the process of trying to score 6 points, the player loses possession of the ball and it grazes the pylon in the front corner of the end zone instead of bouncing out of bounds at the 1-inch line, the offense automatically loses possession to the defense, which instantly gets the ball at its 20.

So why hasn't the rule changed? Every year, the NFL's Competition Committee and its thirty-two teams have the ability to propose potential adjustments to a thick and ever-thickening rule book. It never happens, however.

It never happens for a very basic reason. The worst rule in football has an equal chance of hurting a team and helping a team. For every team that gets screwed out of possession near the opponent's end zone, another team gets the ball at its own 20 when it shouldn't.

Most would think a team that was burned by a bad rule would become the most likely to push to change it. However, plenty of coaches, executives, and owners believe that after ending up on the wrong side of a bad rule, they'll benefit from it the next time it applies in one of their games. Thus, after the Browns lost possession to the Chiefs as receiver Rashard Higgins reached with the ball near the Kansas City goal line during a 2020 divisional round playoff game, the Browns didn't lobby for the rule to change.

That will continue to be the case until the rule determines the outcome of a conference championship game or affects a Super Bowl. Consider the size of the audience watching a Super Bowl. Consider the extent of the broader football knowledge of the millions of casual fans who watch the Super Bowl and few if any other games. Consider their reaction when someone explains the rule to them for the first time. Or at least tries to do so.

That's when the ridiculous nature of the worst rule in football finally will be brought to light. That's when the NFL, as it often does, will react to an embarrassing outcome by changing the rule. And that's when those stewards of the game who refused stubbornly to do anything about the rule will act as if they just realized the problems it causes.

That's how the NFL does business. Instead of creatively and proactively identifying all rules that need to be adjusted in order to avoid a grossly unfair outcome in a Super Bowl or some other significant game, the NFL ignores rules that could lead to a grossly unfair outcome until the grossly unfair outcome happens in a big spot. Then, the rule gets fixed.

So if the rule will eventually be changed after it creates an outcry in a Super Bowl, why not just go ahead and change it before the outcry? As easy as it seems, spotting potential problems and solving them before they become actual problems continues to be one of the NFL's biggest challenges.

PART X
THE FUTURE

THE PROLIFERATION
OF SPORTS BETTING

FOR DECADES, THE NFL had a complicated relationship with gambling. The league craved the extra attention that illegal sports betting brought to the table, but it reserved the right to clutch pearls and/or wag fingers at gambling in most forms. In 2008, for example, the Steelers underwent a dramatic ownership overhaul because some members of the Rooney family had ventured beyond permitted gambling activities (dog racing) and begun investing in prohibited gambling activities (by putting slot machines and casino gambling at their dog-racing tracks).

Through it all, the league treated Las Vegas like the seventh level of hell, refusing to consider staging an exhibition game or the Pro Bowl there—and in 2015 essentially shutting down an effort by former Cowboys quarterback Tony Romo to conduct a fantasy football convention in a gambling-free Las Vegas conference center owned by a casino.

On May 14, 2018, with the stroke of a pen, the US Supreme Court changed everything. In a 6–3 decision, the nine justices deemed unconstitutional a federal law that had prohibited most states from joining the likes of Nevada in legalizing betting on sports.

The ruling didn't open the floodgates; it removed them. Over time, more and more states have begun to realize that legalized sports betting could generate plenty of tax money, especially in communities bordering states that don't have legalized sports betting. That has served only to place more pressure on those states to follow suit with legalized sports betting.

In time, the vast majority of states will develop legalized sports betting programs. It won't be all fifty; even now, only forty-four states have lottery programs. But enough states will legitimize betting on sports to bring a billion-dollar industry out of the shadows and into the kind of ultraviolet light that will make it grow and spread like a highly profitable weed.

The sports leagues initially tried, clumsily, to muscle the various states into surrendering a piece of the action as an "integrity fee." Basically, the people who provide the vehicle for the placing of bets argued that with so much legitimate money riding on the outcome of games such as football, baseball, and basketball, the stewards of the sporting events should get a slice of the take in order to finance broader efforts to ensure that no one gives in to the temptation for shenanigans.

It didn't work. Neither did an effort to pass federal legislation that would have created nationwide sports betting rules, allowing leagues such as the NFL to avoid having to lobby on a state-by-state basis for the most favorable collection of regulations. Instead, sports betting policies and procedures have emerged one state at a time, and as each additional state joins the parade, the cumulative earning potential grows and grows and grows.

And continue to grow it will, to the point at which the NFL and other sports leagues will find a way to earn massive amounts of extra revenue through a collection of partnerships with betting companies— and a wide variety of betting platforms. From in-game betting on a wide range of propositions in the various NFL stadiums to, eventually, in-home betting on items as specific as the outcome of a given play, the pie will grow beyond the size of any conceivable pan into which the NFL could bake it.

Technologically, the challenge is clear. Broadcasters need to be able to send real-time images into homes throughout the country with no delay, thus giving spectators maximum opportunity to dial in a bet before the football is delivered by the center to the quarterback.

Franchises, now with values in the range of $2 billion to $3 billion each, soon will be worth more than $8 billion, as one NFL owner predicted in late 2020. The value will extend not only to the various sports but also to the media companies covering the sports, and any outlet with any substantial audience to which betting products can be directly marketed will have dramatically enhanced value.

This tremendously significant opportunity for the NFL comes with an even bigger challenge. For a league that has developed a reputation for being far more reactive than proactive, it won't be easy to foresee every potential problem that could arise from widespread legalized sports betting. How will the league ensure that players, coaches, and other personnel with valuable inside information won't be corrupted? (More on that in a bit.) How will the league protect players, coaches, and other personnel from racking up debts that could be repaid not by forking over cash but by shaving off points?

The NFL has every reason to anticipate these issues and to solve them. Failure to do so will set the stage for scandal. And scandal will lead to regulation or possibly prosecution.

Consider this. For decades, legalized wagering has occurred through the buying and selling of stock. Prior to the crash of 1929, however, the federal government had created no system for regulating the markets. Five years after the event that triggered the Great Depression, Congress created the Securities and Exchange Commission.

It's arguably inevitable that Congress eventually will establish a federal agency responsible for ensuring the integrity of sports wagering. By taking the best possible care of its own backyard, the NFL has a chance to delay that moment, indefinitely but possibly not permanently.

THE INJURY REPORT

THE NFL'S HISTORICALLY awkward relationship with gambling has included an injury report aimed at creating the impression that inside information regarding the health of players doesn't exist. It always has, however. And it still does.

The injury report provides some information, but not nearly enough. The categories regarding the likelihood of a player being able to play are broad, and there's never any way of knowing with certainty whether and to what extent an injured player actually will be able to play the entire game or whether he'll be at or close to his normal capacity.

At one point, the league had four categories of injury designation: probable, questionable, doubtful, and out. As defined, probable actually meant close to definite. After years of the term causing plenty of confusion, the league simply got rid of it.

Currently, a player with an injury who is listed on the final report prior to a game gets one of four labels: (1) none at all, which means he's good to go; (2) "questionable," which means he's somewhere between 99 percent and 50 percent likely to play; (3) "doubtful," which means he's less than 50 percent likely to play; and (4) "out." Teams tend to most commonly use the "questionable" label, which has been loosely interpreted as a coin-flip proposition and allows for gamesmanship as the game approaches.

For visiting teams, the jig is often up when it's time to travel to the city where the game will be played. If the player actually isn't going to play, he usually doesn't travel—and the team usually downgrades him to "out." The home team has more time to perpetrate the ruse, waiting until ninety minutes before kickoff to place the player on the inactive list for the game.

This approach cries out "inside information," incentivizing efforts by gambling interests to get to the truth wherever and however they can. A player's agent often knows much more about the player's availability than the injury report reflects. Teammates, and sometimes their agents, also know more than the average person. Coaches know more. Trainers know more. And others with access to the team know more.

And so the best and smartest gamblers will cultivate the relationships necessary to get to the truth, especially in situations where the truth otherwise will remain concealed. That's the sweet spot: getting information about a player about whom the information otherwise isn't available.

For its part, the NFL usually looks the other way. Beyond the fact that it's too hard to police thirty-two franchises when it comes to quality and quantity of truthful injury information, the league would prefer not to create the impression that widespread cheating happens when it comes to the injury report. If, for example, Congress knew that most if not all teams strategically fudge the paperwork for football reasons, Congress would become far more likely to create that SEC-style agency charged with regulating pro sports and ensuring the integrity of sports wagering.

The league doesn't always look the other way. Sometimes a player or a team leaves them with no choice.

For example, the 2008 Jets started 8–3 and then fell apart down the stretch. When quarterback Brett Favre, who had been traded by the Packers to the Jets prior to that season, joined the Vikings in 2009, he faced questions about the failure of the Jets to parlay a great start into a playoff berth. Favre justified his dip in performance by explaining that he had a partially torn biceps tendon.

The problem for the Jets became obvious. They had never disclosed that Favre had a biceps or arm injury. The more Favre talked about it, the more glaring the disconnect between the team's past injury reports and Favre's current words became.

Eventually, the NFL had no choice but to take action. The league office fined the Jets $75,000, GM Mike Tannenbaum $25,000, and coach Eric Mangini $25,000.

It happened again in 2019. Steelers quarterback Ben Roethlisberger suffered a season-ending, noncontact elbow injury in Week Two. The elbow had been bothering him. The elbow hadn't been listed on the injury report.

So it was $75,000 for the team (not much inflation over the course of a decade) and $25,000 for coach Mike Tomlin. As with the Jets a decade earlier, the situation gave the league office no choice. (The Lions received similar fines later that year for failing to properly disclose a back injury suffered by quarterback Matthew Stafford. But, frankly, no one really noticed because nobody really cared about the Lions at the time.)

Then came the news, in July 2021, that Buccaneers quarterback Tom Brady had played the entire 2020 season with a torn medial collateral ligament (MCL) in his left knee, but the team had never disclosed that Brady had a knee injury at any point during the season. Brady himself talked about the amount of effort and focus the injury required. Teammate Mike Evans, one of Tampa Bay's receivers and an offensive captain, said on the first day of 2021 training camp that he didn't know Brady had a torn MCL but knew he was "hurt, hurt pretty bad." Regardless of whether the league ever imposed punishment on the Buccaneers for hiding the injury, the point is that the NFL needs to find a way to stop these violations.

They occur often. Too often. In most cases, the league does nothing, and no one ever says much about it. Most fans don't care, and zealous fans of the team in question will attack reporters who push the issue as hall monitors for obsessing over compliance with a rule that everyone violates. As legalized sports betting spreads, it will become harder and harder for the league and its teams to ignore these violations, however.

As explained more fully in a later chapter, the process of acquiring inside information is the potential gateway for infiltrating teams, giving gamblers a reason to create relationships that can blossom into something more than finding out whether the starting quarterback has an injury to his throwing arm that the team isn't talking about. As those relationships grow, real problems can arise—problems that could invite governmental oversight in the form of regulation or, even worse, prosecution.

So what should the league do about this situation? It needs to create far more detailed injury reports, and it should consider having representatives from the NFL constantly confirming that all relevant information has been made available to the betting public in order to dissuade any gamblers from privately trying to ferret out the truth. Whatever it does, one highly placed league executive has told me that the league knows that it must enforce these rules and that it must increase accountability if it hopes to ensure that teams comply.

THE TIM DONAGHY DYNAMIC

GAMBLING, LEGAL OR not, has existed in sports for as long as sports have existed. Gambling, legal or not, invites corruption. Corruption happened for the NBA in 2007 when a scandal emerged regarding a referee named Tim Donaghy, whose gambling habit led to debts and then to the infiltration of gambling interests that pressured Donaghy to use his discretion to guide the final scores of professional basketball games.

The scandal sent shock waves through all sports, especially after Donaghy suggested that the NBA had a role in fixing games in order to extend a playoff series to seven games. (This allegation was never proven.) Additionally, whispers and rumors made the rounds that Donaghy wasn't alone in his effort to fix games. (No one else was ever implicated in the scandal.)

The NFL moved quickly to ensure that it would face no similar issues. Mike Pereira, who served at the time as the NFL's VP of officiating, insisted that the league was clean, that any issues with officiating resulted from error, not foul play. But the risk has remained, in 2007 and every year thereafter.

Legalized gambling doesn't change things because gambling interests—legal or not—will always look for an edge. If NFL officials become involved in gambling and, inevitably, acquire debts that can't easily be satisfied, they will become easy targets for an effort to swap what they can pay for what they can *do*.

In the NFL, penalties happen on virtually every play. The question is whether the officials notice them and act upon them. Holding away from the point of the attack is often overlooked, since it doesn't affect the play. An official looking to alter the outcome of a game could, if he or she so desired, find ways to call or not call enough fouls to have a cumulative effect on the outcome of a game or, more importantly, the application of the point spread.

The league nevertheless believes that it would be harder for football officials to manipulate games than it is for basketball officials. Only the referee (who runs the show) or the umpire (who is in position to call holding fouls) could skew a game one way or the other. Even then, the league office closely monitors every game as it happens.

Besides, the NFL believes that it has properly screened and monitored officials to guard against such situations. The league vets the officials carefully, examining bank accounts and relationships and any and all signs of debt. Also, the league constantly looks for anything that would stand out in relation to betting lines and trends regarding penalty frequency and any other pattern that would cause concern. Still, it's an endless effort to ensure the integrity of officiating, one that has no margin for error, especially with legalized sports betting continuing to spread.

If the NFL had experienced a Tim Donaghy situation before legalized wagering, it would have created a major PR problem. If the NFL experiences a Tim Donaghy problem in a world of legalized wagering, the situation will become much more significant since it will quite possibly impact millions of dollars that were legally wagered in the various states that will eventually have legalized wagering.

It would, quite simply, provide the moment that guarantees federal oversight and regulation of the sport, a development that would rob the league of its highly coveted power to control its own destiny. With a Donaghy-style scandal, the league would experience a worst-case scenario that would entail politicians and bureaucrats determining and enforcing a wide swath of external rules and regulations that will make it much harder, and more expensive, for the NFL to operate.

The league needs to constantly obsess over the possibility that officials will develop gambling habits and in turn become compromised by gambling interests. This requires not only thorough and exhaustive background research for each official but also a relentless and endless effort to continue to ensure that officials who were clean when hired remain that way. All it would take is one rogue official to turn the league upside down; the league must do all it can to prevent that from ever happening.

In a world of legalized gambling, the PR problem becomes ever more pronounced. Plenty of fans are already wired to assume that the fix is in. As the NFL and its teams do more and more business with gambling interests, the conspiracy theories will develop much more credibility. The league and its officials must remain at all times above and beyond even the mere appearance of impropriety.

Preventing such outcomes requires significant resources. That's a commitment the league must make, and the notion of being constantly checked and double-checked is a burden that officials must be willing to bear. It's a line item in the budget the league office must create in order to constantly ensure that the officials are squeaky clean and that the discretion they exercise in officiating turns solely on a legitimate effort to get it right and nothing else.

Too much will ride on ensuring the absence of a Tim Donaghy scandal to not make the investment, to not constantly pester and potentially harass officials to ensure that they aren't compromised in any way, to not make certain that squeaky clean motives, intentions, and behavior always exist in applying the rules to each and every game.

Through it all, it will still take only one. One problem. One issue. One bad apple. One Tim Donaghy. Who will then become even more notorious than Tim Donaghy.

SKY JUDGE

IN ITS OUTDATED approach to officiating games, the NFL continues to rely on a small group of human beings, typically of advancing age, who are interspersed among the gladiators. Secondary to the difficulties inherent to seeing through blurs and flashes, the officials have one goal: to stay alive.

Unsurprisingly, they make mistakes. Often, officials looking directly at a player who, for example, caught a pass and got two feet in bounds, fail to call it correctly. Replay review, through the activation of a convoluted process that often takes too much time, can fix plenty of errors. To truly get all calls right, however, the league needs an intermediate level between relying on the real-time, naked-eye assessments of the folks in black-and-white stripes and the decisions made by the league office based on the fifty-drunks-in-a-bar standard of clear and obvious evidence.

The NFL needs to use a sky judge. Not the half measure that the league adopted for 2021, with the replay assistant having the ability to assist with a small handful of objective calls. The league needs to fully embrace using a separate set of eyes that sees only what the rest of us see on television.

Every game would have an extra member of the officiating crew who would sit in a booth with access to all available camera angles. Typically, the sky judge would be a retired referee who no longer can or will move freely among extremely large, incredibly fast, ridiculously strong men wearing helmets, pads, and cleats. But the sky judge would know the rule book thoroughly, and the sky judge would speak directly to the referee, providing input regarding the play that just transpired.

If the sky judge sees something in the television feed available to anyone and everyone watching at home that conflicts with the ruling that the on-field crew is in the process of making, the sky judge would chime in with guidance based on the available video evidence. The process would bridge the gap between what fans see on TV and what the officials see on the field.

It won't be easy, but it's worth the effort. It won't be cheap, and that's the problem. The NFL, frankly, is cheap. Too cheap. The NFL doesn't believe the benefit of a sky judge justifies the expense. Thus, the NFL would rather save the money and trust the system that has been in place for years.

But even a small increase in the accuracy of calls would justify the expense, especially in an age of legalized gambling. More importantly, the NFL would be creating the impression that it's doing everything it can to ensure that the officials are getting it right. That could delay the eventual, and perhaps inevitable, reckoning that will come in the form of Congress creating a federal agency to regulate football and other sports.

The replay review system would still apply, over and above the work of a sky judge. And perhaps it would be used less frequently, thanks to the opportunity for the sky judge to help the on-field officials correct their mistakes before those mistakes become the basis for replay review.

Although reasonable minds may differ on whether a sky judge can actually make things better, a sky judge definitely can't make things worse. Absent total and complete incompetence, a sky judge would never correct a ruling without seeing, in the same images broadcast to millions of viewers, that a mistake has been made.

A sky judge would be used for anything and everything, even things not subject to replay review, such as pass interference. A sky judge would be another member of the officiating crew with the perspective that comes from watching the game on TV, the same way so many others do. The communications between a sky judge and the referee would be no different than the conversations that happen when multiple members of the crew gather to talk through a ruling on the field.

The NFL has more than enough money to make it happen. The NFL simply needs the incentive to do it. Either the league can develop that incentive by understanding via the application of foresight the upside of implementing a system for enhancing the rulings on the field, or it can do so via the application of hindsight by the Wagering Integrity Commission, or whatever the federal government ends up calling the agency that will be responsible for mandating steps that leagues such as the NFL persistently refuse to take on their own.

Solutions developed internally always work better than solutions developed externally. The sooner the league embraces the full-blown sky judge concept (and not some lame half measure), the sooner the league won't have to worry about someone else embracing the sky judge concept—or some other approach—before it can do so. But since it's too easy (and too cheap) to embrace the way things are and hope that no one forces the league to change these important procedures for getting calls right, the league will be tempted to continue to do nothing at all for as long as possible. Then, when the government begins to press it to implement such safeguards, the league will say it never really considered the concept of having an official who helps officiate every game by seeing everything seen by millions watching the game and ideally, from the league's perspective, the millions betting on it.

PROTECTING INSIDE INFORMATION

GAMBLING CREATES POTENTIAL problems for the NFL beyond the possibility of corrupt or incompetent officials. The possibility of point shaving constantly looms over all sports. In football, however, it becomes harder for any one player (other than a quarterback) to influence the outcome of a game. An equally significant threat comes not from the things that happen on the field but from the knowledge of the things that will happen on the field.

Inside information. Technically known in corporate America as material, nonpublic information. For the same reason that certain facts about a public company can affect its stock price (and thus cannot be disclosed to members of the public), certain facts about a pro football team can provide a very real advantage when it comes to a broad array of available wagers.

As previously discussed, the NFL must require far greater transparency when it comes to injury reports. The potential pitfalls of material, nonpublic information regarding a pro football team arise in other ways as well, given the extent to which sports books plan to eventually expand their betting offerings. In time, fans in stadiums (and, when the technology allows it, fans watching at home) will be able to place bets on each given play, including on propositions as basic as whether it will be a run or a pass. What keeps someone on the sideline who knows what the next play will be from giving hand signals to someone in the stands regarding whether to bet on run or pass? Or what about teams that script the first fifteen or so offensive plays? From coaches to players to janitors, anyone who happens to stumble across the list of plays or any evidence of it has information that becomes extremely valuable to gamblers.

It goes beyond that. Already, wagers can be placed on which quarterback will be the team's starter to begin the season. Some members of an NFL organization will know the answer well in advance. Some, up to and including the owner, have real influence over that decision. A casual conversation among friends regarding the true identity of the starter becomes precisely the kind of information that should not be shared—and thus the kind of information that the league must secure.

Other possible areas in which inside information can make a difference are wagers based on, for example, whether a running back will or won't reach a certain threshold of rushing yards. Those who know the game plan for a given week will know whether it's likely that the target will be matched and exceeded. Likewise, those who know the approach to be taken by the opposing defense will have an edge. In Super Bowl XXV, for example, then Giants defensive coordinator Bill Belichick decided to take the steam out of Buffalo's pass-happy K-Gun offense by making it easier for Bills running back Thurman Thomas to gain rushing yards. New York's defensive players bristled at Belichick's meeting-room suggestion that if Thomas were to gain more than 100 yards rushing, the Giants would win the game. (He did, and they did.) Anyone who caught wind of information of that nature would then be able to bet on the player exceeding the magic number.

The problem of material, nonpublic information also arises with plans for the draft. In 2021, ESPN host Doug Kezirian won more than $300,000 through a series of wagers that Tyson Campbell would be the first safety selected. Although that specific windfall was fueled by BetMGM accidentally listing Campbell as a safety when he was actually a cornerback, it underscored the fact that network reporters can become aware of inside information while doing their jobs. If an ESPN host learned from an ESPN reporter information regarding the round-one draft plans of one or more specific teams, it would be very easy to parlay that knowledge into a major payday via one or more bets based on when and where a player would be selected.

So what can the NFL and the networks do about it? It will require a culture change regarding the manner in which such information is regarded, along with very real disincentives for breaking the rules regarding the manner in which it is handled. Fines won't be enough. The penalties must be real and substantial. And if the league, the teams, the networks, and other media outlets with access to inside information fail to create sufficient internal penalties, the stage will be set for the creation of significant external consequences.

Just one scandal could catch the eye of an ambitious federal prosecutor, who could scour the laws on the books in search of a basis to convene a grand jury. That one scandal also could result in the creation of new laws—along with the ever-present possibility of the establishment of a federal agency charged with regulating the NFL on a broad and comprehensive basis. (That potential development has resided on the league's radar screen for decades, as evidenced by comments made by Commissioner Pete Rozelle to PBS in 1983.) The end result would be the league losing some of the control that it currently has (and wants to keep) over its business.

That's all the more reason for the league to develop its own internal rules and regulations regarding the classification and handling of inside information sooner rather than later. The longer the NFL waits, the more likely it becomes that those rules and regulations will be created by persons other than NFL executives.

THE PLAYOFF SEEDING FORMULA

IN 1972, AFTER the Steelers beat the Raiders in the divisional round of the playoffs thanks to the Immaculate Reception, the Steelers qualified for the AFC Championship. The next Sunday, they hosted the Miami Dolphins. Yes, as unfair as it seems, the 14–0 Miami Dolphins visited the 11–3 Steelers for a berth in Super Bowl VII.

No one complained about it at the time because that was just how it was. Regular-season records did not determine home-field advantage in the playoffs.

That changed in 1975, with home-field advantage from that year forward hinging on how a team had fared in the regular season. While less problematic at a time when each conference had three division champions and one wild-card team, opportunities increased for a team with a losing record to win a division and host one game (or more) against a team with a better record as the playoffs grew from four teams per conference to five in 1978 (three division winners and two wild-card teams) to six in 1990 (three and three) to six under the realigned arrangement of divisions in 2002 (four and two) to seven in 2020 (four and three).

It has happened several times. Most notably, the Seahawks—with a 7–9 record in 2010—won the NFC West and earned a home game against the Saints, who qualified as a wild card with a record of 11–5. Four games better than Seattle, the Saints had to go there for their first playoff game since winning Super Bowl XLIV the prior year.

Seattle benefited from home-field advantage. The crippling noise generated in the team's stadium (designed to ricochet as much sound as possible toward the field) set off nearby Geiger counters during running back Marshawn Lynch's game-clinching 67-yard touchdown run, which he capped with a plunge into the end zone, grabbing his crotch to taunt his opponents and amuse his fans.

Some argued that the outcome proved that the Seahawks were the better team. But it's just as likely that if the Seahawks had had to play the game in New Orleans, the Saints' home-field advantage would have swung the game in their direction. It was the location of the contest that made the difference.

Other instances of a division winner with a nonwinning record hosting a wild-card team with more wins than losses have occurred. In 2011, the 8–8 Broncos (AFC West champions) capped Tebowmania by beating the 12–4 Steelers in overtime. In 2014, the 7–8–1 Panthers (NFC South champions) outscored the 11–5 Cardinals. (It helped that Arizona was down to its third quarterback.) In 2020, Washington won the NFC East at 7–9, capping a year that saw the entire division maligned throughout the season. But for Washington's Week Seventeen win over the Eagles, the Giants would have advanced to the playoffs with a 6–10 record, hosting the 11–5 Buccaneers.

Concerns have persisted that a team that wins a division without a winning record shouldn't host a playoff game. The league traditionally has placed extra importance on a division crown. But with four divisions per conference and four teams per division, what does it mean to be the best of four potentially horrible teams? It's a predetermined placement, independent of any sense of merit-based seeding. All four teams in a given division can stink in a given year, and one of them will still be given a home game in the playoffs.

It won't be easy to get at least twenty-four owners of the NFL's thirty-two franchises to agree to change the current rule. They all have, in theory, a 25 percent chance of hosting a playoff game in every given year. They won't want to dilute that one-in-four shot by applying a caveat based on having a winning record or, possibly, having a better record than the best of the wild-card teams.

Still, the situation creates periodic embarrassment for the league, establishing a storyline based on a team being bad rather than a team being good. The vague possibility of creating a formula for preventing a division winner from hosting a playoff game lingers, but the league never acts on it. The league will from time to time hint that it will, but it ultimately never has.

The best outcome possibly would be to revert to three divisions per conference. Two would have five teams, and one would have six. Winning a division under those circumstances would mean more. Then it would be three division winners and four wild cards in each conference, and chances are that the division winners would each have winning records.

That change is also unlikely. The league likes the current configuration of teams. It's neat. It's tidy. Two conferences. Sixteen teams per conference. Four divisions per conference. Four teams per division. It looks good. Who cares if it doesn't always work right when it's time to seed playoff teams?

That's not a rhetorical question. The answer is obvious. Not nearly enough of the people who own teams or who run the league care about the problem. Until enough do, an obviously unfair dynamic won't change.

EXPANSION

THE NFL LOVES the current number and configuration of its teams. Neat, clean, simple, symmetrical.

An alignment based on a quartet of four-team divisions in each of two conferences arrived in 2002. It hasn't changed for twenty years. That's the league's longest stretch ever of stability and consistency. After the 1970 merger, the league saw new teams arrive in 1976 (two, the Buccaneers and Seahawks), 1995 (two, the Panthers and Jaguars), 1999 (one, via the reconstitution of the Browns), and 2002 (one, the Texans, to balance out the reconstitution of the Browns).

Some in league circles believe that the league won't add any more teams anytime soon, in part because the incorporation of more teams (presumably two) would increase two of the eight divisions to five. Ideally, the league's next expansion (if any) would push the league from thirty-two to forty, with eight five-team divisions and at least sixteen teams in the annual postseason. But that's just too many teams to add at once.

For years, the strongest argument against expansion came from subpar quarterback play. There simply weren't enough good quarterbacks to go around. In truth, there weren't enough bad quarterbacks to go around.

In recent years, more and more young quarterbacks have proven that they can perform at a high level, increasing the supply of competent field generals. From the proliferation of seven-on-seven camps to the willingness of NFL coaches to embrace the offensive systems used by the quarterbacks while in college, incoming quarterbacks have performed better than ever. As a result, fewer NFL teams have found themselves lost and shiftless at the quarterback position.

Then there's gambling. With so much money to be made via wagering on sporting events, the league wants to increase inventory. Through the addition of a seventeenth regular-season game, it has. An eighteenth regular-season game seems inevitable. But inventory can grow without making players on any given team play more games. By adding more teams, the league will necessarily stage more games. Currently, the NFL has 272 regular-season games, with thirty-two teams playing seventeen each. Two more teams would expand the number of regular-season games to 289. Four more teams would grow the regular season to 306. If the NFL ever made it to forty teams and eighteen regular-season games, the league would play a whopping 360 games in every regular season.

A separate challenge is having NFL-ready markets. Currently, the league likes having a small handful of cities that can host NFL teams as leverage for stadium negotiations between teams and their current homes. Putting franchises in London, San Diego, Oakland, Toronto, San Antonio, Austin, and/or St. Louis (or a second team in a city such as Chicago) would diminish that leverage.

That could be a small price to pay for adding so many regular-season games and, in turn, so many opportunities for wagering. Besides, the league will always dredge up some new market that could be the place into which a team could potentially move in order to get taxpayers in its existing market to pay for all or part of a new or renovated stadium.

Ultimately, money drives the issue. If the owners realize that plenty of money can be made by placing more teams in more towns, the NFL will. And it can, thanks to the money that can be generated by gambling.

It all comes back to gambling. To the money that can be made by gambling. More games, more drives, more plays, more opportunities to place bets.

That's why expansion, if not already secretly on the table, soon will be. And the NFLPA would have no objection. More teams mean more jobs mean more union dues.

A larger NFL means more money for everyone. From the cities that used to have NFL teams (St. Louis, San Diego, Oakland) to the cities that could add a second team (Chicago) to the cities that have never hosted a team (San Antonio, Toronto, Orlando, Sacramento, Portland, Raleigh-Durham, Salt Lake City), the NFL has more than enough options for placing new teams while also maintaining just enough extra empty cities to serve as leverage when it's time for current teams to build new stadiums without paying for them.

THE BEST APPROACH
TO OVERTIME

FOR MORE THAN fifty years, the NFL had no procedure for breaking a tie at the end of regulation in a regular-season game. For nearly fifty years since then, the NFL has had a system for breaking ties that fails to give both teams a fair chance to win.

The NFL adopted sudden-death overtime in 1974. For thirty-five years, the team that won the coin toss at the outset of the extra session simply needed to drive into field-goal range, trot out the kicker, put the ball through the uprights, and win the game.

From the 1970s onward, kickers improved. A 40-yard field goal once qualified as an impressive feat. That minimum eventually moved to 50 yards. Coupled with gradual and persistent rules favoring the offense, it became easier and easier for the team that won the toss at the outset of overtime to get in position for a walk-off 3-pointer.

The problem hid in plain sight for decades, but (as usual) the NFL refused to do anything about it until the worst-case scenario unfolded in a big spot. That happened on January 24, 2010, when the Vikings faced the Saints for the NFC Championship. Although the game eventually would become the catalyst for the bounty scandal, the more immediate consequence emerged from the manner in which New Orleans won.

With Minnesota driving for a potential game-winning field goal at the end of regulation, two key moments kept the Vikings from returning to the Super Bowl for the first time since 1976. First, after a timeout with nineteen seconds to play, coach Brad Childress sent twelve men into the huddle. The ensuing penalty pushed the ball from the Saints' 33 to the 38. Then, as quarterback Brett Favre rolled right and easily could have run for some extra yardage before the Vikings called a final timeout and kicked the game-winning field goal, Favre threw the ball across his body toward receiver Sidney Rice. Cornerback Tracy Porter intercepted, and the game headed to overtime.

The home team won the toss. Pierre Thomas returned the ball 40 yards, to the New Orleans 39. A questionable defensive holding foul on third and 6 extended the drive. Later, a questionable pass interference call gave New Orleans a first down at the Minnesota 29. The drive stalled at the Minnesota 22, Garrett Hartley made a 40-yard field goal, and the Saints qualified for their first Super Bowl in franchise history, with the Vikings never getting a chance to possess the ball in overtime.

Although the potential for such an outcome had existed for three and a half decades, the NFL had never addressed the situation. After it happened in a conference championship game, the NFL moved quickly to change the rules.

The league opted for a clunky partial solution. If the team with first possession in overtime scores a field goal and not a touchdown, the other team has a chance to tie the game with a field goal or win it with a touchdown. If the other team matches a field goal with a field goal, overtime then converts to sudden death, with the team that had the first overtime possession getting the ball next. If the team with first possession in overtime scores a touchdown, the game ends at that point.

Initially, the new rule—passed by owners after the coaches were literally sent to the golf course—applied only to the postseason. The league later extended it to the regular season since coaches wanted the same procedure to apply regardless of whether the situation happened in a playoff game.

Although this partially preserves the sudden-death element of overtime (a factor that the league regards as very important), it's still not fair to both teams. The team that kicks off should have a chance to match a touchdown. However, change is unlikely because change already should have happened. In Super Bowl LII, the Patriots capped a comeback for the ages to tie the Falcons. Then, New England won the coin toss to start overtime, drove down the field, and scored a game-winning touchdown. Few argued that the Falcons and league MVP Matt Ryan should have had a chance to match the score. Two years later, the Patriots forced overtime in the AFC Championship against the Chiefs. Then, New England won the coin toss to start overtime, drove down the field, and scored a game-winning touchdown. More, but not nearly enough, argued that the Chiefs and league MVP Patrick Mahomes should have had a chance to match the score.

The league remains unwilling to change. A revolutionary spot-and-choose proposal from the Ravens in 2021 (one team picks the location where the ball would be placed to start overtime, and the other team chooses to play offense or defense) got very little traction. The NFL has shown no inclination to adopt college football's approach, with the teams alternating possessions from the opponent's 25-yard line until someone emerges with the lead. However, there's a basic equity that applies in those situations; both teams have the same chance under the same circumstances to score a field goal or a touchdown.

As the NFL looks for ways to connect with younger fans and to make the game more exciting, the league should consider an idea crafted by PFT and adopted by the short-lived second iteration of the XFL. The league should implement a contest of 2-point conversions, with both offenses alternating at either end of the field through three or five efforts each to put the ball into the end zone. Whoever has scored more points at the conclusion of the three or five frames wins the game. If the game is still tied, it continues until one team converts and the other fails to do so.

Making the concept even more compelling would be the placement of both offenses and both defenses on opposite ends of the field, with the action ping-ponging from one end to the other, allowing for thirty or forty seconds between plays. It would introduce a gripping element of controlled chaos into a sport that already entails plenty of that, and it would make overtime games the kind of must-see event that, as word spreads of a looming 2-point shootout on social media and elsewhere, would cause viewers—and gamblers—to flock to their televisions for the opportunity to watch—and to bet on—each attempt to punch in the ball from the 2.

Such ideas will always meet stodgy, old-school resistance. However, the gambling angle for each snap in overtime makes it something the league should embrace.

Will the offense score or not? Which player will score? Will it be a run or a pass? Who will make the tackle? Will there be an interception or a fumble recovery? Money will flow on every potential permutation as the adrenaline of the players, the coaches, the fans in attendance, and the viewers at home pumps through their capillaries and, for many, loosens their wallets.

Remember this idea. Eventually, gambling will make it a reality. And, yes, I'd bet a lot of money on that.

PROTECTING THE
MENTAL HEALTH OF PLAYERS

THROUGHOUT SOCIETY, GREATER sensitivity has emerged regarding the question of mental health. The stigma has largely evaporated, and meaningful conversations regarding anxiety, depression, and other similar conditions have commenced.

That same sensitivity has applied to NFL players, with one important caveat. To the extent that this conversation entails striking a balance between mental health and mandatory media access to players, some simply refuse to even consider crossing that bridge.

Decades ago, the NFL decided that requiring players and coaches to speak to reporters helps the sport because it gives reporters content for stories that they can then write in newspapers or magazines. At one point in the NFL's existence, that approach made perfect sense because the NFL didn't enjoy the immense popularity it now does.

Today, reporters will write and talk about endless aspects of the NFL with or without players and coaches being forced to show up at press conferences and answer questions. Today, reporters no longer serve as the exclusive liaison between team and fan.

Routinely, players communicate directly with fans on social media. Teams communicate directly with fans through websites owned and operated by the NFL and its thirty-two franchises. Reporters have very real value when it comes to the quotations secured and observations made in a locker room after a game, but if the mental health of players is to be taken seriously, the question of whether it always makes sense to force players to face questions in the immediate aftermath of a game must be addressed.

The stakes of football contests continue to increase. A sufficiently big mistake in a sufficiently significant game by a player already drifting toward the potential end of his career in a given city can become the final straw. Should every player in those situations be expected to immediately face a stream of questions, some of which may lack the appropriate recognition of the fact that although it is "just a game" on the surface, for the player, it means so much more?

The template for taking a stand became obvious in early 2015 when the league threatened former Seahawks running back Marshawn Lynch with a significant financial penalty if he failed to participate in the Super Bowl XLIX media-day press conference. Lynch showed up, took every question, and answered each one with some variation of "I'm just here so I won't get fined." On at least one other occasion, Lynch engaged in similar behavior, saying "Thank you" or otherwise providing nonresponsive answers to questions from reporters until they gave up.

Reporters who fret that players, if given the option of not speaking to the media, would opt in droves to not do so ignore that glaring loophole. The league can't force the players to be cooperative or informative or entertaining. The league can only force them to be present and to provide a response, no matter how disconnected it may be from the question.

Most players want to speak to reporters. Most players understand that this helps the development of their personal brands, which can result in plenty of additional income. Most realize that being regarded as affable or funny or insightful can pave the way for a postfootball career in the media.

So let the ones who see the value in talking do so, and leave the ones who don't want to talk alone. While a more delicate balance that takes into account a given player's actual mental health status arguably would provide a better barometer for who should and shouldn't speak, the better approach would be to make it completely and totally voluntary for players.

Many will still talk. And reporters will still have plenty of things about which to write or to speak. The idea that members of sports media represent the sole custodians of some sacred truth grossly overstates our role and our value. Yes, we ferret out stories that enhance the enjoyment of following the sport. But these aren't national secrets or strategic decisions or matters of life and death. Before insisting that the private industry of pro football be as open and transparent as public offices and functions, a small dose of perspective is in order. And that perspective includes considering the impact of forcing players who are paid for their athletic abilities to become involuntary participants in an outdated system for promoting a sport that currently requires no promotion.

GLOBAL DOMINATION

STARTING WITH THE 1958 NFL Championship between the Colts and the Giants (an overtime game that wasn't decided on the first possession of the extra session), pro football began its climb toward becoming the most popular sport in America. Once regarded as falling somewhere between college football and pro wrestling, the NFL had finally found its footing, thanks to TV.

The game translated very well to television. It looked good. It sounded good. It felt right. And it thrived. As the NFL grew and the AFL arrived and the NFL eventually embraced the competition (and absorbed it), the Super Bowl era dawned, the two leagues merged, and the NFL continued to grow and to grow and to grow in popularity, not just bypassing baseball but leaving it in the stray dirt of an umpire's brush.

Once the NFL climbed to the top of the domestic hill, it set its sights on a much larger mountain.

Soccer was, is, and undoubtedly will continue to be, for decades to come and beyond, the most popular sport on the planet. Given the way pro football resonates in America, however, the NFL decided to try to aggressively export the product. And the best way to get fans in other countries fully engaged is to take the sport to them.

Starting in 2007, the NFL began playing regular-season games every year in London. Over time, the annual allocation grew from one to four, with the Jacksonville Jaguars becoming the franchise that goes each and every year. (In 2020, the Jaguars would have played two games in London but for the pandemic.)

The London games do well, selling out quickly and usually generating much more money than they would have made if played in the designated home team's usual American city. The local news coverage in England continues to languish, however, with NFL stories relegated to third-tier status. Still, English NFL fans have become extremely passionate, as the sport has slowly generated more of a following among people who follow their own version of football far more zealously than their American counterparts do.

The league tries to tease them with the promise of more. Whether it's the vague suggestion that a team will move to London or the even more vague notion that a Super Bowl could be played there, the league dangles such possibilities (typically in and around the playing of games in London) in order to drive more and more and more interest.

So will a team ever move to London? Some within the league's power structure believe that if Jaguars owner Shad Khan ever wants to do it, enough other owners would let him. It makes more sense, however, to have two teams do so rather than just one. A geographic rivalry would accelerate the organic interest in the sport, and London currently has two different venues (Tottenham Hotspur Stadium and Wembley Stadium) that are suitable for NFL games.

Challenges would quickly emerge. From tax rates to the dollar-pound exchange to players not wanting to live in London to players not wanting to leave their families in London for extended road trips (when crossing the Atlantic, they'd stay in the United States for two or three games at a time), the NFL would have to give the London team(s) extra draft picks or cap space to balance out the inherent competitive imbalance. If/when, however, the London team(s) thrive, some would argue that they get too much in the way of extra draft picks or extra cap space.

Money always finds a way. Moving a team to London would result in a lot more money for the NFL—especially if the team that relocates comes from a small market that fails to consistently fill its home stadium. The notion of London relocation continues to have a "when" not "if" feel, even though the "when" may still take a while.

As for a Super Bowl in London, that will never happen. It will never happen for one very important reason. The 6:30 p.m.-ish Eastern Time kickoff of the game would time-zone to an 11:30 p.m.-ish kickoff in London. Also, even though the vast majority of NFL fans will never actually attend a Super Bowl, the notion of sending the ultimate American sporting event to another country instantly infuriates those who will still watch it on TV, even if it were played on the moon.

Unless and until the NFL moves a team, or two, to London, the number of games played there every year will slowly grow until fans there get the equivalent of eight small boxes of cereal shrink-wrapped into one pack. Different teams, different players, different matchups, but perhaps in time it could host a full slate of eight or nine games, the same that an American city with a single franchise would host.

It's not just London that will see more and more NFL games. Mexico City has hosted multiple games, and the NFL constantly flirts with the idea of taking games elsewhere. The seventeenth regular-season game, added in 2021, gives the league up to sixteen games that could be played in neutral sites all over the world.

That's ultimately where the NFL wants to be. All over the world. It already has a global presence. It hopes, even if it takes one hundred years or longer, to achieve global domination.

CORPORATE OWNERSHIP

THE GREEN BAY model of corporate ownership happened at a time of desperation triggered by extreme financial struggles. Corporate ownership could eventually spread in the NFL at a time of desperation triggered by extreme financial success.

As franchise values continue to grow—and gambling will make them spike in the direction of $10 billion—it will become increasingly difficult for families that own teams to plan for the payment of estate taxes when the primary owner passes. On several occasions over the years, families have sold a team because they lacked the ability to satisfy the government without turning the football asset into cash. That problem will be no easier to solve as the value of franchise equity continues to inflate.

A separate problem will eventually arise when it's time to sell a team. The greater the value, the higher the price will rise. The higher the price, the harder it will become to find someone who can buy it.

Eventually, the NFL may run out of wealthy businesspeople who have earned billions in other lines of work and who have yet to realize, as mentioned earlier, that the only thing better than being rich and famous is being rich. Then again, if teams eventually carry a ten-figure price tag, few potential buyers who have that kind of money will be anonymous.

Of course, as those individuals buy teams and the value keeps climbing, the dilemma will eventually play out for *that* owner's family. For those with enough money to afford a franchise worth $10 billion or more, will there be enough money to pay the ultramassive estate taxes that will attach when the asset is inherited without selling all or part of the team?

The snowball effect of franchise value growth could, over time, force the NFL to explore more creative structures. One possibility is to continue to shrink the minimum share that a majority owner must hold. (Already, it's well below 50 percent.) Another possibility is to take the ownership of NFL teams corporate, allowing each of these major, multibillion-dollar businesses to behave as multibillion-dollar businesses usually do, with publicly traded shares and boards of directors and CEOs.

Arguably, the sport would be better off with corporate control. The long-standing model of franchise ownership has resulted in a fascinating, and for plenty of fans maddening, dichotomy between intricate, specialized football operations and the de facto monarchies that run them. When Jerry Jones bought the Cowboys in 1989, he didn't know a damn thing about running an NFL team. But he owned it, so he ran it. And he made himself the GM despite zero experience managing a professional football team (or any sports team) because he could.

For other family-owned teams, a similar problem arises when control of the franchise passes from one generation to the next. What qualifications does the child of an NFL owner possess to run a team other than shared DNA? To be sure, plenty of sons and daughters have proven that they can and will serve as capable stewards of the teams they inherit. Plenty of others have not.

But what other multibillion-dollar concern operates with such a roll of the dice from parent to child? Although NFL franchises essentially print money thanks to ticket sales and TV deals, bad management results in bad teams.

Of course, the good teams don't mind having a healthy complement of bad owners, at least to the extent that bad owners screw up only their own teams and not the rest of the league. It becomes easier for the good teams to stay good if enough of the other teams stay dysfunctional.

For example, more than a few owners don't live and work in the cities where their teams are located. As one team owner who shows up every day for work at his team's facility has said regarding the dynamic of absentee owners, "I love competing against them."

It nevertheless can hurt the sport to have a cluster of owners whose management of the team invokes another word beginning with "cluster."

Yes, the NFL has thrived through decades of less-than-stellar family-based management of certain franchises. How much better would the NFL be if all ownership groups ran their businesses at a high level? Failures in football will necessarily result in other types of failures, keeping the broader business from being as financially viable as it could be.

Corporate ownership would change that, in theory. Decisions would be made not by a person who happened to benefit from the lottery ticket fueled by the right combination of egg and sperm but by someone who has, through education, experience, and achievement, earned the right to make those decisions. It could introduce a more thorough sense of parity to the sport, giving more teams a legitimate chance to contend and giving more teams a chance to ultimately play in meaningful games in January and February.

Regardless of whether corporate ownership would become a positive or a negative for the game, it could be an inevitable product of the massive success the NFL has enjoyed over the years. At some point, there simply may not be enough people with enough money to continue the family-business model that has created for the NFL equal measures of charm and consternation.

ALTERNATIVE LEAGUES

FRUSTRATED AND UNDERMINED by the AFL, the NFL eventually absorbed it. In more than fifty years since then, no other league has even come close to getting the NFL to flinch.

Threats have definitely emerged. The WFL in the mid-1970s bought up a bunch of star NFL players (such as Larry Csonka), but the upstart league quickly collapsed. The USFL tried to create a spring complement to the NFL but also captured some NFL-caliber talent, such as Herschel Walker. A fateful decision to move the season to the fall (widely attributed to a man who would go on to become the American president) coupled with a disastrous courtroom Hail Mary aimed at leveraging a merger ended the USFL.

And so ended any real threats to the NFL. The league created its own spring league in 1991. The World League of American Football, with teams in the United States, Canada, England, Germany, and Spain, sputtered after two seasons, returned in 1995 as a six-team, Europe-only venture, became NFL Europe in 1998, shifted the second "e" to an "a" (after all, when in Roma) in 2006, and went out of business in 2007.

Many have since bemoaned the absence of a developmental league since players, coaches, executives, and officials got valuable experience in the NFL-owned minor league. The NFL's owners, however, weren't willing to burn money on a zero-sum game. If, for example, Kurt Warner doesn't become Kurt Warner given the absence of opportunities in a lesser league, someone else will have his roster spot—and someone else will lead a team to a championship, as Warner did in 1999. The supply of interested applicants for all NFL jobs will always exceed the demand. Why waste money to give fringe candidates a chance to supplant those who are otherwise good enough?

If the NFL could run a spring league or other minor league profitably, the NFL would do it in a heartbeat. If some entrepreneur were able to run a spring league or other minor league profitably, the NFL would write a check for the operation in a heartbeat. No one can make a spring league or other minor league work.

The AAF tried in 2019. It quickly failed. The XFL tried twice, in 2001 (it failed after one season) and in 2020 (it failed during its first season back, thanks to the pandemic). With Dwayne "The Rock" Johnson buying the XFL's carcass, the third time could be a charm. Or not. And the USFL may be making another comeback. Or not.

Legalized gambling boosts the potential for an alternative pro football league because people need things on which to bet. However, people already have plenty of things on which to bet in the spring. Will they flock to football wagering after football season has ended?

That's the core question that proprietors of spring football leagues seem to consistently ignore. Most football fans want football in football season. As a result, an alternative league quite possibly would thrive during football season, on the nights when the NFL isn't playing games.

How about an in-season Tuesday-Wednesday league? Football fans who watch football during football season would give it a chance. Football bettors would have a way to build on their weekend wins or to chase their losses. Games could even be played on Fridays and Saturdays, territory the NFL must avoid due to the broadcast antitrust exemption, which protects high school and college football from early September through early December. An alternative league would not be bound by that limitation.

An alternative league also would not be bound by other limitations. Many have complained in recent years about the NFL's shift toward safety, which has taken many big hits out of the sport. Fans keep watching because there's no other choice when it comes to professional football. What if someone were to launch a professional football league that turned back the clock to the 1990s, the 1980s, the 1970s?

What if a new league embraced full-contact, no-holds-barred football with no rules against helmet-to-helmet hits, no enhanced protections for defenseless players, reduced restrictions on contact with quarterbacks, and more? No player who signed up for that sport could claim he didn't know the risks, and every player would sign a contract fully documenting that awareness and, in consideration of employment, waiving all legal rights arising from the argument that the league had failed to inform him of the risks or otherwise failed to protect him from injuries that reasonably and foreseeably flow from the game.

The barriers would be less legal than moral. In our current political climate, however, it's stunning that someone hasn't sufficiently bristled at blue-state football by bringing back the red-state style. For the NFL, that could be the biggest business risk to its ongoing dominance of the American football market. If someone with $10 billion to spend decides not to buy an NFL team but to start something like the Patriot Football League, that league could find instant popularity with anywhere from one-third to one-half of the country.

That would be enough to make the owner of the PFL rich. And it would be enough to take a bite out of the NFL's ever-burgeoning brand.

Of all the challenges the NFL faces, this is the one over which it has the least control. Short of lobbying state and federal legislators to outlaw certain football tactics (which would be worth a try), the NFL would have to hope that the same thought processes that have divided the country won't conquer pro football as we know it.

ACKNOWLEDGMENTS

Before the summer of 2019, I'd heard from time to time some version of "You should write a book about the NFL." I didn't want to. Pretty much every day since November 1, 2001—and every single day without interruption since January 1, 2004—I've written anywhere from ten to twenty articles about the NFL at PFT. The idea of carving out time to write even more about the NFL made no sense and held little appeal. But I still kept hearing it. Maybe I did this so it would stop.

Whatever the reason, I'm glad I did it. I knew all along that, if we determined an approach and crafted an outline, the book would write itself. I say "we" because once David Black agreed to represent me, his patient guidance and advice helped me take the things I've learned about the NFL over two decades and arrange them in a way that would convey compelling information in a manner that makes sense. After Public-Affairs expressed interest in the idea and Ben Adams became involved in further shaping the outline, it quickly moved toward a final form. We had ten sections with ten or more topics per section; the writing became the easy part. And the fun part. For many of the topics covered in the book, I had to refresh my memory by reading articles from PFT and elsewhere. Some things I'd never known or had forgotten to the point that there was no memory to refresh.

The entire team at PublicAffairs made the experience not just easy but enjoyable. From production editor Kelly Lenkevich to copy editor Connie Oehring to marketing director Lindsay Fradkoff to publicist Jocelynn Pedro, their efforts made the book and the efforts to market it better. Through it all, I didn't know what to expect, and I constantly braced for something that would make me ask why in the hell I'd agreed to do this. That never happened, not a single time.

Ben Adams also challenged me to harvest from these various old stories some new information. That part of the project became the most rewarding. For many of the items, the passage of time and the relentlessly comprehensive nature of NFL news gathering has left nothing fresh to discover. For plenty, I still found nuggets that had never before seen the light of day.

Like the vast majority of modern NFL reporting, the new information came from anonymous sources who provided information in exchange for a promise to not disclose their names, all of which would be instantly recognizable to a zealous NFL fan. Some spoke on the record, including my *PFT Live* partner Chris Simms and former Raiders CEO Amy Trask, who was an early adopter of PFT—and who has never hesitated to point out that owners and others with positions of power and influence in NFL circles have regularly frequented PFT for news, information, and analysis about the sport pretty much since the day PFT launched.

Without my colleagues at PFT and NBC, the entire enterprise would be little more than a solitary man with a messy office that may or may not contain a chicken. Michael David Smith, Peter King, Charean Williams, Josh Alper, Myles Simmons, Curtis Crabtree, and previous contributors such as Gregg Rosenthal and Darin Gantt have helped PFT become a comprehensive, one-stop destination for anything and everything happening in the NFL. On the TV/radio/podcast side, Simms has helped me learn much more about the game from a quarterback's perspective, and Matt Casey, Rob Hyland, Pete Damilatis, Kristen Coleman, and previously Rob "Stats" Guerrera have helped me look smart (or perhaps not quite as dumb) on many, many occasions. At the executive level at NBC (you may think I'm just sucking up here, and you may be right), Mark Lazarus, Pete Bevacqua, and Sam Flood have supported PFT's mission of transparency, accuracy, honesty, and authenticity to the audience—even when those things sometimes rankle folks within the NFL's power structure.

But for Rick Cordella and former NBC exec Kevin Monahan, there's a good chance that the entire enterprise would still be little more than a solitary man with a messy office that may or may not contain a chicken. Cordella persuaded PFT to partner with NBC in 2009, and Monahan was instrumental in blending the NBC and PFT cultures in a way that made the relationship seamless.

My business partner, Larry Mazza, has helped guide PFT through the ever-changing landscape in which media companies operate. His focus on issues unrelated to the creation of content have allowed me to focus almost exclusively on reporting, writing, and talking about football.

My wife, Jill, and my son, Alex, deserve a ton of credit, too. Jill carefully reviewed an early draft of this book, spotting plenty of typos and providing the valuable perspective of a casual football fan. Also, they have unconditionally supported me during the many hours I've devoted to all PFT-related endeavors over the past twenty years.

I've dedicated *Playmakers* to my parents. Like so many children of Italian immigrants, they wanted to give me a chance to realize the dream that their parents came to America to pursue. My parents sparked my interest in pro football (my mom may have been a bigger fan than my dad), and they both died before I wandered into this business. I often wonder what they would think of the strange but memorable way the dominoes have fallen in the last two decades. Their reaction probably would mesh with something a family friend, herself an Italian immigrant, said when visiting us a couple of years ago during the holidays: "If-a your mother was alive, she'd-a be dead."

© Jill Florio

Mike Florio is the creator and owner, in partnership with NBC Sports, of ProFootballTalk.com, one of the leading NFL news organizations in America. He hosts a daily show, *PFT Live* on NBCSN, which has a radio simulcast on SiriusXM. During the NFL season, he also appears weekly on the *Sunday Night Football* broadcast. With regular appearances on national and local sports radio programs around the country and more than 1.7 million followers on Twitter, Florio is among the most prominent football commentators working today.

PublicAffairs is a publishing house founded in 1997. It is a tribute to the standards, values, and flair of three persons who have served as mentors to countless reporters, writers, editors, and book people of all kinds, including me.

I. F. STONE, proprietor of *I. F. Stone's Weekly*, combined a commitment to the First Amendment with entrepreneurial zeal and reporting skill and became one of the great independent journalists in American history. At the age of eighty, Izzy published *The Trial of Socrates*, which was a national bestseller. He wrote the book after he taught himself ancient Greek.

BENJAMIN C. BRADLEE was for nearly thirty years the charismatic editorial leader of *The Washington Post*. It was Ben who gave the *Post* the range and courage to pursue such historic issues as Watergate. He supported his reporters with a tenacity that made them fearless and it is no accident that so many became authors of influential, best-selling books.

ROBERT L. BERNSTEIN, the chief executive of Random House for more than a quarter century, guided one of the nation's premier publishing houses. Bob was personally responsible for many books of political dissent and argument that challenged tyranny around the globe. He is also the founder and longtime chair of Human Rights Watch, one of the most respected human rights organizations in the world.

·　　·　　·

For fifty years, the banner of Public Affairs Press was carried by its owner Morris B. Schnapper, who published Gandhi, Nasser, Toynbee, Truman, and about 1,500 other authors. In 1983, Schnapper was described by *The Washington Post* as "a redoubtable gadfly." His legacy will endure in the books to come.

Peter Osnos, *Founder*